RAISING THE BAR

RAISING THE BAR

better drinks better entertaining

NICK MAUTONE WITH MARAH STETS

PHOTOGRAPHS BY METTE RANDEM

ARTISAN NEW YORK

To my dad, Nick, Sr., who never cared what I did as long as I did my best. Wish you were here.

9 Introduction

15 Home Bar Basics

35 The Best Ingredients

71 Favorite Classic Cocktails

109 Specialties of the House

139 Bubblies and
a Bit of Decadence

153 Nogs, Grogs, and
Other Holiday Warmers

169 Summer Splurges

191 Knockout Punches

201 The After-Party

213 Morning Glories and
Tonics to Cure What Ails You

225 Java Heaven
and Spiked Tea Time

237 Nonalcoholic Refreshers

249 Snacks and Hors d'Oeuvres

276 Mail-order Sources

277 Bibliography

279 Index

THE INTIMATE RELATIONSHIP BETWEEN THE BAR AND THE KITCHEN IS PARAMOUNT whether in a restaurant or at home. Cocktails are part of a meal and thus part of the overall entertaining experience. A lengthy career spent in restaurants has ensured that when mixing a cocktail I am never focused solely on that drink; I am always acutely aware of the food that will be served either with or around it.

The restaurants I worked in over the last twenty years have set the standard for food and for drink. As a manager at New York's Gotham Bar and Grill I trained and coached the bartenders, often tweaking drinks with unexpected flavors from the kitchen. Working with Alfred Portale, Gotham's amazing chef, I learned about the importance of using fresh ingredients and proper technique. Portale's intense concentration of flavors and his emphasis on balance continue to be an inspiration to me.

At Hudson River Club, where the always innovative Waldy Malouf was chef, I began matching my drinks to the seasons, just as he does his food.

Danny Meyer and Tom Colicchio, the talented owners of Gramercy Tavern, and Claudia Fleming, the restaurant's award-winning former pastry chef, always focus on excellence. The purity of flavors and use of incredible raw product were enhanced by chefs who partnered with me on creating a cocktail program that bridged the gap between great house-made cocktails and fine dining.

INTRODUCTION

In fact, it was kitchen leftovers that transformed one of my signature cocktails into something exquisite. I entered the kitchen at Gramercy Tavern one morning and found one of the chefs about to discard the remaining bits of oven-dried tomato chips that had garnished roasted striped bass the night before. These slow-roasted slices of plum tomatoes are both sweet and savory, a melt-in-your-mouth highlight of that roasted fish dish. I rescued the tomato chips and took them to the bar. That night, the tomato chips were floating atop the Basil Martini (page 126), adding a flash of color and delicate flavor to this distinctive cocktail specialty. Utilizing leftovers is one of the hallmarks of my cooking and cocktail making; I do not like to waste anything. I think of ways to use items that might otherwise be discarded. Extra pumpkin from making soup can enrich Holiday Eggnog (page 155). Extra stewed fruit from dessert can be blended into a mulled wine (see pages 160 and 162). Peaches, plums, and berries can be turned into fabulous cordials (see pages 66 and 67).

. . . it is all about the people you're serving and exceeding their expectations.

My approach to cocktail making—a focus on balance of flavor and respect for the ingredients that make a drink—is as intense as that of any chef. From when the ingredients are purchased to the moment a cocktail is served to one of my guests, the result must meet the same exacting standards as any dish served in a great restaurant. Unfortunately, too many bars, restaurants, and even people who entertain at home don't feel that way. This is not to say that cocktails must be complicated or difficult to make to be delicious. On the contrary, sometimes the simplest drinks are the most elegant and tasty. The Classic Martini (page 73), for example, is as simple as it gets: gin or vodka with vermouth served very cold with a perfect garnish.

Nothing gives me more pleasure than sharing a meal, a drink, and great conversation with friends and family. My approach to entertaining is straightforward: I plan my meals and beverages somewhat thematically. I like to match the before-dinner drinks to the meal and the wine to be served with it. I try to surprise my guests with new and different drinks at unexpected times. For example, most people serve Bloody Marys (pages 215 to 217) at brunch. This is a wonderful and classic combination, but there are others, such as the Tangerine Dream (page 220), to enhance a brunch that will surprise your guests and excite them as well. I keep a well-stocked bar at home so I can usually accommodate my guests' imbibing pleasures. I prefer to plan out an occasion, including the drinks everyone will have, in advance. Before a summer evening grilling outdoors, I often serve Blackberry Coolers (page 185) with hors d'oeuvres. As my guests arrive, we share drinks perfectly matched to our evening. Then we move on to the main meal, for which I will generally open a good bottle of wine during the first course. While cocktails are a passion, I adore wine with my meals and feel that this is a natural progression for a great dinner. At this point my guests will have finished their before-dinner drinks and had some food, so they can easily switch over to wine, which allows me to spend more time with them.

I try to surprise my guests with new and different drinks at unexpected times.

In order to accommodate all of your guests' particular preferences, you should always keep some basics on hand. For liquors, keep your favorite brands of vodka, gin, rum, tequila, scotch, bourbon, sweet and dry vermouth, and triple sec always at the ready. For extra ingredients, keep olives, bitters, superfine sugar, Tabasco, and kosher salt on hand. Of course, there are hundreds and hundreds of liquors, cordials, and brandies that you could stock, but these basics and extras make literally hundreds of different drinks to satisfy your guests' cravings.

The rules for pairing wine with food apply to cocktails as well: The cocktail should complement the food, by offering a counterpoint to the dominant characteristics of the food. For example, match rich, creamy foods with cocktails that have bountiful acidity and are full-flavored. The acid cuts through the fats and cleanses the palate. Salty foods demand contrasting elements such as sweetness to balance out the salt. Most cocktails are served before dinner because they are perfect palate openers. Some cocktails are great after dinner when they act as a digestif or even as dessert. I generally do not serve cocktails with the main meal because as good as cocktails are, their place is before or after the main meal, rarely during it. Of course there are exceptions: The Watermelon Cooler (page 184) goes incredibly well, much better, in fact, than most wines, with great barbecue.

When introducing a wine to your meal after your cocktails, always remember that balance is the key. Great wines (no matter what the price) act as a condiment to the meal. If you have served strong cocktails before dinner, try to serve a light wine such as a crisp Alsatian or New York

Riesling with your first course. If your cocktails were light and the meal permits, you could enjoy a richer chardonnay with the appetizer. Remember, the idea is not to get people drunk but to enhance their meal.

Often, when I go to friends' houses or they come to mine, we mix a full batch of margaritas or a pitcher of martinis instead of making single drinks. The recipes in this book are geared to serving groups; most of them will be for four, six, or eight servings and are easily doubled, tripled, or even quadrupled for larger groups. Many of the recipes offer time-saving tips or notes on planning ahead so that you can spend more time partaking of your preprandials instead of making them.

The recipes in this book are geared to serving groups. Most of the recipes will be for four, six, or eight servings, and are easily doubled, tripled, or even quadrupled for larger groups.

One universal rule for enjoying company is to prepare as much in advance as possible. For drinks that have both an alcohol and nonalcohol base, mix each component of the drink in a separate container, without any ice, well in advance and store them sealed in the refrigerator. When your guests arrive you can then mix the two in the correct proportions without any fuss. Even easier are drinks that can be mixed in one container, such as Manhattans (page 77). If you are having a group over, prepare a pitcherful of Manhattans for eight, or even more, servings and store it tightly sealed in the refrigerator, without ice, until ready to serve. When ready, you can stir or shake one or two servings at a time, allowing you to efficiently serve drinks to order.

Whenever I make a large batch of a drink such as the Mojito (page 88) that includes muddled ingredients, I muddle the ingredients with a mortar and pestle or in a large bowl with a wooden spoon and then divide the ingredients evenly among the glasses. I also freeze my fresh-squeezed juices. If I am having a group over on Saturday, I may squeeze all the juices on Wednesday and freeze them immediately. Allow the juice to thaw in the refrigerator overnight before using. The freezing does not negatively affect the juice and you are still serving a freshly prepared product that will improve the flavor of your drinks.

A well-made cocktail enhances conversation and stimulates fun, but this does not mean that every drink needs to be alcoholic. There are times when nonalcoholic recipes are desired, so this book includes a chapter (pages 239 to 247) for those times. Sharing a drink means sharing the responsibility. Never overpour or urge guests to drink. Everyone's tolerance for alcohol is different. Guests should always feel comfortable, and free to either refuse or request an additional round.

As I like to base my cocktails on what I am eating or how I am entertaining, I have organized the chapters in this book thematically as well. For example, "Bubbles and a Bit of Decadence" includes sparkling cocktails and some others for a bit of luxury; "Summer Splurges" encompasses those drinks that work best during the warmer months; and so on. If you are looking for a drink based on a specific liquor, such as vodka, simply look in the index, where you will find the recipes organized by base liquor.

I hope you enjoy this book and use it to share many great days and nights entertaining friends and family.

17 **A FOCUS ON BALANCE**

18 **THE RIGHT TOOLS**

21 **THE RIGHT TECHNIQUES**

23 **THE RIGHT GLASSWARE**

26 **THE RIGHT BOOZE**

32 **OTHER INDISPENSABLE ITEMS**

HOME BAR BASICS

UNDERSTANDING THE BASICS IS THE KEY TO BEING SUCCESSFUL IN ANY endeavor. Chefs cannot rise to greatness if they cannot properly execute the fundamental techniques of cooking: searing, braising, sautéing, sauce making, and baking. Perfecting these and other basic techniques and using superior ingredients and the proper tools are fundamental to creating an extraordinary meal. And so it is with mixing drinks. Great cocktail making employs many simple techniques, easy-to-use tools, and quality ingredients.

This chapter focuses first on what is perhaps the most important element of a great cocktail: balance. Without balance a drink might be too sweet, too sour, or even just too big, but it is easy to avoid these excesses and get a grasp on how a properly balanced drink should taste. Next featured are a few basic tools and techniques that facilitate efficient and fun cocktail making. The Right Glassware (page 23) will help you identify which glass in your cupboard is best suited to the drinks being served. And finally, The Right Booze (page 26) is a straightforward guide to stocking your liquor cabinet with a few well-chosen basics.

Consider this chapter a brief but thorough course in great cocktail making. Taking a little time with these home bar basics before tackling the recipes that follow will enhance your experience and improve your results, for on these pages are the necessary building blocks to transform you into a master home bartender, and that's when the fun really begins!

A Focus on Balance

The first rule of cocktail making is that balance is everything. One way to define balance is "a state in which the elements form a satisfying and harmonious whole and are in proportion to one another."

In imbibing, balance might be viewed as the ratio of acid to sweetness to alcoholic strength. In the case of wine, those that are too low in acid taste "flabby," wines that are too high in alcohol taste "hot" or medicinal, and wines that are too high in sugar or too low in acid or alcohol taste cloying. These same principles hold true for cocktails. For example, in a margarita, too much tequila will cause it to taste hot and perhaps bitter, too much lime juice makes it taste overly acidic, too much triple sec makes it much too sweet.

Determining balance in your drinks will also help you understand the characteristics of liquors and mixers. For example, some bourbons are sweeter than others. If you use them in an old-fashioned, you may require less sweet vermouth. Other bourbons are higher in alcohol, and when using them you may choose to add more water. Certain recipes in this book recommend a specific brand of liquor for the distinct sweetness, dryness, or extra kick it provides.

Personal preference also comes into play when making cocktails. I generally like my drinks on the sweeter side. When I am out, I take the time to inform the bartender what my preference is, and when at home, I make my drinks according to my tastes: Martinis have a little more dry vermouth, Manhattans a dash more sweet vermouth, and margaritas contain a bit of extra triple sec. The choice is yours: Just be sure to work toward a balance of acid, sweetness, and alcoholic strength.

If you are a newcomer to mixing your own cocktails, I suggest you make the recipes in this book as they are written. Once you have tasted the drink, you can determine if you prefer it sweeter, stronger, or lighter.

Also important is the size of the final drink. Remember that bigger is not necessarily better. In fact, many of the recipes in this book have lesser yields, for drinks that are often as small as 3 ounces. This allows you to sip a perfectly made, balanced cocktail ice cold. If it were any larger, the cocktail would become warm and insipid before the drinker could finish it. The more cocktails you prepare, the more comfortable you will become with determining your own specific sense of balance.

LEFT TO RIGHT: Antique sterling jigger, antique elephant shaker, cobbler shaker, antique pewter jigger, Boston shaker set

The Right Tools

You don't need much in the way of expensive equipment to mix great drinks. There are many good inexpensive starter kits on the market that contain shakers, strainers, jiggers, bar spoons, and a paring knife. Eventually, however, you will probably want to add an assortment of shakers and pitchers of different sizes and styles to help you entertain with a little flair. Aside from the household basics—a bottle opener, can opener, and corkscrew—here are some other tools you will need:

SHAKERS

There are two types of cocktail shakers: the cobbler shaker and the Boston shaker. Either one works well, although each has particular features that make it useful. Specifically, the cobbler comes in varying sizes, from 8 to 16 to 24 ounces and even larger. These variations allow for different drink sizes and some flexibility when presenting and serving cocktails. For the shaking and stirring technique, see page 21.

An elegant-looking tool, the cobbler shaker is usually stainless steel and consists of a base shaker topped by a snug-fitting top with a built-in strainer. A smaller cap is either screwed onto the top or simply fits snugly. To use a cobbler, fill the base shaker with ice and the cocktail ingredients. Place the top on with the cap in place. Shake well, remove the cap, and strain the drink into a glass.

The Boston shaker is the one most bartenders use. It is a little more versatile than the cobbler, but by the same token, it is slightly more difficult to use. The Boston is composed of two tumblers. One tumbler is metal and holds roughly 26 to 30 ounces. The other tumbler is glass and generally holds 16 ounces. To use a Boston, fill the glass tumbler with ice and the cocktail ingredients. Place the metal tumbler on top and gently but firmly give it a tap or two to seal the two tumblers together. Hold the bottom of the glass tumbler in the palm of one hand while pressing the metal shaker with the palm of the other and shake vigorously. Invert the shaker on a counter so that the metal half is on the bottom. Hold the seal between the two shakers with one hand; two fingers should be on the glass and two fingers on the metal. Hold firmly and, with the heel of your other hand, tap the rim of the metal shaker. This should break the seal. If it does not, tap it again. Remove the glass shaker carefully. Place a strainer over the top of the metal tumbler and pour.

STRAINERS

The Hawthorn strainer and the julep strainer each serves its own purpose, and both are necessary if using a Boston shaker set. The Hawthorn strainer has a metal coil on its underside, and the julep strainer is solid metal with holes throughout. The Hawthorn is used for shaken drinks and works with the metal tumbler, and the julep strainer is used for stirred drinks and is used with the glass tumbler.

JIGGERS

Jiggers are basically tiny measuring cups. The most common jiggers have a long handle with two cups of different sizes that measure 2 ounces or less, but my favorite jigger is a small, shot glass–size measuring cup with measurements ranging from ¼ to 1 ounce and their equivalencies in teaspoons, tablespoons, and milliliters all etched on its side.

COCKTAIL SPOONS

Cocktail spoons are used to stir a drink in a pitcher or shaker. The same rules apply to stirring as to shaking: Stir until the outside of the shaker is frosted and beaded with sweat, ten to fifteen seconds. When entertaining, I love to stir a pitcher of Manhattans or martinis slowly while chatting with my guests. It sets a relaxed mood for the whole party, and it makes me feel like William Powell in *The Thin Man*.

NUTMEG GRATER
This tool is indispensable for garnishing drinks such as hot toddies or punches such as Whiskey and Ginger Punch (page 198) with freshly grated nutmeg.

KNIVES
For cocktail making, you will need a paring knife for cutting your lemons, limes, and oranges and a chef's knife for cutting large fruit such as pineapples. Paring knives usually come with a 4-inch blade that tapers to a sharp point. I prefer an 8-inch chef's knife for better control.

CHANNEL KNIVES AND ZESTERS
A channel knife has a rounded or rectangular metal head with a small curved blade and a hole on either the side or the top. This is used for producing long citrus-peel swirls. Sometimes the tool is double-headed, with a channel knife on one end and a zester on the other. A zester is a small hand tool with five or six tiny holes at the end of what looks like a palette knife. The holes are used to produce very fine threads of zest.

MUDDLERS
Bar muddlers are used for mashing fruit, sometimes with sugar, to extract juice. They are also used for bruising soft fruit, such as cherries, and herbs, such as mint, as with a Mojito (page 88) or Lime Tequilla Frappé (page 177). The best muddlers are made of soft, unvarnished wood and are generally 6 inches long with a flat end on one side. They are very inexpensive, but if you cannot readily find one, a wooden spoon will do. For the muddling technique, see page 22.

JUICERS AND REAMERS
I strongly recommend purchasing a citrus juicer. As you will see in the next chapter, I place great importance on fresh-squeezed juices. The models on the market today offer a great value, and many allow you to select the amount of pulp you would like to retain. Make sure to get a model that is large enough to handle grapefruit as well as lemons and limes.

Although you do not *need* a juice extractor for cocktail making, it is a wonderful luxury, especially if you use and love fresh pineapple, mango, peach, and apple juices.

In addition, always keep a wooden citrus reamer on hand. This handy little device has a pointed, riveted end that you twist into a citrus half to extract the juice. It is great if you have to juice just a few lemons or limes.

COCKTAIL PITCHERS

Tall, elongated, and somewhat narrow, cocktail pitchers range in size from 1 to 2 quarts. They have a pinched and rolled rim that keeps ice from coming out with the drink. Standard cocktail pitchers also come with a long glass stirrer for elegant cocktail mixing. Gallon-size glass pitchers and several plastic pitchers with tight-fitting lids are also good to have on hand. When entertaining for a group, I sometimes forgo the elegance of cocktail shakers and pitchers and mix my drinks in large Tupperware-type pitchers with lids. This allows me to shake a large number of drinks for six or even eight guests in one batch.

The Right Techniques

There are very few strict rules for mixing drinks and with just a bit of practice you can easily master them all.

SHAKING AND STIRRING

When shaking your drinks, follow this simple but important rule: Shake vigorously until the outside of the shaker is frosted and beaded with sweat. The shaker should be so cold that it is almost painful to hold. This will generally take ten to fifteen seconds. Most important, maintain a consistent and constant rhythm while shaking to ensure the drink is mixed effectively.

As for shaking versus stirring, it is my opinion that drinks that are all or mostly liquor, such as a martini (see page 73), should be stirred; drinks that contain juice, egg, or other heavy ingredients should be shaken. The simple reason for this is texture: In cocktails that are primarily or all liquor, stirring produces a more delicate texture; shaking produces a slight effervescent or hazy effect that many people don't like. For juice-based or weightier drinks, shaking emulsifies the cocktail, ensuring a smooth, even texture. It will also produce a lovely froth that floats on top.

For very weighty drinks, such as a Bloody Mary (page 215) or those based on fruit purees, a technique called rolling is the best method for mixing and can be done only in a Boston shaker. Rolling consists of pouring a drink back and forth between the two tumblers. This thoroughly combines heavy juices such as tomato with other ingredients without producing a foamy texture that is unpleasant in these types of drinks.

MUDDLING

To muddle, place the fruit, herbs, sugar, or other ingredients to be muddled in the bottom of a large glass or shaker. Using the flat end of the muddler, firmly press and twist the tool, crushing and breaking down the fruit or herb to release as much juice and essential oil as possible. If bruising an herb, do not press quite as hard, for you do not want to pulverize it.

RIMMING

Rimming a glass with sugar, salt, or spices ensures that every sip of the cocktail is a multilayered experience. Salt on the rim of a glass filled with sweet Margarita (page 81) is probably the best-known example of how two distinct textures and flavors in your mouth at one time can equal a sublime drink.

The key to proper rimming is to keep the granules on the *outside* of the glass. Too many granules on the inside of the rim mean that each time the drinker tips his glass, the garnish falls into the cocktail, eventually throwing off the balance of flavors in the whole drink. A common, but incorrect, method is to moisten both the inside and the outside of the glass rim and then dip the whole glass upside down into the sugar or salt, thereby coating the inside as much as the outside of the rim. The *correct* method is to pour the sugar or salt onto a small plate. Rub the juicy side of a wedge of lemon, lime, or other citrus fruit on the *outer* edge of the rim— not along the inside. Holding the glass at an angle, roll the outer edge of the rim in the salt or sugar until it is fully coated.

FLOATING

Floating is a technique that has both aesthetic and practical benefits. Brightly colored syrups, cordials, or cream may be floated on a cocktail, such as the Zombie (page 86), giving an attractive layered look to the drink and dividing the drink into two distinct levels in the drinker's mouth. There are two ways to float one liquid on top of the other. You may place the bowl of a spoon upside down over the cocktail and pour the cream or syrup slowly over it, allowing the liquid to gently spread over the top of the drink. Alternatively, you can pour the liquid to be floated into the bowl of a spoon and gently "drop" it onto the drink.

The Right Glassware

Feel free to improvise when it comes to glassware. While there is a glass for every type of cocktail and each one is designed to enhance a specific drink, it is just not practical to own them all. If you do not have a margarita coupe, for example, a wineglass will work fine. An old-fashioned glass can easily double for a whiskey-tasting glass. The most important rule in glassware isn't about the glasses at all. It is about what you serve *in* the glass—a high-quality, freshly made, well-balanced beverage.

The photograph above highlights sixteen different glasses for wine, cocktails, and straight spirits. While you do not need all of these glasses, you should keep the following basics on hand: old-fashioned glasses, highball glasses, martini glasses, all-purpose wineglasses, champagne glasses, beer glasses, and perhaps dessert wine or port glasses.

1. OLD-FASHIONED OR "ROCKS" GLASSES can range from 8 to 12 ounces and are used for spirits served over ice, or "on the rocks." Generally they are short and round or, in some cases, rounded squares.

2. HIGHBALL GLASSES are tall and round and are used for drinks containing soda as well as liquor. Most highballs hold 10 to 16 ounces of liquid. Their extra height keeps the bubbles of the soda intact for a longer period than a shorter, wider glass would. *Collins glasses* are even taller and narrower and are often frosted like the one shown here. They are used for the classic Tom Collins (page 84), of course, and are also excellent for serving other tall drinks, such as the Singapore Sling (page 84).

3. COCKTAIL OR MARTINI GLASSES are used for cocktails served "up," or without ice. Holding the glass by its long stem prevents the heat of your hand from warming the drink. Cocktail glasses can be as small as 3 ounces and as large as 10 ounces. Serving "up" drinks in smaller-size glasses not only ensures that the drink will remain cold, but also keeps you and your guests from overindulging. Large martini glasses are great for show, but 6, 8, or 10 ounces of straight liquor is a lot to handle all at once. Here, we are showing a classic 6-ounce version and an elegant antique 3-ounce size.

4. ALL-PURPOSE WINEGLASSES are good for more than just wine. They are perfect for frappés, delicate-tasting drinks, and some frothy, juicy drinks. I often use an all-purpose wineglass for margaritas served "up." Choose one that holds 6 to 8 ounces, which will give you versatility. The stem keeps your hand off the bowl of the glass, and its roundness keeps the froth of a properly shaken drink elegantly floating on top.

5. CHAMPAGNE GLASSES also come in a variety of styles and sizes. I prefer a champagne flute that is shaped like an elongated wineglass. This versatile style is great for serving sparkling wine as well as cocktails made with it. Choose a champagne glass that, like the all-purpose wineglass, holds 6 to 8 ounces to accommodate either sparkling wine or a cocktail.

6. BEER GLASSES can be as varied as wineglasses. The two shown here are a beer mug and a pilsner glass. A tall, heavy-bottomed beer mug is the most practical choice. Choose one that is at least 12 ounces, the average size for a bottle of beer, and not more than 16 ounces, which gives you room for a big head on your beer or for ice if you are using the glass for another type of drink. The mug keeps the beer cold, of course, and it can also double as a specialty glass for big summer coolers and frozen drinks. A pilsner glass's footed bottom and elegant stemmed shape are perfectly suited to lighter, crisper beers, as well as for serving effervescent cocktails such as the Dark and Stormy (page 94).

7. DESSERT WINEGLASSES OR PORT GLASSES are used for sweeter after-dinner wines and cordials. This glass, which resembles a small wineglass, is also great for whiskey sours and other elegant frothy drinks served "up."

8. WHISKEY-TASTING GLASSES are specialty items used to serve whiskeys neat or straight and unchilled. In some respects, they act like a brandy snifter: The bulbous bottom aerates the whiskey and allows the volatile vapors to dissipate.

9. BORDEAUX OR CABERNET GLASSES are used for full-bodied and tannic red wines, such as cabernet sauvignon, the most common grape variety in Bordeaux. The rounded bottom and elongated top and shoulders allow the wine to aerate and "soften." This means that the harsh tannins and acids dissipate while the fruit and softer tannins remain.

10. BURGUNDY OR PINOT NOIR GLASSES are for the lighter, softer red wines. These wines need to develop their aromas, which dissipate too quickly. Therefore, the glass is very wide at the bottom, then turns inward at the edge to trap and heighten the aroma of the wine, allowing the perfume of the lighter grapes to stay in the glass and not aerate too quickly.

11. MONTRACHET GLASSES are used for full-flavored and full bodied white wines such as Montrachet, Chablis, and California chardonnay. These wines benefit from the glass's wide, open shape, which allows air to enter and soften the acidity while enhancing the fruit.

12. AROMATIC WHITE WINEGLASSES are used for slightly sweet or fruit-forward wines such as Riesling that do not need to aerate. These smaller glasses keep the focus on the freshness of the wine, and the outward angling of the edge lets the wine hit the tongue in just the right spot for our taste buds to sense sweetness.

13. BRANDY SNIFTERS are specialized glasses that enhance the flavor and aroma of fine cognacs, Armagnacs, and brandies. The wide, bulbous bottom allows a great deal of air to hit the brandy, softening the harsh alcoholic vapors and enhancing the caramel notes in the brandy.

14. SHERRY COPITAS are very similar to port glasses but are slightly taller and narrower. This shape enhances the delicate aromas of sherries, allowing their complex scents and flavors to gently scoot up the glass.

15. GRAPPA OR EAU-DE-VIE GLASSES enhance the pronounced and assertive flavors of grappa with their tall, narrow shape. These glasses are generally small in volume, typically around 3 ounces or so. Most eaux-de-vie are very potent and drunk at the end of a meal when, presumably, wine or other alcohol has already been imbibed, so a little goes a long way. This glass also makes a very acceptable cordial glass. Also shown is a smaller antique cordial glass that will work with grappa or cordials just as well.

16. IRISH COFFEE MUGS are perfect for all manner of coffee drinks, nogs, grogs, and other hot beverages.

IN ADDITION it is helpful to have a *punch bowl* or large pitcher, as well as large glasses for serving tall frozen drinks. *Hurricane glasses,* shaped like hurricane lamps, typically hold around 15 ounces and are perfect for tropical drinks. *Tall cooler* or *iced-tea glasses* hold 16 to 20 ounces.

The Right Booze

Whole books have been written about many of the liquors essential to the home bar. I could not possibly discuss all the spirits here, so I'll distill them for you (excuse the pun), keeping to the basics and a few extras. Whenever I call for a spirit or ingredient not discussed here, I explain it in the "Straight Up" notes in the recipes that include it.

When stocking your bar, start with the basic spirits: vodka, gin, whiskey, rum, tequila, brandy, sweet and dry vermouth, and curaçao. From these you can make literally hundreds of great cocktails.

When choosing liquor for your home bar, do not use price as your only guide. Price alone does not ensure quality. Imported spirits generally cost more than similar domestic spirits because of the duties and import taxes, but imports are not always better. Tasting as many brands of liquor as possible is the best way to decide what you like. Within each category of liquor there are many different styles. Scotch, for example, can be either blended or single malt, and its flavor can range from smooth to smoky to salty. Moreover, within these styles the level of alcohol can vary. Bourbon is a great example of this: It comes in 86-proof versions as well as in 101-proof versions. (Proof is the measure of alcohol in liquor, and the number is always double the percentage of alcohol. In other words, if a liquor is 80 proof, it is 40 percent alcohol.) Both are great, but they appeal to different people for different reasons. Over time you will find the types you like and that work well for your entertaining style and your budget.

VODKA

Vodka was first produced in Russia at the end of the ninth century. Although Poland claims to have distilled it as early as the eighth century, the liquor was distilled wine, so it would actually have been more of a brandy. Either country, however, could lay claim to its name, which comes from the Russian word *voda* or the Polish *woda,* both of which mean "water."

Vodka is a rectified spirit (distilled three times) produced from grain or potatoes. Ninety percent of the vodka produced is grain based. Occasionally, and mainly in Europe, rice or molasses is used. Though colorless and odorless, vodka has a subtle taste. I find that potato-based vodkas, such as Pekonica from New York State and Luksusowa from Poland, have very distinctive flavors. Some vodkas are distinguished by their texture, which ranges from oily to watery. Taste and texture vary from producer to producer, and experimentation and sampling are the best way to decide what you like. Vodka is great to sip ice cold on its own and is wonderful mixed with other ingredients.

GIN

Gin seems to be going through a minor resurgence. In the 1920s and 1930s, at the height of the age of the cocktail, it was more often than not the drink of choice. But through the middle of the twentieth century, as vodka saw its star rise, gin fell out of favor because many people were afraid of its strong, pronounced flavor. Now, thanks to innovative bartenders, bars and restaurants have brought gin drinks back to front and center.

Gin is a distillate of cereal grains, especially corn and barley, although wheat and rye are also used. It is distilled three times (rectified), and during the distillation process aromatic herbs and spices called botanicals are infused into the base neutral spirit. All gin includes juniper, which gave the liquor its name: The Dutch who created gin in the sixteenth century called it *genievre,* which means "juniper." Other herbs and spices in the blend can include, but are not limited to, coriander, angelica, orange peel, lemon peel, cardamom, cinnamon, grains of paradise (a spice in the ginger family), cubeb berries (similar to black pepper berries, but primarily used for pickling and gin making), and nutmeg. Most gins contain six to ten different botanicals in the blend.

The two most prominent styles of gin are Dutch and London dry. Dutch gin is 70 to 80 proof (35 percent to 40 percent alcohol) and is made from rye, corn, and barley and distilled in pot stills. The botanical blend is added during fermentation, and the finished gin is aged in oak casks. This gin is excellent on its own or as a mixer. London dry gin is triple distilled and higher in alcohol than Dutch gin. The botanicals are added during the distillation process when the base spirit is actually in a vapor form before recondensing. This is a perfect martini gin or great as a mixer.

WHISKEY

Whiskey comprises a large, diverse family of spirits. Whiskeys are defined by several factors, including their three basic ingredients: grain, yeast, and water. Within these three ingredients are many variations that create a diverse array of end products. The type of yeast or base grain (corn, barley, rye, or wheat) and the water source have a dramatic effect on taste.

WHISKEY is thought to have first been created by the Irish in the twelfth century. The word *whiskey* derives its name from the Gaelic term *usque baugh* (oos-keh-baw), which means "water of life." *Blended whiskey* is the term for whiskeys that are made to promote a house style. These are generally a mix of whiskeys from different distilleries, each with a distinctive characteristic that gives its flavor to the final blend. Some give their whiskeys more smoke, others more sweetness or body. It is up to the master blender to determine how much of each goes into the final blend.

IRISH WHISKEY is based on malted barley and sometimes rye. Malting is a process by which the grains are allowed to partially germinate, thereby converting the natural starches to sugar, which in turn changes to alcohol. The malted grains are dried in a kiln before mashing and fermenting. The whiskey then undergoes its three-part distillation. After distillation, it is aged in casks until the desired house style is achieved.

SCOTCH goes through the very same process, with one exception: The malted grain is dried over peat fires, which give scotch its signature smoky profile. Scotch is often aged in old bourbon or sherry casks, and in some cases certain distilleries use both. These used barrels impart much subtler flavor than new, unused casks. Irish whiskey tends to be a bit mellower and sweeter than scotch, which has more bite and that smoky note.

BOURBON, which derives its name from Kentucky's Bourbon County, is made primarily from corn—up to 80 percent of the mash is corn, with the balance rye or wheat. The mash in any one bourbon is either of two types: sweet mash, a fresh mashed grain to which yeast is added to kick off the fermentation, or sour mash, which uses the residual mash from the prior fermentation to kick off the next batch. After fermentation, the base is distilled three times and allowed to age in new charred oak barrels. The charring of the barrels gives bourbon its smoky-sweet nose, and their being new adds to the pronounced sweet and sometimes vanilla notes in the end whiskey. Tennessee whiskey is similar in every way to bourbon except one: It undergoes filtration through charcoal before being aged in the charred oak barrels. This filtration process takes at least ten days.

RYE WHISKEY is made with a minimum of 51 percent rye by law. It is similar to bourbon, but has a more pronounced savory, spicy note.

RUM

Rum is made from molasses, sugarcane juice, or cane syrup. It was an important staple of Colonial America, and the first New World fortunes were often made by the rum producers of the British West Indies. There are three basic kinds of rum: light-bodied, medium-bodied, and heavy-bodied. Light-bodied rum, also called white or silver, is aged for up to one year in casks and is filtered before bottling, which makes the rum fairly neutral. Medium-bodied rum, often called gold or amber, is aged in wood longer than light rum and often has added caramel for even color. This rum is richer and smoother than light rum. Heavy-bodied rum has two distinctly different subcategories: blended rums and well-aged sipping rums. Blended rums are dark and heavily colored and have a distinct weight in the mouth. The well-aged sipping rums are kept in casks much longer than all other rums and take on a brandylike flavor; they are distinctive and should be sipped on their own, not mixed in drinks. Rum is produced all over the Caribbean and West Indies, with each island producing its own distinctive rums. Have some fun and treat yourself to an island comparison.

TEQUILA

Tequila, an interesting, delicious spirit, is made from the heart, or *piña*, of the blue agave cactus. Mexican law very strictly regulates the different categories of tequila, the main two of which are mixto and 100 percent agave. Mixto, as it sounds, is a mix: 51 percent agave mash and up to 49 percent other sugars, such as cane or beet; 100 percent agave is distilled solely from the blue agave plant. Within both mixto and 100 percent agave, there are four main subcategories: *blanco, joven abocado, reposado,* and *anejo. Blanco,* white, silver, or *plata* all mean the same thing: tequila that is aged fewer than sixty days in wood. *Joven abocado* is also known as gold tequila. The color comes from other flavoring and coloring agents. *Reposado* means "rested" in Spanish. These tequilas must age at least sixty days in wood, and many are aged at least a year; they can also have flavoring and coloring agents. *Anejo* means "aged," and by law it must spend at least a year in wood, though most actually spend a longer time. One hundred percent agave *anejo* is my favorite tequila. It has pronounced added complex earth notes and while it has a bite, the extra aging in wood mellows the sharp or bitter tones.

BRANDY

BRANDY is a broad term, encompassing a large family of spirits that includes many different and distinctive types. It is basically the fermented and distilled juice of grapes, apples, pears, plums, peaches, or almost any other fruit grown. More often than not, when we say *brandy,* we are referring to grape brandy, as that is the most prominent of all brandies. Any other type will be referred to by its fruit, such as apricot brandy, or by its stylistic name, such as calvados, which is apple brandy from Normandy, France. All brandies can be used in cocktail making, and you will see a variety of grape, apple, and other fruit brandies called for throughout this book.

Grape brandies are produced in many countries and in many styles, with the largest producers being France and Spain. Grape brandy starts out as wine, which is distilled and then aged in oak. The term *brandy* comes from the Dutch term *brandewijn,* meaning "burnt wine." It is blended, adjusted with water to the correct alcoholic strength, and often enhanced with caramel or other agents to produce a consistent house style.

In France there are two main types of aged grape brandies: cognac and Armagnac. The differences are actually quite pronounced.

COGNAC, based on a wine made from the ugni blanc grape, is distilled twice in pot stills and then aged in new white oak casks from the Limousin and Tronçais forests. It is aged and blended in a slow process that marries small proportions of older stocks with younger stocks to produce a consistent house style. The age of a cognac is indicated on its label by one of four designations. *V.S.* means "very superior." V.S. cognacs (which may alternatively be labeled Three-Star) are the youngest and are good values. *V.S.O.P.* means "very superior old pale." These are older than V.S. and more expensive. *Extra* and *Reserve* are placed on labels that include the house's oldest stocks of brandy and are the most expensive.

ARMAGNAC starts as a blended wine made mostly from the ugni blanc grape along with a variety of other grapes local to southwestern France, where the brandy is produced. It is distilled in a continuous still and is aged in black oak casks from the Monzelun forest. Armagnac's labeling is similar to cognac's: V.S., V.S.O.P., Extra, and Hors d'Age. The key difference is that Armagnacs are almost always older and can be vintage dated, meaning the wine from a specific harvest was used to create the brandy. To me, Armagnacs have a little more bite and more pronounced flavor than cognacs. Both are excellent, but one is not necessarily a substitute for the other.

SPANISH BRANDY is often a better value than other brandies on the market—half the cost of an equivalent bottle of V.S.O.P. cognac; the quality is generally high; and the flavor quite unique. Spanish brandies are made in the solera system, a complex method that is used to produce all the wonderful brandies and sherries from Spain. New brandy is placed in barrels in the front of a row or on top of a stack. Many decades' worth of older brandy is in barrels either behind or below the new barrels. Each year, small amounts of older brandy are added to the new, and sometimes some of the newer brandy is added to the barrels of older brandy. This continues for many, many vintages until the master blender determines the brandy is ready, and it is bottled. Spanish brandy is delicious. It is a little mellower and sweeter than other brandies and makes a great mixer.

CALVADOS is apple brandy from the Normandy region of France. Fermented apple cider is double distilled, then aged in wooden casks. It must spend at least one year in cask, and the average for good calvados is ten to fifteen years. Many are aged as long as thirty, forty, or fifty years. In the United States, we have a great apple brandy called applejack. Most people consider calvados to be the best apple brandy, and for sipping they might be right, but for cocktails applejack is a wonderful substitute.

VERMOUTH

Vermouth is a fortified and aromatized wine. The name comes from the German word *Wermut,* which means "wormwood," a plant that has a narcotic effect and was used in the early blends of many beverages— in general it is no longer used. Vermouth is made by infusing a base wine with roots, herbs, flowers, and even bark along with brandy and unfermented grape juice for sweetener. The mixture is then pasteurized, cold stabilized to remove impurities, filtered, and bottled. There are many different styles of aromatized wines and vermouths. Some are great for mixing, such as the basic sweet and dry vermouths. Others, such as Lillet or Dubonnet, Punt e Mes, Carpano Antiqua, and many others can also be served chilled on their own as an apertif. Vermouths are fairly inexpensive, considering that you use very small amounts in your cocktails. Take time to experiment with some of the better vermouths on the market and find your favorites. I keep several different varieties of both white and sweet vermouths on hand.

CURAÇAO

Curaçao comes in several different guises, and in any form it is indispensable to the home bar. Orange curaçao is a cordial made from the bitter oranges of the Caribbean island Curaçao. It was originally produced in France and is now made all over the world. Triple sec, mentioned throughout this book, is a type of curaçao. Cointreau, a French liqueur, is widely considered the best curaçao on the market. You can find white, orange, and blue curaçao. The only difference among the three is the addition of food coloring. For the most part, curaçao is used as a sweetener and flavoring agent for cocktails; it is almost never drunk neat.

Other Indispensable Items

BITTERS

One hundred years ago a cocktail would not have been a cocktail without the addition of bitters, an infusion of alcohol, herbs, spices, fruits, and roots. Bitters were, and are, indispensable to great cocktail making. Apothecaries throughout the country used to make their own bitters, and all claimed theirs to be "the tonic to cure what ails you." It's true that bitters and soda will settle the stomach, but beyond that, I'm not sure they're quite the cure-all they were once touted to be. Today there are three types of bitters: Angostura, Peychaud's, and orange. The three are quite different and not necessarily interchangeable. All are great balancers in a cocktail.

ANGOSTURA BITTERS, produced since 1830, derive their name from the Venezuelan town of Angostura (long since renamed Ciudad Bolívar). These bitters were developed by Dr. J.G.B. Siegert and were used as a curative for various ailments. Angostura bitters are the most widely used bitters among the three. They are also the darkest and most strongly flavored. The flavor of Angostura bitters is strong and herbaceous, with great acidity, just a hint of sweetness, and, of course, an appealing bitterness.

PEYCHAUD'S BITTERS were first produced in New Orleans by Antoine Amedee Peychaud in the early 1800s. He billed his bitters as the cure for just about whatever ailed you. Peychaud's bitters have a distinctive cherrylike flavor and go particularly well with rum and sweeter cocktails for balance. They are of medium weight and color, compared to Angostura bitters.

ORANGE BITTERS' light color and sublime bitter orange flavor enhance many different beverages. Orange bitters were once much more widely produced than they are today, but they're still fairly easy to find (see Mail-order Sources).

HOT SAUCES

Hot sauces are used mainly in the Bloody Mary (page 215); however, they are a wonderful way to add a drop of heat and complexity to any drink. Adding a dash of hot sauce to a vodka martini gives you a delicious quick version of the once-popular cajun martini. Hot sauce is a mash of peppers and salt that is aged in oak barrels for at least two years. Vinegar and perhaps more salt is added to the resulting liquid. Tabasco brand is the quintessential hot sauce and the most widely used and sold in America. It is a wonderful product made from tabasco peppers. Other styles of hot sauce are flavored with garlic, onions, and spices. Some use different peppers, such as the habanero, which is extremely hot, or the chipotle, which is smoky. Try a few kinds and use your favorite.

WORCESTERSHIRE SAUCE

Like hot sauce, Worcestershire sauce is mainly used in the Bloody Mary (page 215), but it can add a wonderful savory, meaty note to any cocktail— try adding a few drops to a Dirty Martini (page 74). Worcestershire sauce is a blend of vinegar, salt, many spices, garlic, herbs, peppers, tamarind, molasses, and other ingredients. The most prominent brand is Lea & Perrins, although with the growth of steak houses in the United States, other proprietary brands are quickly becoming available.

37 **WATER AND ICE**

38 **FRESH CITRUS JUICES**

38 **GARNISHES**

49 **HOMEMADE GARNISHES**

49 OVEN-DRIED TOMATO CHIPS

50 QUICK CARROT PICKLES

51 VERMOUTH-SOAKED OLIVES

52 COCKTAIL ONIONS

53 MARASCHINO CHERRIES

54 WHIPPED CREAM

55 **SYRUPS FROM SCRATCH**

56 SIMPLE SYRUP

56 BROWN SUGAR SYRUP

57 MINT SYRUP

58 VANILLA SYRUP

59 GINGER SYRUP

59 RUM SYRUP

60 VODKA SYRUP

60 RED WINE SYRUP

61 PINEAPPLE SYRUP

62 BERRY SYRUP

62 SPICED SYRUP

64 GRENADINE

65 **SOUR MIX**

65 LEMON OR LIME SOUR MIX

66 **CORDIALS AND BRANDIES**

66 BLACKBERRY CORDIAL

67 CRANBERRY CORDIAL

68 PEACH BRANDY

69 LIMONCELLO

THE BEST INGREDIENTS

WHEN ASKED WHAT MAKES THEIR COOKING SO WONDERFUL, GREAT CHEFS invariably stress using the freshest, most seasonal ingredients before they discuss their cooking style. Similarly, great winemakers refer to grapes picked at the peak of ripeness before revealing their winning winemaking methods. Both often add something about letting the natural flavors of the ingredients speak for themselves. So it is with great mixologists as well. Marrying the freshest, most natural juices and mixes with high-quality liquors heightens the cocktail experience for you and your guests. And while it is true that there are some wonderful prepared and packaged cocktail ingredients on the market—and I will recommend specific products whenever possible—I urge you to make your own juices, syrups, and mixes for maximum results.

Many of these juices, mixes, syrups, and garnishes can be prepared far in advance to save time. The syrups will last for several weeks in the refrigerator. Fresh citrus juices can be frozen for up to one month, and the Lemon or Lime Sour Mix (page 65) can be frozen for several months. I keep my refrigerator and freezer stocked with items I've prepared in advance, and when I'm entertaining, I even prepare most garnishes a few hours before the event. I like to get as much done in advance of my guests' arrival as possible so that I can enjoy the party right alongside them.

On the other hand, for anything that isn't done in advance, I bring my guests into the kitchen or bar with me to lend a hand. Many enjoy juicing the lemons or limes for our preprandials while I prepare the hors d'oeuvres. Some like learning the tricks of the trade, and most just love being a part of the process and are happy to help.

Water and Ice

Every cold cocktail depends on ice in some form or another, whether it's seen, as when the cocktail is served "on the rocks," or unseen, as when the drink is shaken or stirred with ice before being strained into a cocktail glass. It follows that the quality and clarity of the water used to make those cubes is vital. Tap water can often taste "fuzzy." Using an inexpensive water filter ensures a clean, clear quality to your drinking water and ice cubes.

On the other hand, for ease of use, you can't beat a refrigerator with a built-in ice maker that continuously provides instant crushed ice and a large quantity of ice cubes. Those ice cubes, however, are oftentimes small, oddly shaped, and cloudy and that makes a difference. If a cube is too small and fragile, it melts too quickly, diluting the drink and not keeping it cold for as long as it should. Cloudy cubes can be an indication that the water used has minerals and metals that can affect the taste of the drink. The cloudiness can also come from the rapid freezing of water. To achieve crystal-clear cubes—ideal for translucent drinks such as martinis on the rocks—fill the ice cube trays with *hot* water, filtered if possible. The longer freezing time allows the molecules to bond and solidify more slowly, thereby eliminating the cloudiness associated with faster freezing.

When entertaining a large group, opt for convenience and go with the ice-maker cubes. For a smaller group, keep three sizes of ice cube trays in the house and use different sizes for different drinks. For straight liquor served on the rocks, use the largest size available. For mixed drinks served on the rocks, such as an old-fashioned, use large cubes. For highballs and coolers, use smaller (not tiny) cubes that will fit more closely in the taller, narrower glass. And finally, for frappés and fun, slushy drinks, only crushed ice will do. To crush ice, put large cubes in a towel and whack the towel several times with a hammer (expel aggressions while entertaining guests!). Or buy an ice crusher; several moderately inexpensive models on the market are quite effective. If you do not have an ice crusher, crush the ice in advance and store in the freezer in a plastic bag. When you are ready to use it, gently drop the ice on the counter a few times to loosen.

For perfectly fitted, slow-melting ice cubes that will keep your drinks cold without diluting them, fill disposable plastic cups that fit just inside your rocks glasses with about 2 inches of hot water, filtered if possible, and freeze. When you're ready to serve the drinks, remove the frozen cups from the freezer and let them sit on the counter for a minute, then slide one "cup cube" into each rocks glass, pour the drink over it, and serve.

Fresh Citrus Juices

Nothing compares to the taste of freshly squeezed lemon, lime, orange, and grapefruit juices. The big question with fresh citrus juices is whether to leave the pulp in or strain it out. When it comes to straining the pulp for cocktails, the rules vary depending on how much juice goes into the drink. For highballs with lots of juice, such as the Blood Orange Sunrise (page 220) or the Bitter Pill (page 183), or when making Lemon or Lime Sour Mix (page 65), strain the pulp out. When less juice is called for, as in the Salty Dog (page 132) or the Pompano (page 131), leave the pulp in.

A good option for fast results is an electric citrus juicer. Most have settings to allow for more or less pulp. If you opt for less pulp, I recommend pouring the residual pulp into a fine-mesh strainer over a bowl and using a rubber spatula to scrape the pulp around the strainer to extract as much of the juice as possible.

When choosing citrus for juicing, pick the fruit with the thinnest skins, as they have more "meat" inside and therefore more juice to extract. Do not refrigerate citrus destined for juicing, as cold fruit yields less juice. Freshly squeezed juice should be stored in the refrigerator, for if left out, it will quickly sour. It can also be frozen for up to one month, especially convenient when you'll be needing a large quantity of fresh juice, as for the Lemon or Lime Sour Mix (page 65).

Nature is rarely consistent, but for the purposes of this book, you can safely assume the following:

1 lime = 1 ounce juice

1 lemon = $1\frac{1}{2}$ ounces juice

1 orange = $3\frac{1}{2}$ ounces juice

1 grapefruit = $6\frac{1}{2}$ ounces juice

1 quart juice = 5 large grapefruit, or 10 large oranges, or 24 to 30 large lemons or limes

There is a complete list of equivalent measurements on page 46.

Garnishes

Resist the temptation to garnish for garnish's sake, whether on a plate or in a glass. A garnish should be a fundamental part of the beverage—something that actually enhances the overall product visually, texturally, and flavorfully, taking into consideration the drink's proper balance. Two general rules for garnishing drinks include, first, using fresh or high-quality preserved ingredients—nothing ruins a good drink more than lifeless, shriveled adornment—and second, adding enough garnish to make it relevant—it should complement and even enhance the flavors of the drink. Be sure that all cleaning, drying, and cutting of garnishes is completed before you start mixing the drink. If you mix the drink before all of this prep work is done, the ice will begin to melt and water down the drink.

Here are the basics on garnishes and how to use them:

CITRUS TWISTS, ZEST, SWIRLS, AND WEDGES

To keep citrus twists, zest, swirls, and wedges fresh for a few hours, place them in a small cup or bowl, generously moisten a paper towel with ice water, and lay it flush against the top of the garnish.

TWISTS are 1- to 1½-inch-long oval or rectangular slivers of lemon, lime, orange, grapefruit, or other citrus rind. Twists are, in fact, twisted over a cocktail, releasing their essential oils into the drink. Thicker-skinned, evenly colored fresh, ripe fruits produce more of the fruit's essential oils than thin-skinned ones yield.

To make twists, start by cutting off the "polar" nubs at each end of the fruit. Then place the fruit on one flat end and use a paring knife to gently cut off a slice of the rind, starting at the top and working your way downward. Try not to get too much of the bitter white pith. Alternatively, you may use a vegetable peeler. Hold the fruit firmly in the palm of your hand. Starting at one end and cutting straight toward the other end, carefully and steadily remove a slice of the rind.

To get the most flavor out of the twist, hold it between both hands an inch or two over the cocktail, pith side up. Gently twist the ends in opposite directions, releasing the essential oils. Rub the skin side onto the rim and inner lip of the cocktail glass, then drop the twist so that it floats on the drink. This will allow the essential oil to sit on top of the cocktail and give it the citrus flavor you want without getting lost.

ZEST is either fine strands or finely grated rind of citrus fruits. Zest is dropped in a cocktail or steeped in liquor to add subtle citrus flavor, producing less essential oil than a twist, but more intrinsic fruit aromas.

For zest used to flavor salt or sugar for rimming a glass, or to sprinkle on top of a cooler, use a fine-toothed cheese grater or nutmeg grater. Hold the whole fruit in your hand and gently grate off the outer skin of the fruit, leaving the bitter white pith.

For a longer, more substantial zest to be used as you would a twist, use a citrus zester. This small hand tool has five or six tiny holes at the end of what looks like a palette knife. Holding the fruit firmly in your hand, dig the small holes into the skin of the citrus fruit and scrape off long, fine strands.

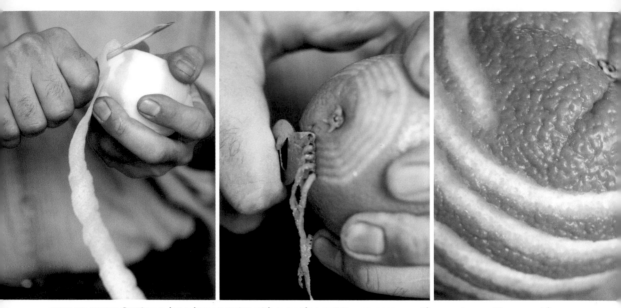

LEFT TO RIGHT: **Cutting a long lemon twist with a peeler, cutting an orange with a zester, cutting a swirl**

Long zest works best in hot, healing drinks, such as the Green Tea Toddy (page 235), because it constantly releases gentle, aromatic whiffs of citrus.

SWIRLS, often called horseneck garnish, are long strips of zest cut from the circumference of the fruit so they have a curly, springy look. They add flavor and a festive feel to your drink. Long swirls (3 to 4 inches long) are generally used in tall, cooler-type drinks. Shorter swirls are used in drinks served in rocks glasses or are perched on the edge of a cocktail served straight up.

You can use two different tools to make swirls. A channel knife has a rounded or rectangular metal head with a small curved blade and hole on either the side or the top. Sometimes the tool is double-headed, with a channel knife on one end and a zester on the other. To use a channel knife, hold the citrus fruit firmly in your hand, dig the curved blade into its skin, and pull it around the circumference (instead of from top to bottom).

You can also use a vegetable peeler, which will make wider swirls than the channel knife. Hold the citrus fruit firmly in one hand, dig the peeler into the skin of the fruit, and peel around the circumference of the fruit.

WEDGES are either used to garnish the top of a drink or are muddled (see page 22) in the drink. The two types of wedges are cut differently, but the same rule applies: Use good, fresh, ripe fruit.

Generally, the only citrus fruit cut into garnish wedges are lemons or limes. Oranges and grapefruit are too large for this sort of presentation. To prepare these wedges, cut off the nubs at each end of the fruit, then cut it in half lengthwise. Lay the two halves flat side down on the cutting board and, holding the knife at a 45-degree angle, cut each half lengthwise into three wedges. Trim the pithy core and scrape any seeds from each wedge.

For muddling wedges of lemon or lime, cut off the nubs at each end of the fruit, then cut it in half lengthwise. Lay the two halves flat side down on the cutting board. Cut each in half lengthwise, then turn the wedges 90 degrees and cut the halves in half once again. Trim the pithy core and scrape any seeds from each wedge.

For muddling wedges of orange, cut off the ends of the fruit. Slice it into rounds, then cut each round in half or in quarters.

SUGAR, SALT, AND SPICES

Sugar, salt, and spices are perhaps the most dramatic garnishes in terms of their overall effect on the look, and especially the flavor, of the finished cocktail. It's therefore quite important to use the highest-quality products you can find. See the technique for rimming a glass on page 22.

SUGAR is processed many different ways, and each type has its role in cocktails. White sugar comes in three forms: regular granulated, superfine, and powdered confectioners' sugar. Granulated is the most common type, perfect for coating, or "rimming," a glass's rim. Superfine sugar is ground into very fine granules. If you can't find it, process granulated sugar in the food processor for the same effect. Confectioners' sugar is ground to a powder and has cornstarch added to keep it fluffy and light. Superfine and confectioners' sugars dissolve very quickly when shaken or stirred with other ingredients, so they are useful in drinks that are being made "à la minute," or at the moment you're serving them (a common practice in good bars and restaurants). On the other hand, they are not good for rimming a glass.

Next there are the flavorful brown sugars, of which turbinado is a favorite for drinks. Turbinado is granulated sugar that still has some molasses (hence its brown color), but not as much as regular light or dark brown sugars, so it is less moist and sticky than these. Its texture is very similar to kosher salt: big grains that are fairly even in size. The grains are gently abrasive when they touch your lips but dissolve quickly, releasing their flavor. The color, texture, and flavor of turbinado make it more interesting than regular granulated sugar, so I prefer it for rimming glasses.

The more common light or dark brown sugar can also be used for rimming a glass, but it takes a bit of practice to get it right. Its high molasses content makes it sticky, so when rimming, you will need to work more diligently to achieve an even coating. Your efforts will be well rewarded, however, as brown sugar has great flavor and texture; it is especially wonderful with drinks based on fall fruits such as apples and pears, including the Apple Crush (page 112).

KOSHER SALT AND SEA SALT are best for garnishing. Regular table salt and kosher salt are mined as large rocks or crystals, which are then ground to various sizes. In a pinch, table salt will work fine for rimming a glass, but coarser salt works better as a garnish. The larger grains of kosher salt have more complex flavors and give a rimmed glass a more frosted look. Sea salt often takes on the color and flavor of the minerals in the water from which it comes. It comes in many colors: white, gray, red, and even black. Sea salt is by far my favorite salt to use in cocktails—it has more mineral flavor and also an uneven texture that is appealing—but it can be expensive, so use it prudently. Note that specific types of salt are called for in each recipe: *Salt* refers to ordinary table salt; kosher and sea salts are called for by name.

SPICES such as ground black pepper, allspice, juniper, mace, cinnamon, and nutmeg can be used to garnish drinks. The key to using spices in cocktails is to use them sparingly. Used judiciously, they add extra dimension to the drink, but overused, they can become overpowering, adding bitterness and astringency.

The best way to garnish with spices is either to mix them with sugar for rimming the glass—this balances their bitterness—or lightly sprinkle or grate them over a cocktail, as with the Planter's Punch (page 87), served with freshly grated nutmeg.

FRUITS, VEGETABLES, AND HERBS

Fruits, vegetables, and herbs add not only flavor to a drink, but texture and color as well.

PINEAPPLE WEDGES are used for all sorts of summer and tropical cocktails, especially rum-based drinks. To prepare pineapple wedges, cut the top off a pineapple. Lay the pineapple on its side and cut ³⁄₄-inch round slices. Lay each slice flat on the cutting board and cut it into six or eight wedges, depending on the size of the pineapple. Cut a slit into the point or side of each wedge to prop it on the edge of the glass.

BERRIES, when in season in spring and summer, enhance the look of any drink. Choose fruit that is bright and uniformly colored. If the stem end of the berry is white, as with a strawberry, it is usually less flavorful than a berry with even color. Avoid off-season berries produced in hothouses or shipped in from other countries; they're rarely very flavorful. Dried fruit

CLOCKWISE FROM TOP LEFT: Turbinado sugar, Hawaiian red Alaea sea salt, kosher salt, gray sea salt, dark brown sugar, confectioners' sugar, rock salt

CLOCKWISE FROM TOP LEFT: Vermouth-Soaked Olives (page 51), caper berries, Oven-Dried Tomato Chips (page 49), Quick Carrot Pickles (page 50), Cocktail Onions (page 52), Maraschino Cherries (page 53), Candied Grapefruit Peel (page 149) is usually a better alternative than fresh off-season fruit, and frozen fruit is more than acceptable in flavored syrups and some garnishes. Wash fresh berries just before using them by rinsing under a gentle stream of cold water and laying them flat in a single layer on paper towels to dry.

To use berries as garnish, either float them on top of the cocktail or spear them like an olive. You can also make a small slice in the narrow end of a large berry, such as a strawberry, and place it on the rim of the glass.

If you have extra berries that you are afraid will spoil, turn them into drunken berries to extend their life. Place them in a container with a tight-fitting lid and add rum, vodka, or even gin to cover them by 1 inch. Cover them tightly and refrigerate for up to 2 weeks. Turn them into a summer highball by dropping a few berries in a glass with a bit of the liquor, adding some ice, and topping it off with seltzer.

OLIVES can be as important as the liquor in some drinks, especially martinis. When choosing from the many types of olives available, always buy the best quality. Use either fresh, large, green olives or salty, black, dry-cured olives. For sublime martini olives, soak them in vermouth and spices (see page 51)—the juice adds a spicy, salty vibrancy to the Dirty Martini (page 74).

ONIONS can mean the difference between a mediocre drink and a sublime one. Just ask a Gibson (page 75) drinker, for no one better understands the value of a good cocktail onion. You can often find a good brand of pickled or cured pearl onions in the section of your grocery store where olives are sold. When choosing prepared cocktail onions, try to avoid ones that are simply brine cured, as they have no flavor. If you cannot find a good brand, make homemade, easy-to-prepare Cocktail Onions (page 52). They are delicious and well worth your time.

CAPER BERRIES are the fruit of the caper bush, *Capparis spinosa*, grown widely throughout Europe and the Middle East. It is a sprawling and tenacious plant whose unopened buds are pickled and sold as the familiar small *capers*. Caper *berries*, sold pickled or brined, resemble a large grape with a long stem and are olive green in color. They make an excellent garnish for the Bloody Mary (page 215) or Rosmarino (page 129), or any cocktail that can be improved by their assertive and refreshingly bitter flavors.

HERBS add complexity to cocktails, and when savory herb-based drinks are served before a meal that features the same or a similar herb, they complement the food perfectly. The bases of many of the drinks in this book are herb infusions. Herbs, especially mint, can also be used in some muddled drinks (see page 22) and a few others make especially good garnishes, such as fresh bay or basil leaves floating on a martini (see page 22). When using herbs in a drink, pick the freshest, most vibrant ones you can find, rinse them gently in very cold water, then lay them on a towel to dry. When muddling herbs, remember that it is not necessary to pulverize them; you want only to gently bruise the herb so that its essential oils are released.

MEASUREMENTS AND CONVERSIONS

Most of the recipes in this book measure liquids in ounces, which is common practice when mixing drinks. Use this chart to find the equivalent for measurements; they are rounded off for ease of use.

LIQUID (VOLUME)

AMERICAN	IMPERIAL	METRIC
⅛ tsp (1 dash)		
¼ tsp		1.25 ml
½ tsp		2.5 ml
1 tsp		5 ml
½ Tbs (1½ tsp)	¼ fl oz	7.5 ml
1 Tbs (3 tsp)	½ fl oz	15 ml
1½ Tbs (4½ tsp)	¾ fl oz	
2 Tbs (⅛ cup)	1 fl oz	30 ml
3 Tbs	1½ fl oz	45 ml
3½ Tbs	1¾ fl oz	
¼ cup (4 Tbs)	2 fl oz	60 ml
⅓ cup (5 Tbs)	2½ fl oz	75 ml
⅜ cup (6 Tbs)	3 fl oz	90 ml
½ cup (8 Tbs)	4 fl oz	125 ml
¾ cup (12 Tbs)	6 fl oz	175 ml
1 cup (16 Tbs)	8 fl oz	250 ml
1½ cups	12 fl oz	350 ml
1 pint (2 cups)	16 fl oz	500 ml
3 cups	24 fl oz	750 ml
1 quart (4 cups)	32 fl oz	1 liter
1 gallon (4 quarts)	128 fl oz	4 liters

SOLID (WEIGHT)

US/UK	METRIC
½ oz	15 g
1 oz	30 g
2 oz	60 g
3 oz	90 g
4 oz	115 g
5 oz	140 g
6 oz	170 g
7 oz	200 g
8 oz	225 g
9 oz	250 g
10 oz	300 g
11 oz	325 g
12 oz	340 g
13 oz	375 g
14 oz	400 g
15 oz	425 g
1 lb	450 g

OVEN TEMPERATURES

FAHRENHEIT	GAS MARK	CELSIUS
250	½	120
275	1	140
300	2	150
325	3	160
350	4	180
375	5	190
400	6	200
425	7	220
450	8	230
475	9	240
500	10	260

A NOTE ABOUT IMPERIAL MEASUREMENTS

If converting the measurements called for in this book to Imperial, or British, measurements, note the following:

1 US cup = 8 ounces
1 Imperial cup = 10 ounces
1 US pint = 16 ounces
1 Imperial pint = 20 ounces
2 US tablespoons = 3 Imperial tablespoons

Adjust the measurements called for in this book downward accordingly when preparing these recipes using implements based on the Imperial system.

Homemade Garnishes

In addition to the previously mentioned garnishes, there are a few that can be made easily in your own kitchen. The investment in time will more than pay off in taste. Rather than a typical celery stick for the Bloody Mary (page 215), Quick Carrot Pickles (page 50) make a far more interesting counterpoint to the spicy tomato mixture. Two drinks specifically developed around homemade Maraschino Cherries (page 53) are the Maraschino Old-fashioned (page 131) and the nonalcoholic Maraschino Muddle (page 246). Try the Cocktail Onions (page 52) and Vermouth Soaked Olives (page 51) in your next martini (page 73) or Gibson (page 75). And, finally, homemade Whipped Cream (page 54) is an indispensable topping for hot drinks such as Kentucky Cappuccino (page 230) and Chestnut Hot Chocolate (page 164).

Oven-Dried Tomato Chips

Makes about 1 dozen chips, enough for 12 drinks

These slow-roasted, intense-flavored tomatoes produce a tangy, sweet garnish. The chefs at Gramercy Tavern garnished roasted fish with these, and it was there that I discovered the magic they brought to the Basil Mary (page 215). They'll do the same for just about any savory drink.

PLANNING AHEAD Can be made up to 24 hours in advance and stored in a single layer on wax paper at room temperature or in the refrigerator.

Preheat the oven to 200°F. Line a baking sheet with parchment paper. Arrange the tomato slices on the baking sheet.

Roast the tomato in the oven until the slices are dry to the touch and can be picked up between thumb and forefinger without breaking, 1 to 2 hours, depending on the ripeness of the tomato.

When they are done, remove the tomato chips from the oven and allow them to cool on the baking sheet until just above room temperature, about 15 minutes. Using a thin spatula, gently lift the chips off the sheet and transfer to a plate covered with wax paper.

Just before using, sprinkle with salt to taste.

1 large tomato, sliced crosswise into ⅛-inch slices

Kosher salt

Quick Carrot Pickles

Makes 2 dozen pickles, enough for 24 drinks
(photograph on page 48)

2 dozen baby carrots, trimmed, with green stems attached

1½ cups sherry vinegar, white wine vinegar, or cider vinegar

1 cup water

½ cup sugar

1 tablespoon salt

½ teaspoon coriander seed

¼ teaspoon fennel seed

¼ teaspoon mustard seed

12 allspice berries

12 peppercorns

6 juniper berries

2 whole star anise

2 whole cloves

1 dried chile

1 bay leaf

These tasty pickled carrots are a delicious and colorful alternative to onions or olives in martinis, to celery stalks in the Bloody Mary (page 215), and the perfect accompaniment to the Greenmarket Gibson (page 123). This recipe is very forgiving, so don't worry if you don't have every spice it calls for. Feel free to use more or less of one or another based on what you have on hand. Try adding a handful of trimmed baby radishes to the recipe—they're fantastic in just about any vodka drink.

There will be a lot of pickling liquid with the carrots. Use some of this liquid to replace some of the vinegar or other acid in salad dressing or as part of the base mix in a Bloody Mary.

PLANNING AHEAD Can be made up to 1 month in advance and stored in the refrigerator.

Bring a large pot of water to a boil. Prepare an ice bath in a large bowl. Add the carrots to the boiling water and blanch for 30 seconds. Drain the carrots in a colander, then immediately place them in the ice bath.

Place all of the remaining ingredients in a medium saucepan and bring to a boil.

Drain the carrots from the ice bath and add to the saucepan. Turn off the heat. Allow the carrots to cool in the cooking liquid, 15 to 20 minutes.

Transfer the carrots and liquid to a container with a tight-fitting lid and store in the refrigerator.

Vermouth-Soaked Olives

Makes 35 to 40 large olives or 45 to 50 small to medium olives, enough for 20 to 25 drinks

These olives make a great addition to a tray of noshes before dinner, or a simple accompaniment to a hunk of pecorino and some sopressata. And for garnishing martinis, there simply is no comparison to the jarred and brined variety.

PLANNING AHEAD If you use large, firm, green olives—those that have a waxy look—you can make this recipe up to 1 week in advance. If you use softer green olives—those that look slightly shriveled, with papery-looking skin—make them no more than 24 hours in advance or they will plump up too much.

Place the water, salt, red pepper flakes, peppercorns, garlic, rosemary, and thyme in a small saucepan. Bring to a boil, then immediately remove the pan from the heat. Add the vermouth and olive oil and stir well.

Let cool to room temperature. Stir in the olives and transfer to a container with a tight-fitting lid. Refrigerate until ready to use.

1 cup water

¼ cup salt

1 teaspoon red pepper flakes

1 teaspoon peppercorns

6 cloves garlic

1 branch fresh rosemary or 1 teaspoon dried rosemary

1 branch fresh thyme or ¼ teaspoon dried thyme

1 cup vermouth

½ cup extra virgin olive oil

1 pound pitted large green olives

Cocktail Onions

Makes 2 to 4 dozen onions, depending on the size of the onions, enough for 12 to 24 drinks

1 pound pearl onions

½ cup sherry vinegar or white vinegar

½ cup cider vinegar

½ cup water

½ cup salt

¼ cup sugar

½ teaspoon mustard seed

24 juniper berries

12 peppercorns

6 allspice berries

1 rosemary branch or
1 teaspoon dried rosemary

1 dried chile pepper

1 cup dry vermouth

Store-bought cocktail onions, which are generally brined, or stored in salt and water, have a salty, one-dimensional flavor, and not much in common with onions. These cocktail onions, on the other hand, actually taste like onions, and their flavor is maximized with spices, vermouth, and a tangy acidity from the vinegar. Try them in your next Gibson (page 75) and you'll never go back to the store-bought variety again.

PLANNING AHEAD Can be made up to 1 month in advance and stored in the refrigerator.

To peel the onions, place them in a large bowl and pour boiling water over them just to cover. Let stand for 1 minute. Drain and rinse under cold running water. Using a paring knife, cut off the root ends of the onions and peel off the thin outer skins.

Add all of the remaining ingredients except the vermouth to a medium saucepan and bring to a boil.

Add the onions to the saucepan, reduce the heat, and simmer for 2 minutes. Remove the pan from the heat and allow the onions to cool in the liquid.

Stir in the vermouth. Transfer the cooled onions and liquid to a container with a tight-fitting lid. Store in the refrigerator.

Maraschino Cherries

Makes 2 to 3 dozen cherries, enough for 12 drinks

A world apart from the cloying, artificially red maraschino cherries available at the supermarket, this homemade version requires very little effort. Though it is used sparingly, the grape juice adds body and complexity to the syrup, enhancing the flavor and color of the cherries and balancing out any unripe undertones. The star anise adds a hint of the exotic; if it's unavailable, cardamom or cinnamon can be used instead. Almond, a traditional pairing with cherry, adds a mellow roundness to the cherries. The melding of these flavors happens during the long steeping in the refrigerator. These maraschino cherries are the inspiration for the creation of the Maraschino Old-fashioned (page 131) and the nonalcoholic Maraschino Muddle (page 246). They're also fantastic over ice cream or a slice of warm, toasted pound cake. During the winter when fresh cherries are not available, substitute frozen cherries.

PLANNING AHEAD Can be made up to 2 weeks in advance and stored in the refrigerator. The cherries are ready as soon as they are cool but are better if steeped at least 24 hours.

In a nonreactive saucepan, add the water, grape juice, sugar, lemon juice, salt, and star anise. Place over medium-high heat and bring to a boil. Reduce the heat and simmer the mixture until the sugar has dissolved.

Add the cherries and almond extract. Simmer on low heat for 10 minutes or until the cherries have exuded some of their juice and the syrup has taken on a distinctly cherry flavor. Be careful not to overcook. The point is not to actually cook the cherries, but to heat them in the syrup just long enough to bring out their essence.

Remove the pan from the heat, transfer the cherries and the syrup to a bowl, and let cool to room temperature. Transfer to a container with a tight-fitting lid, cover tightly, and refrigerate. The longer the cherries steep, the more flavorful they will become.

QUICK MARASCHINOS When fresh cherries are at their ripest and juiciest during the summer, you can easily prepare quick homemade maraschinos. Sprinkle a handful of pitted cherries with a teaspoon or two of sugar, stir, and refrigerate for 1 hour before garnishing.

1½ cups water

½ cup red grape juice (use 100% juice)

1 cup sugar

3½ ounces fresh lemon juice (from approximately 3 lemons)

Pinch of salt

1 whole piece star anise

1 pound sweet cherries, pitted

1 teaspoon almond extract

Whipped Cream

Makes 2 cups whipped cream, enough for 8 large dollops

2 cups cold heavy cream

2 tablespoons sugar

1 teaspoon vanilla extract

Vanilla "Cocoa" (page 164) topped with whipped cream

Whipped cream is an indispensable topping for nogs (pages 155 to 157), and for coffee drinks, such as Christmas Eve Chocolate (page 163). Whipped cream lends itself to numerous improvisations. I prefer the cream to be whipped until fairly stiff—too soft and it won't hold up in a hot drink, collapsing into a milky coating. For perfectly whipped cream, use the freshest cream possible and use it right from the refrigerator so it is at its coldest. It also helps to chill both the mixing bowl and the whisk or whisk attachment beforehand.

PLANNING AHEAD If possible, place the mixing bowl and whisk in the refrigerator at least 1 hour before whipping the cream. Whipped cream can be made several hours in advance and kept, covered, in the refrigerator.

Add the cream right from the refrigerator to a chilled bowl. Using a whisk or an electric mixer, start whipping the cream on high speed. When the cream begins to stiffen, add the sugar and vanilla. Continue whipping until soft peaks form, turning the mixer down slightly as the cream gets stiffer.

Use immediately or scrape down the sides of the bowl, place plastic wrap flush against the surface of the whipped cream, and refrigerate for several hours.

TANGY WHIPPED CREAM Add 2 tablespoons cold sour cream to the heavy cream before you start whipping. This tangier flavor is especially good in Hot Chocolate Chocolate (page 163).

CHOCOLATY WHIPPED CREAM Sift 2 tablespoons unsweetened cocoa into the sugar before beating it into the cream for a subtle chocolate flavor that goes well with any coffee drink (pages 228 to 232) or Chestnut Hot Chocolate (page 164).

SPICED WHIPPED CREAM Sift 1 teaspoon cinnamon into the sugar before beating it into the cream to add an exotic note to any coffee drink (pages 228 to 232) or the Thanksgiving Nog (page 156).

BACK LEFT TO RIGHT: **Spiced Syrup (page 62)**, **Ginger Syrup (page 59)**, **Vanilla Syrup (page 58)**, **Pineapple Syrup (page 61)**, **Berry Syrup (page 62)**, **Simple Syrup (page 56)**, **Mint Syrup (page 57)**; FRONT: **Red Wine Syrup (page 60)**

Syrups from Scratch

Simple syrup allows sugar, which has been heated in water and dissolved, to blend more easily than granulated sugar into iced tea, coffee, and lemonade. They may also "float" on top of a cocktail (see page 22 for the proper floating technique). The use of different sugars, herbs, and fruits adds zest and complexity to any nonalcoholic drink or cocktail. Berry, cherry, mint, or ginger syrups can be used to create your own cocktails or flavored margaritas or sours. Since the syrups last several weeks in the refrigerator, you can use part of a batch and save the rest for later. Just be sure that you store the syrup in a glass or stainless steel container. You can use plastic, but it must be very clean or, preferably, brand new, because plastic absorbs flavors, some of which are quite difficult to eliminate entirely, even with scrupulous cleaning. Delicate syrups will take on those flavors; this is not as much of an issue with heartier syrups, such as those made with vodka.

Simple Syrup

Makes 2 cups syrup (photograph on page 55)

2 cups sugar

1 cup water

This recipe for plain sugar syrup provides the base for most of the syrup recipes that follow.

PLANNING AHEAD Can be made up to 2 weeks in advance and stored in a very clean container in the refrigerator (see page 55).

Place the sugar and water in a small saucepan and stir to combine. Bring to a gentle boil over medium-high heat. Reduce the heat and simmer until the sugar is completely dissolved and the syrup is slightly thickened, about 3 minutes.

Remove from the heat and let cool. Transfer the syrup to a container with a tight-fitting lid, cover, and refrigerate until ready to use.

Brown Sugar Syrup

Makes 2 cups syrup

2 cups brown sugar

1 cup water

Brown sugar syrup's rich flavor blends well with dark rum and adds a chocolaty note to whatever drink it is blended with. It must be used judiciously, however, for its potency can actually overpower the other ingredients in a drink. Use it in hot beverages such as Kentucky Cappuccino (page 230) or Mocha Rum Toddy (page 230).

PLANNING AHEAD Can be made up to 2 weeks in advance and stored in a very clean container in the refrigerator (see page 55).

Place the sugar and water in a small saucepan and stir to combine. Bring to a gentle boil over medium-high heat. Reduce the heat and simmer until the sugar is completely dissolved and the syrup is slightly thickened, about 3 minutes.

Remove from the heat and let cool. Transfer the syrup to a container with a tight-fitting lid, cover, and refrigerate until ready to use.

Mint Syrup
Makes 2 cups syrup (photograph on page 55)

Use this staple drink ingredient to sweeten iced tea and Limeade (page 241) or just about any cocktail or highball made with rum, gin, or vodka. You'll find it called for specifically in the Tea & Whiskey Highball (page 180).

PLANNING AHEAD Can be made up to 2 weeks in advance and stored in a very clean container in the refrigerator (see page 55).

Place the mint, sugar, and water in a small saucepan and stir to combine. Bring to a gentle boil over medium-high heat. Reduce the heat and simmer until the sugar is completely dissolved and syrup is slightly thickened, about 5 minutes.

Remove from the heat and let cool. When the syrup is cool, remove the mint and reserve it for another use (see Trick of the Trade and Bonus from the Bar). Transfer to a container with a tight-fitting lid, cover, and refrigerate the syrup until ready to use.

1 bunch mint, approximately 3 ounces, rinsed, with roots trimmed

2 cups sugar

1 cup water

TRICK OF THE TRADE

The reserved cooked mint can be stored for up to 1 day in the refrigerator. Pull off some of the large leaves and add them right to your highball for color and more flavor. Or you can use the whole bunch of mint in the recipe below.

BONUS FROM THE BAR

MINT RUB FOR GRILLED CHICKEN OR LAMB Chop the cooked mint leaves from the mint syrup and place them in a small bowl. Add ½ teaspoon each of cumin, salt, and ground black pepper, ¼ teaspoon cayenne pepper, ⅛ teaspoon ground allspice, ¼ cup olive oil, and the freshly squeezed juice of 2 lemons and mix well. Rub on 4 lamb chops or 4 bone-in chicken breast halves, refrigerate for 30 minutes, and grill.

Vanilla Syrup

Makes 2 cups syrup (photograph on page 55)

2 cups sugar

1 cup water

1 whole vanilla bean

This subtle variation of simple syrup can be used interchangeably with the basic version. Vanilla syrup can be used for sweetening Lemonade (page 239), Limeade (page 241), or other nonalcoholic beverages and wherever a hint of vanilla flavor might brighten a cocktail. It works particularly well with rum and brandy drinks.

PLANNING AHEAD Can be made up to 2 weeks in advance and stored in a very clean container in the refrigerator (see page 55).

Place the sugar and water in a small saucepan and stir to combine.

Split the vanilla bean in half lengthwise. With the back of a small knife, scrape out the seeds and add the seeds and the bean halves to the saucepan.

Bring to a gentle boil over medium-high heat. Reduce the heat and simmer until the sugar is completely dissolved and the syrup is slightly thickened, about 3 minutes.

Remove from the heat and let cool. When the syrup is cool, remove the vanilla bean halves (don't discard them; see Bonus from the Bar) and transfer it to a container with a tight-fitting lid, cover, and refrigerate until ready to use.

BONUS FROM THE BAR

VANILLA ACCENTS Let the used vanilla bean halves dry overnight on paper towels. (They can be stored for up to 2 weeks, lightly wrapped in paper towels and placed in an airtight container.) To add a subtle vanilla flavor to your coffee, add them to the filter with the ground coffee and brew a potful as you normally would. Or toss them into the sugar jar, where they will add a wonderful aroma to the sugar.

Ginger Syrup

Makes 2 cups syrup (photograph on page 55)

Ginger syrup is the base for the Gin-ger & Tonic (page 130). It is perfect in all tea drinks and blends incredibly well with whiskey. Try combining it with green tea and lemon for great relief from the common cold.

PLANNING AHEAD Can be made up to 2 weeks in advance and stored in a very clean container in the refrigerator (see page 55).

Place all ingredients in a small saucepan and stir to combine. Bring to a gentle boil over medium-high heat. Reduce the heat and simmer until the sugar is completely dissolved and the syrup is slightly thickened, 2 to 3 minutes.

   Remove from the heat and remove and discard the ginger pieces. Let cool, then strain the syrup into a container with a tight-fitting lid, cover, and refrigerate until ready to use.

2 cups sugar

1 cup water

One 3-inch length of gingerroot, peeled and cut into six ½-inch pieces

2 tablespoons fresh lime juice (from approximately 1 lime)

Rum Syrup

Makes 2 cups syrup

The rich taste of dark rum makes this syrup far more than a simple sweetener in a drink. Use it in the Sparkling Rum Runner (page 143) and in the Triple Rum Martini (page 132), or in place of simple syrup in other rum-based beverages where it will really enhance the drink.

PLANNING AHEAD Can be made up to 6 weeks in advance and stored in a very clean container in the refrigerator (see page 55).

Place the sugar and rum in a small saucepan and stir to combine. Bring to a gentle boil over medium-high heat. Reduce the heat and simmer until the sugar is completely dissolved and the syrup is slightly thickened, about 3 minutes.

   Remove from the heat and let cool. Transfer the syrup to a container with a tight-fitting lid, cover, and refrigerate until ready to use.

2 cups sugar

1 cup dark rum

Vodka Syrup

Makes 1 cup syrup

2 cups sugar

1 cup vodka

Hard syrups (those made with spirits) have a more pronounced bite than their nonalcoholic cousins. This syrup adds a subtle sweetness to vodka cocktails without losing the essential vodka flavor. Use it in the Goose Berry (page 210) and in recipes that call for moistening or soaking cake layers or cookies.

PLANNING AHEAD Can be made up to 6 weeks in advance and stored in a very clean container in the refrigerator (see page 55).

Place the sugar and vodka in a small saucepan and stir to combine. Bring to a gentle boil over medium-high heat. Reduce the heat and simmer until the sugar is completely dissolved and the syrup is slightly thickened, about 3 minutes.

Remove from the heat and let cool. Transfer the syrup to a container with a tight-fitting lid, cover, and refrigerate until ready to use.

VANILLA VODKA SYRUP Use vanilla vodka in place of the regular vodka.

CITRUS-FLAVORED VODKA SYRUP Use lemon- or orange-flavored vodka in place of the regular vodka.

Red Wine Syrup

Makes 3 cups syrup (photograph on page 55)

2 cups red wine

2 cups sugar

Use a fruity, medium-bodied wine, such as California merlot or Spanish Garnacha. A heavy Bordeaux, bold zinfandel, or Shiraz may be overpowering. Try this syrup in a Brandywine Sour (page 151) or the Park Avenue (page 146).

PLANNING AHEAD Can be made up to 3 weeks in advance and stored in a very clean container in the refrigerator (see page 55).

Place the red wine and sugar in a small saucepan and stir to combine. Bring to a gentle boil over medium-high heat. Reduce the heat and simmer until the sugar is completely dissolved and the syrup is slightly thickened, about 15 minutes.

Remove from the heat and let cool. Transfer the syrup to a container with a tight-fitting lid, cover, and refrigerate until ready to use.

Pineapple Syrup

Makes 3½ cups syrup (photograph on page 55)

So much more luscious than simple pineapple juice, pineapple syrup transforms many nonalcoholic drinks into something really special. It's also great served with rum and lemon juice. The leftover pineapple can be used as a topping for ice cream or the base of a delectable glaze for baked ham (see Bonus from the Bar).

1 small pineapple

3 cups sugar

1½ cups water

PLANNING AHEAD Can be made up to 1 week in advance and stored in a very clean container in the refrigerator (see page 55).

Use a large chef's knife to cut the green leaves off the top of the pineapple, then cut a thin slice off the bottom. Stand the pineapple upright on a cutting board and slice the rind off the fruit using a gentle downward sawing motion and cutting away as little of the flesh as possible. There are likely to be small "eyes" left behind, which can be removed with a paring knife. Cut the pineapple lengthwise into quarters. Cut away and discard the tough core from each quarter and chop the remaining fruit into 1-inch chunks.

Place the sugar, water, and pineapple in a medium saucepan and stir to combine. Bring to a gentle boil over medium-high heat, stirring regularly.

Reduce the heat and simmer until the pineapple has a glossy, candied look and has exuded its juice, about 15 minutes.

Remove from the heat and let cool. Once the syrup is cool, strain it into a container with a tight-fitting lid, cover, and refrigerate until ready to use. Save the pineapple for another use.

HARD PINEAPPLE SYRUP Substitute light or dark rum for the water for an alcoholic syrup with very complex flavors. It also gives you delicious rum-soaked pineapple.

BONUS FROM THE BAR

BAKED HAM PINEAPPLE GLAZE Finely chop the cooked pineapple from the syrup and place in a bowl. Add one 4-ounce can of chipotle peppers, ¼ cup cider vinegar, 6 cloves finely minced garlic, 1 teaspoon each of ground cumin and black pepper, ½ teaspoon each of salt, cayenne pepper, and onion powder, ¼ teaspoon each of ground cloves, allspice, and cinnamon, and stir well. Coat the ham with the glaze 20 minutes before the end of baking.

Berry Syrup

Makes 2¼ cups syrup (photograph on page 55)

2 cups sugar

1 cup water

1 pint berries, rinsed and stemmed

Use this syrup to create all types of seasonal daiquiris or use it in place of grenadine in punches and sunrises, such as the Bitter Pill (page 183).

PLANNING AHEAD Can be made up to 1 week in advance and stored in a very clean container in the refrigerator (see page 55).

Place the sugar and water in a small saucepan and stir to combine. Bring to a gentle boil over medium-high heat.

Stir in the berries and reduce the heat. Simmer until the syrup has taken on the color and aroma of the berries, about 10 minutes.

Remove from the heat and let cool. Strain the syrup through a fine-mesh strainer, pressing the berries to extract their juice, into a container with a tight-fitting lid. Discard the berries. Cover the syrup and refrigerate until ready to use.

HARD BERRY SYRUP To make hard berry syrup for use as a float on a cocktail or as a mixer, substitute brandy, light rum, vodka, or eau-de-vie for the water.

Spiced Syrup

Makes 2 cups syrup (photograph opposite and on page 55)

1 cup water

12 whole cloves

1 or 2 whole star anise

⅛ teaspoon ground cinnamon

2 cups sugar

In this syrup, cloves, star anise, and cinnamon add a little boost of flavor. Use this in the Clove Martini (page 136) and Sunday Ham (page 136).

PLANNING AHEAD Can be made up to 4 weeks in advance and stored in a very clean container in the refrigerator (see page 55).

Place the water, cloves, star anise, and cinnamon in a small saucepan and stir to combine. Bring to a gentle boil over medium-high heat. Reduce the heat and simmer for 2 minutes. Add the sugar and simmer until the sugar is completely dissolved and the syrup is slightly thickened, about 2 minutes more.

Remove from the heat and let cool. Remove the cloves and star anise with a slotted spoon. Transfer the syrup to a container with a tight-fitting lid, cover, and refrigerate until ready to use.

Grenadine

Makes 2½ to 3 cups grenadine

6 pomegranates

2 cups sugar

2 cups water

True grenadine syrup is made from pomegranate juice. It is used as a sweetener and coloring agent for many cocktails and punches, perhaps most famously lending its red hue to the Shirley Temple and the tequila sunrise. Unfortunately, most of the grenadine on the market is made from corn syrup and artificial coloring. With a little searching, you can find a real version, but making your own is quick and easy. This grenadine is a clear red color, but not as intense as the artificially colored versions. If you want deep red grenadine, substitute 1 cup of cranberry juice for 1 cup of the water.

PLANNING AHEAD Can be made up to 2 weeks in advance and stored in a very clean container in the refrigerator (see page 55).

Cut the pomegranates into quarters and remove the fruit with a paring knife, discarding the skin. Add the fruit to a medium saucepan with the sugar. Muddle the two together (see page 22) to extract the juice from the pomegranate.

Stir in the water and bring to a gentle boil over medium-high heat. Reduce the heat and simmer, stirring regularly, for about 10 minutes.

Remove from the heat and let cool. Strain the syrup into a container with a tight-fitting lid; discard the fruit. Cover and refrigerate until ready to use.

TRICK OF THE TRADE

Store the syrup in a squeeze bottle so you can quickly add a measure to the Jack Rose (page 95) or a "float" (see page 22) to the Lava Flow (page 88).

Sour Mix

Sour mix is called for in so many cocktails that it makes sense to prepare a quantity of it in advance to keep on hand. Sour mix is a vital component in classic drinks such as the Tom Collins (page 84), Classic Daiquiri (page 83), and in some signature drinks, including the Pear Cobbler (page 111) and Brandywine Sour (page 151).

Lemon or Lime Sour Mix

Makes 6 cups mix, enough for 12 to 24 drinks, depending on the cocktail

Egg whites, which help emulsify the ingredients, are traditional in sour mix. You can use fresh egg whites or liquid or powdered pasteurized egg whites. This recipe halves or doubles perfectly.

PLANNING AHEAD This mix can be made several days or even several weeks in advance and frozen. It will keep safely in the refrigerator. For longer-term storage, you can juice all the fruit in advance and freeze the juice in a tightly sealed container for up to one month. Transfer it to the refrigerator to defrost at least 24 hours before using.

Juice the fruit and pour the juice through a fine-mesh strainer into a bowl. Using a rubber spatula, scrape the pulp through the strainer to ensure that you get every drop of juice. Discard the pulp. You should have 1 quart of juice, which generally requires 24 to 30 lemons or limes. Use more if needed.

Add the egg whites and syrup and whisk thoroughly.

Strain the mixture once more through a fine-mesh strainer into a container with a tight-fitting lid. Taste the mix. It should taste true to the fruit but with a hint of sweetness. If you prefer it sweeter, add more syrup. Depending on the time of year, the acid and sugar in the lemons and limes can vary, so adjust syrup as needed.

Cover and chill thoroughly before using.

1 quart freshly squeezed and strained lemon or lime juice (from 24 to 30 lemons or limes)

1 cup egg whites, from approximately 8 large eggs or 6 to 7 jumbo eggs

1 cup Simple Syrup (page 56), or more to taste

TRICK OF THE TRADE

Try replacing the simple syrup in sour mix with any of the flavored syrups. For example, use Pineapple Syrup (page 61) in the lime sour mix for a more tropical style, or use Vanilla Syrup (page 58) in the lemon sour mix to give it a mellow yet exotic flavor.

Cordials and Brandies

Nothing could be easier than making homemade cordials, and few formulas so completely transcend the sum of their parts: Combine fresh seasonal fruit such as peaches, plums, cranberries, and berries with liquor, and you've got a concoction that will serve as a digestif elegant enough for your finest dinner parties, a mixer for any number of great cocktails, coolers, or punches, or a housewarming or holiday gift that will keep giving long after you've gone home. Just to clarify terms, I call any of these macerations made with brandy a "brandy" and everything else a "cordial."

TRICK OF THE TRADE

Try to buy whatever spirit is called for in exactly the quantity called for. Then save the bottle and pour the prepared cordial or brandy into it for easy storage and inspired holiday gift giving.

Blackberry Cordial

Makes 1 liter

16 ounces fresh blackberries, rinsed if necessary

2 cups sugar

One 1-liter bottle dark rum

Ripe, deep purple blackberries have a great deal of acidity and well-balanced sweetness, making for a delicious cordial.

PLANNING AHEAD The maceration requires 7 days in the refrigerator. The cordial can be made up to 1 month in advance and stored in the refrigerator.

Place the blackberries and sugar in a medium saucepan and stir to combine. Let stand at room temperature for 10 minutes to help extract the juice from the berries.

Stir 2 cups rum into the blackberries and sugar. Bring to a boil over medium heat. Reduce the heat and simmer until the berries begin to break apart, about 10 minutes.

Remove the saucepan from the heat. Allow the mixture to cool to room temperature. Transfer the mixture to a large pitcher with a tight-fitting lid. Add the remaining rum (save the bottle) and stir well. Cover and refrigerate for 7 days.

Strain the mixture through a fine-mesh strainer. Discard the berries. Pour the cordial into the reserved bottle and store in the refrigerator.

Cranberry Cordial

Makes 2 liters

Cranberry cordial has a bright, clear, burgundy-hued color with a pure cranberry flavor and a slight backbite.

PLANNING AHEAD The maceration requires 2 days in the refrigerator. The cordial can be made up to 1 month in advance and stored in the refrigerator.

Place the sugar, water, and cranberry juice in a large saucepan over medium-high heat. Bring to a boil, stirring constantly. Once the sugar has dissolved, stir in the cranberries and reduce the heat.

Simmer, stirring regularly, until the cranberries begin to pop, 8 to 10 minutes. Remove the pan from the heat and continue to stir the cranberries, thoroughly mashing them with the spoon. Let cool.

Transfer the cooled cranberries to a large pitcher or jar with a tight-fitting lid. Pour in the vodka and stir well (save the vodka bottles for storing the cordial later on). Refrigerate for 2 days, stirring occasionally.

Pour the cranberry mixture through a colander into a large bowl or second pitcher. Using a rubber spatula, press the pulp against the sides of the colander to extract as much of the cordial as possible. Discard the pulp.

Strain the mixture a second time through a fine-mesh strainer. Using a rubber spatula, scrape the sides of the strainer to allow the cordial to flow through freely. You may see some light pulp. This will settle over time.

Pour the cordial into the reserved bottles and store in the refrigerator.

2 cups sugar

1 cup water

1 cup cranberry juice

24 ounces fresh cranberries, rinsed

Two 1-liter bottles vodka

Peach Brandy

Makes 1 liter

1 pound fresh peaches
(4 to 6 large or 6 to 8 small or
medium), cut into 1-inch chunks

2 cups sugar

One 1-liter bottle brandy

1 vanilla bean

1 whole star anise

In addition to flavoring brandy, the drunken peaches
and plums in this recipe and variation are sublime over
ice cream or even served alone, topped with a dollop of
whipped cream.

PLANNING AHEAD The maceration requires 7 days in the
refrigerator. The brandy can be made up to 1 month in
advance and stored in the refrigerator.

Place the peaches and sugar in a medium saucepan and stir
well. Let stand at room temperature for 10 minutes to help
extract the juice from the peaches.

Stir 2 cups of the brandy into the peaches. Bring to a boil
over medium heat. Reduce the heat and simmer until the
peaches are somewhat translucent, about 15 minutes.

Remove the saucepan from the heat. Split the vanilla bean
in half lengthwise and add it to the pot with the star anise.
Allow the mixture to cool to room temperature.

Transfer to a large pitcher with a tight-fitting lid. Add the
remaining brandy and stir well (save the brandy bottle for
storing the brandy later). Cover and refrigerate for at least 7
days.

Strain the mixture through a fine-mesh strainer. Save the
peaches for another use (see above). Pour the brandy into the
reserved bottle and store in the refrigerator.

PLUM BRANDY Replace the peaches with 1 pound of fresh black
or red plums and omit the vanilla bean and star anise.

Limoncello

Makes 1 liter

Limoncello's vibrant lemon flavor, subtle sweetness, good acidity, and hint of bitterness make it an incredible digestif as well as a perfect mixer with other liquors and juices. You can also make this with oranges, limes, and even clementines. Keep a bottle on hand in the freezer, where it will remain liquid but slushy.

PLANNING AHEAD The maceration requires 7 days in the refrigerator. The limoncello can be stored indefinitely in the freezer.

Juice the lemons and reserve the juice for another purpose. Cut the remaining rind into quarters.

Place the lemon rind and sugar in a large pitcher with a tight-fitting lid and stir well, using a spoon to break up the lemons to help extract any remaining juice.

Add the vodka or grappa (save the bottle for storing the limoncello later) and stir well.

Cover and refrigerate for 24 hours, then stir well and taste, adding more sugar if necessary.

Refrigerate for 6 days more, stirring every day.

Strain the mixture through a fine-mesh strainer, pressing the lemons against the sides of the strainer to extract all of the limoncello. Pour into the reserved spirit bottle and store in the freezer.

12 lemons

1½ cups sugar

One 1-liter bottle vodka or grappa

73 CLASSIC MARTINI	89 COSMOPOLITAN	100 GIN RICKEY
74 MARTINEZ	89 STINGER	100 DEBONAIRE
74 DIRTY MARTINI	90 PIÑA COLADA	101 BLOODLESS MARY
75 GIBSON	90 BLACK RUSSIAN	102 MOSCOW MULE
76 VESPER	91 SAZERAC	102 AMERICANO
76 SILVER BULLET	91 SIDECAR	102 FLORIDITA
77 MANHATTAN	93 ROB ROY	103 KNICKERBOCKER
79 DRY MANHATTAN	93 THE BRONX	103 WARD 8
79 PERFECT MANHATTAN	94 DARK AND STORMY	103 VALENCIA
81 MARGARITA	94 RAMOS GIN FIZZ	104 SOURS
82 FROZEN PRICKLY PEAR MARGARITA	95 NEGRONI	104 CAIPIRINHA
	95 JACK ROSE	106 RUSTY NAIL
83 CLASSIC DAIQUIRI	96 OLD-FASHIONED	106 SWIZZLE
83 BRANDY ALEXANDER	97 MINT JULEP	107 SCARLETT O'HARA
84 SINGAPORE SLING	98 MAI TAI	107 RHETT BUTLER
84 TOM COLLINS	98 MAIDEN'S PRAYER	107 BETWEEN THE SHEETS
86 GIMLET		
86 ZOMBIE		
87 FLIP		
87 PLANTER'S PUNCH		
88 MOJITO		

FAVORITE CLASSIC COCKTAILS

JUST WHAT MAKES A COCKTAIL A CLASSIC? THE *AMERICAN HERITAGE DICTIONARY* lists several definitions of *classic,* including "of the highest rank or class," "serving as the established model or standard," and "having lasting historical, cultural or literary associations." Combine these three definitions and you get a sense of what a classic cocktail is. Some—the nearly 125-year-old Ramos Gin Fizz (page 94) and the 200-year-old Mint Julep (page 97)—are considered historical classics by virtue of the fact that they have demonstrated staying power. The Cosmopolitan (page 89) is a good example of a drink that has established classic cultural significance by way of repeated guest appearances in movies and on television. Some cocktails, such as the Classic Martini (page 73), have it all.

Classic cocktails also lead to inspiration. They encourage us to create new tastes, textures, and approaches to the standards. From these classics, basic techniques are learned and mastered and an exponential number of new cocktails are invented. The Margarita (page 81), for example, is a perfect balance of sweetness and acidity. Such perfection makes it easy both to isolate one component and substitute another in its place, and to add favorite flavors to tailor a drink to your own taste. Using sour mix in place of lime juice creates a Frothy Margarita (page 81). I was inspired to add one of my favorite flavors, prickly pear, to this frothy version, and suddenly I had the unusual and quite delicious Prickly Pear Margarita (page 82). This flexibility is what makes the classics so inspiring.

The drinks in this chapter are those I turn to again and again. They are all perfect for entertaining and, I hope, will tempt you to take the next step of creating your own signature cocktails.

Classic Martini

Makes four 4-ounce drinks (photograph also on page 70, left and right)

The martini is the world's most celebrated cocktail. No other drink inspires such heated debate over both its master and its method. The original martinis were made from gin, as vodka was not really introduced into the United States until the 1930s. A vodka martini is more subtle and cleaner tasting, while a gin martini has more pronounced aromatics and a bigger bite. A martini is not a martini without at least a drop of vermouth—how much or how little is purely a matter of taste. The less vermouth, the drier the martini. On the topic of stirring versus shaking, I prefer to stir martinis. In my opinion, clear liquor drinks without juice, such as the martini, should be stirred, as shaking tends to give them a fuzzy texture. The classic garnish for a martini is an olive. Try using the homemade Vermouth-Soaked Olives (page 51) or try a fresh bay leaf for a distinctive touch.

PLANNING AHEAD Place the cocktail glasses in the freezer or refrigerator 30 minutes before serving.

Fill a tall pitcher with ice and add the gin or vodka and vermouth.

Stir 50 times.

Strain into cocktail glasses, add olives or bay leaves, and serve.

14 ounces gin or vodka

2 ounces dry vermouth

8 cocktail olives or 8 Vermouth-Soaked Olives (page 51) or 8 fresh bay leaves for garnish

GLASSWARE Cocktail glasses (see page 24), chilled

Martinez

Makes four 4-ounce drinks

6 ounces gin

6 ounces sweet vermouth

2 ounces maraschino liqueur
(see Straight Up)

4 teaspoons Simple Syrup
(page 56)

4 teaspoons Cointreau

4 dashes Angostura bitters

4 lemon twists (see page 39)
for garnish

GLASSWARE Cocktail glasses
(see page 24), chilled

Jerry Thomas, the great bartender at the Occidental Hotel in San Francisco, created this drink in 1864 for a gold miner on his way to Martinez, California—or so the story goes. Since some of the original ingredients are either no longer available or extremely hard to find, I have updated this version for today's tastes.

PLANNING AHEAD Place the cocktail glasses in the freezer or refrigerator 30 minutes before serving.

Fill a pitcher with ice and add all the ingredients except the lemon twists. Stir vigorously until the pitcher is beaded with sweat and frosty.

Strain into cocktail glasses, garnish with the lemon twists, and serve.

STRAIGHT UP

Maraschino liqueur is a clear, sweet liqueur made from marasca cherries. It is commonly used to sweeten punches as well as cocktails and was very popular in the nineteenth and early twentieth centuries.

Dirty Martini

Makes four 4-ounce drinks

12 ounces gin or vodka

3 ounces dry vermouth

4 teaspoons brine from olives

8 cocktail olives or
8 Vermouth-Soaked Olives
(page 51) for garnish

GLASSWARE Cocktail glasses
(see page 24), chilled

A salt-lover's paradise in a glass, the dirty martini was popularized by Franklin Delano Roosevelt, who served it to Joseph Stalin at the Tehran Conference during World War II. The olive brine adds a flavorful, savory note and appealing texture to the drink.

PLANNING AHEAD Place the cocktail glasses in the freezer or refrigerator 30 minutes before serving.

Fill a tall pitcher with ice and add the gin or vodka, dry vermouth, and olive brine. Stir vigorously until the pitcher is beaded with sweat and frosty.

Strain into cocktail glasses, drop in the olives, and serve.

Gibson

Makes four 4-ounce drinks (photograph also on page 70, center)

You can use store-bought onions rather than homemade, but it is very important that you don't skimp on their quality when making this drink, for the Gibson is all about the onion.

PLANNING AHEAD Place the cocktail glasses in the freezer or refrigerator 30 minutes before serving.

Fill a tall pitcher with ice and add the gin or vodka, dry vermouth, and onion brine. Stir vigorously until the pitcher is beaded with sweat and frosty.

Strain into cocktail glasses, drop in the onions, and serve.

12 ounces gin or vodka

4 ounces dry vermouth

1 teaspoon brine from onions, optional

8 Cocktail Onions (page 52) or use store-bought for garnish

GLASSWARE Cocktail glasses (see page 24) chilled

Vesper

Makes two 3½-ounce drinks

3 ounces vodka

1 ounce gin

½ ounce Lillet Blanc
(see Straight Up)

2 orange twists (see page 39)
for garnish

GLASSWARE Cocktail glasses
(see page 24), chilled

I could not resist including this recipe, the original James Bond martini, as it first appeared in Ian Fleming's *Casino Royale,* the first of the Bond books. It was changed to a plain vodka martini for the movies.

PLANNING AHEAD Place the cocktail glasses in the freezer or refrigerator 30 minutes before serving.

Fill a cocktail shaker with ice and add the vodka, gin, and Lillet. Shake vigorously until the outside of the shaker is thoroughly beaded with sweat and extremely cold to the touch.

Pour into cocktail glasses, garnish with orange twists, and serve.

STRAIGHT UP

Lillet Blanc is an aromatized wine from France made from sauvignon blanc and sémillon grapes. The base wine is mixed with a maceration of different fruits and brandy. It is a wonderful aperitif best served cold garnished with a slice of orange.

Silver Bullet

Makes four 4-ounce drinks

Ice for serving

1 ounce scotch

12 ounces gin or vodka

3 ounces dry vermouth

4 lemon twists (see page 39),
for garnish

GLASSWARE Cocktail glasses
(see page 24), chilled

The silver bullet is another variation on the classic martini, enhanced by a dash of scotch on top, which adds a mellowing hint of smokiness.

PLANNING AHEAD Place the cocktail glasses in the freezer or refrigerator 30 minutes before serving.

Place a couple of ice cubes in each glass. Add a ¼-ounce splash of scotch to each glass.

Fill a tall pitcher with ice and add the gin or vodka and dry vermouth. Stir vigorously until the pitcher is beaded with sweat and frosty.

Strain into cocktail glasses, garnish with the lemon twists, and serve.

Manhattan

Makes two 3-ounce drinks (photograph on page 78)

The original Manhattan, created in 1874 at the Manhattan Club in New York, was made with sweet vermouth and rye, which produces a smooth, mellow cocktail. Over time, multiple variations of the Manhattan have developed, with tweaks to both the whiskey and the vermouth, so that today you can have a classic sweet Manhattan, made with only sweet vermouth; a Dry Manhattan (page 79), made with only dry vermouth; or a Perfect Manhattan (page 79), made with equal amounts of both. And as bourbon has become increasingly popular over the last few decades, it has found its way into the Manhattan in place of the rye whiskey, giving a richer cocktail with more bite and a hint of smokiness. Make yours according to your taste—sweet, dry, or perfect—and with either bourbon or rye. No matter what style you prefer, don't be afraid to use the bitters, as they make the drink fuller and more flavorful.

Fill a pitcher with ice and add the whiskey, sweet vermouth, and bitters. Stir vigorously until the outside of the pitcher is thoroughly beaded with sweat and is extremely cold to the touch.

Place a maraschino cherry in each cocktail glass. Strain the drink over the cherries and serve immediately.

TRICK OF THE TRADE

If using homemade Maraschino Cherries (page 53), I add a drop of the maraschino liquid to the Manhattan for an extra hint of fruit.

$4\frac{1}{2}$ ounces rye or bourbon whiskey

$1\frac{1}{2}$ ounces sweet vermouth

2 dashes Angostura bitters

2 Maraschino Cherries (page 53) or use store-bought for garnish

GLASSWARE Cocktail glasses (see page 24)

Dry Manhattan

Makes two 3-ounce drinks

Dry Manhattans make a great palate opener before dinner. Substituting Lillet Blanc for the vermouth adds a distinctive orange note and more fruitiness. Also, try using an orange twist instead of lemon.

Fill a pitcher with ice and add the whiskey, dry vermouth, and bitters. Stir vigorously until the outside of the shaker is thoroughly beaded with sweat and is extremely cold to the touch.

Strain into cocktail glasses, then twist the lemon over each drink and drop it in. Serve immediately.

4½ ounces rye or bourbon whiskey

1½ ounces dry vermouth
or Lillet Blanc
(see Straight Up, page 76)

2 dashes Angostura bitters

2 lemon twists (see page 39)
for garnish

GLASSWARE Cocktail glasses
(see page 24)

Perfect Manhattan

Makes two 3-ounce drinks

Adding both sweet and dry vermouth makes the perfect Manhattan a complex marriage of flavors. For a truly unique drink, substitute cherry brandy for the sweet vermouth. The result is a dry fruit flavor that is both refreshing and palate cleansing.

Fill a pitcher with ice and add the whiskey, dry vermouth, sweet vermouth, and bitters. Stir vigorously until the outside of the shaker is thoroughly beaded with sweat and is extremely cold to the touch.

Strain the drink into cocktail glasses, twist the lemon over the drink, and drop it in. Serve immediately.

4½ ounces rye or bourbon whiskey

¾ ounce dry vermouth

¾ ounce sweet vermouth or
cherry brandy

2 dashes Angostura bitters

2 lemon twists (see page 39)
for garnish

GLASSWARE Cocktail glasses
(see page 24)

Margarita

Makes four 4½-ounce drinks (photograph opposite, back)

The margarita is among the most popular drinks ever. One reason for the demand is that it goes so well with food. The margarita's balanced blend of sweet-tart earthiness and acidity cuts through the richness and spice of many foods.

Pour the salt onto a small plate. Cut the reserved lime rind as necessary and rub the juicy side along the outer edge of the lip of each coupe—not along the inside of the rim. Holding each coupe at an angle, roll the outer edge of the rim in the salt until it is fully coated.

Fill a cocktail shaker with ice and add the lime juice, tequila, and Cointreau. Shake vigorously until the outside of the shaker is beaded with sweat and frosty.

Strain into the salted coupes, garnish with lime rounds, and serve.

FROTHY MARGARITA Prepare the Margarita, substituting 4 ounces Lime Sour Mix (page 65) for the lime juice.

FROZEN MARGARITA Prepare the Margarita, placing the tequila, Cointreau, and lime juice in a large pitcher without ice and stirring to mix. Process in a blender in batches, using 1 cup of crushed ice and 4½ ounces of mix per serving. Blend until smooth and pour into salted coupes.

GRAND MARGARITA Grand Marnier has a much more pronounced orange flavor and more intensity than Cointreau. Prepare as usual, using Grand Marnier in place of the Cointreau. Garnish with orange zest. See photograph on page 82.

Kosher salt for rimming the glasses

4 ounces fresh lime juice (from approximately 4 limes), some lime rind reserved for rimming the glass

8 ounces tequila

6 ounces Cointreau

4 lime rounds for garnish

GLASSWARE Margarita coupes or cocktail glasses (see page 24)

Frozen Prickly Pear Margarita

Makes four 6½-ounce drinks (photograph on page 80, front)

2 prickly pears (approximately 8 ounces total)

¼ cup sugar

Kosher salt for rimming the glasses

Lime wedge for rimming the glasses

2 cups ice

8 ounces tequila

6 ounces Cointreau

4 ounces Lime Sour Mix (page 65)

GLASSWARE Margarita coupes or cocktail glasses (see page 24)

Prickly pears add an unexpected twist to a typical margarita. They are in season from fall through spring. Note that you will need a blender to make this drink.

To prepare the prickly pears, cut off each end and then slice lengthwise down one side of the fruit, cutting just through the skin. Peel off and discard the skin, then cut the pear into bite-size chunks, discarding the seeds. Place the fruit in a bowl with the sugar and stir vigorously to mix; the prickly pears will break down quite a bit. Let sit for 10 minutes. Stir vigorously again, then strain into a bowl, pressing the fruit against the sides of the strainer to extract as much juice as possible. Set the juice aside and discard the pulp.

When ready to serve, pour the salt onto a small plate. Rub the juicy side of the lime wedge along the outer edge of the lip of each coupe—not along the inside of the rim. Holding each coupe at an angle, roll the outer edge of the rim in the salt until it is fully coated.

Transfer the prickly pear juice to a blender and add the ice, tequila, Cointreau, and sour mix. Blend thoroughly. If you prefer a thicker drink, add more ice to taste.

Pour into the salted coupes and serve immediately.

Classic Daiquiri

Makes four 3½-ounce drinks

The daiquiri was created in Cuba and named after the town of the same name. Its beauty is in its simplicity: Rum, lime, and sugar come together in a succulent and refreshing beverage. The daiquiri took off after it was discovered by Ernest Hemingway, whose favorite variation was called the Papa Dobles and included a few drops of maraschino liqueur (see Straight Up, page 74) and a dash of grapefruit juice.

Fill a cocktail shaker or tall pitcher with ice and add the rum and sour mix. Shake or stir vigorously until the shaker or pitcher is beaded with sweat and frosty and the mixture is frothy.

Strain into cocktail glasses, float a lime slice on top of each, and serve.

VARIATIONS ON THE DAIQUIRI Try one of these simple embellishments to make the classic Daiquiri extra special.

Rim the cocktail glasses with sugar (see page 22) and fill them with crushed ice before straining the daiquiri into them.

Add 2 ounces maraschino liqueur or Cointreau before shaking or stirring the mixture.

After floating the lime slice on top, add a few drops of Grenadine (homemade if desired, page 64) or Berry Syrup (page 62) on top.

8 ounces light rum

8 ounces Lime Sour Mix (page 65)

4 thin, round lime slices for garnish

GLASSWARE Cocktail glasses (see page 24)

Brandy Alexander

Makes four 4-ounce drinks

Once a very popular late-night drink, this is one of the most decadent yet simplest cocktails ever created. It's fantastic served for dessert with biscotti.

Fill a cocktail shaker with ice and add the brandy, crème de cacao, and cream. Shake vigorously until the outside of the shaker is beaded with sweat and frosty.

Pour into the cocktail glasses, grate fresh nutmeg on top, and serve.

8 ounces brandy

4 ounces white crème de cacao

4 ounces heavy cream

Fresh grated nutmeg for garnish

GLASSWARE Cocktail glasses (see page 24)

Singapore Sling

Makes four 7½-ounce drinks (photograph opposite, left)

Ice for serving

8 ounces gin

2 ounces Cherry Heering
(see Straight Up) or cherry brandy

2 ounces fresh lemon juice
(from approximately 2 lemons)

2 ounces Simple Syrup (page 56)
or Pineapple Syrup (page 61) or
Ginger Syrup (page 59)

16 ounces club soda

4 orange slices for garnish

4 Maraschino Cherries
(page 53) or use store-bought
for garnish

GLASSWARE Highball glasses
(see page 23)

If you look up this recipe in a hundred different cocktail books, you'll get a hundred different versions. Some recipes call for the addition of ½ ounce Bénédictine (an aromatic French cordial) or ½ ounce Cointreau to each serving for sweetness and complexity. Others call for a dash of pineapple juice or bitters. I have even seen some that call for all of the above. I use my version mainly as a cordial or after-dinner drink. It is also an excellent mixer.

Fill the highball glasses with ice.

Fill a cocktail shaker with ice and add the gin, Cherry Heering, lemon juice, and syrup. Shake vigorously until the outside of the shaker is thoroughly beaded with sweat and is extremely cold to the touch.

Strain into the highball glasses and top each with 4 ounces of soda. Garnish with the orange and cherry and serve.

STRAIGHT UP

Cherry Heering is a Danish cherry liqueur invented in the late nineteenth century. It is generally easy to find and quite delicious. If you cannot find Cherry Heering, use cherry brandy instead.

Tom Collins

Makes four 7½-ounce drinks (photograph opposite, right)

Ice for serving

8 ounces gin

6 ounces Lemon Sour Mix
(page 65)

16 ounces club soda

4 orange slices for garnish

4 Maraschino Cherries
(page 53) or use store-bought
for garnish

GLASSWARE Collins glasses
(see page 23)

The Tom Collins takes its name from the Old Tom sweetened gin originally used to make this simple cocktail such a wonderful light aperitif.

Fill the collins glasses with ice.

Fill a cocktail shaker with ice and add the gin and sour mix. Shake vigorously until the outside of the shaker is thoroughly beaded with sweat and is extremely cold to the touch.

Strain into the glasses. Top off with club soda, garnish each with an orange slice and a cherry, and serve.

RUM COLLINS Prepare the Tom Collins, replacing the gin with dark rum.

Gimlet

Makes two 3½-ounce drinks

4 ounces gin

3 ounces Rose's lime juice

GLASSWARE Cocktail glasses
(see page 24)

The gimlet was created by mixing gin and Rose's Lime Cordial (sweetened lime juice) in the nineteenth century when limes were eaten by English sailors to help prevent scurvy. The gin was added to—well—help the lime go down, of course.

Fill a cocktail pitcher with ice and add both ingredients. Stir vigorously until the outside of the shaker is beaded with sweat and frosty.

Strain into cocktail glasses and serve.

Zombie

Makes six 7-ounce drinks

10 ounces fresh orange juice
(from approximately 3 oranges)

4 ounces fresh lemon juice
(from approximately 3 lemons)

4 ounces fresh lime juice
(from approximately 4 limes)

6 ounces apricot brandy

6 ounces dark rum

6 ounces light rum

2 ounces Grenadine
(page 64) or use store-bought

½ ounce Angostura bitters

Crushed ice for serving

3 ounces 151-proof rum for floating
(optional)

Fresh mint leaves for garnish

6 pineapple wedges
(see page 42) for garnish

GLASSWARE Hurricane glasses or
cooler glasses (see page 25)

Depending on whom you ask, the creation of the zombie is alternately credited to Trader Vic, the legendary restaurateur, and Don the Beachcomber, another restaurateur who traveled the beaches of the world. Either way, the zombie is the perfect way to kick off a summer barbecue.

Fill a large pitcher with ice and add the citrus juices, apricot brandy, dark rum, light rum, grenadine, and bitters. Stir briskly until the pitcher is beaded with sweat and frosty.

Fill the glasses with crushed ice and strain over the cocktail.

If desired, float ½ ounce 151-proof rum on top of each cocktail. Garnish each with several mint leaves and a pineapple wedge and serve.

ZOMBIE PUNCH Double the recipe and serve in a punch bowl; this yields approximately twenty-four 4-ounce punch cup servings.

Flip

Makes four 3-ounce drinks

The flip originated in America during Colonial times. It was served as a hot nog and included beer along with the spirits, egg, and sugar. Over time the beer became less common and the flip evolved into a cold drink. I serve flips at brunch, where they marry well with egg dishes and are incredible with my Sunday roast ham. You can also serve them with dessert, or even *for* dessert.

Fill a cocktail shaker with ice and add all ingredients except the nutmeg. Shake several times just to blend.

Strain into glasses and grate fresh nutmeg on top. Serve.

VARIATION For a more complex and truly special flip, replace the 4 ounces each of brandy and port or Madeira with 2 ounces each of bourbon, rum, port, and Madeira.

4 ounces brandy

4 ounces port or Madeira
(see Straight Up, page 137)

4 teaspoons sugar or brown sugar

4 large eggs or 8 tablespoons
Egg Beaters or other pasteurized
egg product

Fresh nutmeg for garnish

GLASSWARE Small wineglasses or
sherry copitas (see page 25)

Planter's Punch

Makes six 7-ounce drinks

Planter's punch is a unique mixture of savory and sweet, a balance that makes the drink particularly well suited to serve with grilled fish. Topping the drink off with nutmeg may seem incidental, but it makes the flavor of the drink more distinctive.

Fill the hurricane glasses with ice.

Fill a large pitcher with ice and add all the ingredients except the garnishes. Stir briskly until the pitcher is beaded with sweat and frosty.

Strain the cocktail into the glasses. Grate a pinch of fresh nutmeg over the top of each drink, garnish with the orange and cherry, and serve.

Ice for serving

6 ounces dark rum

6 ounces light rum

3 ounces triple sec

12 ounces fresh orange juice
(from approximately 4 oranges)

12 ounces pineapple juice

3 ounces fresh lime juice
(from approximately 3 limes)

1 ounce Grenadine
(page 64) or use store-bought

1 teaspoon orange bitters
(see Mail-order Sources) or
Angostura bitters

Freshly grated nutmeg for garnish

6 orange slices for garnish

6 Maraschino Cherries
(page 53) or use store-bought
for garnish

GLASSWARE Hurricane or
cooler glasses (see page 25)

Mojito

Makes four 8-ounce drinks

12 fresh mint sprigs

4 ounces Simple Syrup
(page 56)

4 ounces fresh lime juice
(from approximately 4 limes)

Ice for serving

8 ounces white rum

24 ounces seltzer

GLASSWARE Highball glasses
(see page 23)

The mojito was the original drink of the Cuban working class. A cooling, thirst-quenching mojito was a great way to end the day. The current formalized recipe was created at the La Bodeguita hotel in Cuba, one of Hemingway's haunts. If you prefer this drink short and stronger, cut the seltzer to 4 ounces or omit it.

In each of the highball glasses place 2 mint sprigs, 1 ounce syrup, and 1 ounce lime juice. Muddle the ingredients together (see page 22).

Add ice and 2 ounces rum to each glass and stir to blend.

Fill each glass with seltzer, garnish with the remaining mint, and serve.

Cosmopolitan

Makes two 4-ounce drinks

No one truly knows where the *über*popular Cosmopolitan came from. The only thing that can be stated with any certainty is that it appeared after citrus-flavored vodkas first arrived on the market in the 1980s. If it wasn't a classic already, the women of *Sex and the City* certainly did their part to make it one.

Fill a cocktail shaker with ice and add all the ingredients except the orange twists. Shake vigorously until the outside of the shaker is frosted and beaded with sweat.

Strain into cocktail glasses, garnish with the orange twists, and serve.

3 ounces citron vodka

2½ ounces triple sec

2 ounces cranberry juice

½ ounce fresh lime juice (from approximately ½ lime)

2 orange twists (see page 39) for garnish

GLASSWARE Cocktail glasses (see page 24)

Stinger

Makes four 3-ounce drinks

An old boss of mine claimed that this drink got its name when a fairly inebriated customer walked into a Lower East Side speakeasy late at night just after Prohibition ended and told the bartender that he only wanted one for the road, something that "stings like a bee." The barman complied with this strong, minty cocktail.

Fill the rocks glasses with crushed ice.

Fill a cocktail shaker with ice and add the brandy and crème de menthe. Shake vigorously until the shaker is beaded with sweat and frosty.

Strain the cocktail into the rocks glasses and serve.

Crushed ice for serving

8 ounces brandy

4 ounces white crème de menthe

GLASSWARE Rocks glasses (see page 23)

Piña Colada

Makes eight 17-ounce drinks

32 ounces pineapple juice

24 ounces Coco Lopez cream of coconut or 16 ounces Coco Lopez cream of coconut and 8 ounces heavy cream

12 ounces light rum

8 ounces Myers's rum

8 cups crushed ice

8 pineapple wedges (see page 39) for garnish

GLASSWARE Hurricane glasses or other large specialty glasses (see page 25), chilled

Created in the 1950s at the Caribe Hilton in Puerto Rico, nothing evokes island paradise better than the piña colada. Seventeen ounces may seem like a huge drink, but remember that each cocktail has 8 ounces of ice and only 2½ ounces of rum. Replace 8 ounces of the cream of coconut with heavy cream to yield a smoother, richer drink. Use spiced rum instead of the Myers's rum for a little more complexity. Note that you will need a blender to make this drink.

PLANNING AHEAD It's best if the ingredients are well chilled before mixing, or you can combine all but the crushed ice (see page 37) and the garnish up to 8 hours in advance and refrigerate it until you are ready to blend. If you have time, prechilling the glasses will help keep the piña colada from melting too fast.

Mix all ingredients except the crushed ice and pineapple wedges in a large pitcher. If desired, cover and refrigerate for up to 8 hours.

When ready to blend, do so in batches, using 1 cup of crushed ice and 9 ounces of mix per serving. Process in a blender on medium speed until smooth.

Pour into glasses, garnish each with a pineapple wedge, and serve.

Black Russian

Makes two 3-ounce drinks

Ice for serving

3 ounces Kahlúa

3 ounces vodka

GLASSWARE Rocks glasses (see page 23)

This is one of the greatest after-dinner drinks of all time. The vodka cuts the sweetness of the coffee-flavored Kahlúa enough to keep the drink from being cloying.

Fill the rocks glasses with ice.

Fill a cocktail pitcher with ice and add the Kahlúa and vodka. Stir vigorously until the outside of the shaker is beaded with sweat and frosty.

Strain into the glasses and serve.

Sazerac

Makes four 3-ounce drinks

Created in the 1830s by New Orleans apothecary Antoine Peychaud, this drink was originally made with brandy, absinthe, and a dash of Peychaud's own secret bitters. The drink later gained its name and popular reputation thanks to the owner of Sazerac Coffee House, who made it only with Sazerac de Forge et Fils brandy. I have seen the Sazerac made with either brandy or whiskey, or even with both.

Add a few ice cubes and a splash of Pernod to each glass. Stir and set aside.

Fill a pitcher with ice and add the brandy, syrup, and Peychaud's bitters. Stir well until the outside of the pitcher is beaded with sweat and frosty.

Remove the ice and pour out the liquid from the cocktail glasses. Add a couple of fresh ice cubes to each. Strain the drink into the glasses, garnish with the lemon twists, and serve.

Ice for serving

Splash of Pernod (see Straight Up, page 221) or Ricard

8 ounces brandy, rye, or bourbon

2 to 2½ ounces Simple Syrup (page 56) or Berry Syrup (page 62)

24 dashes Peychaud's bitters

4 lemon twists (see page 39) for garnish

GLASSWARE Cocktail glasses (see page 24)

Sidecar

Makes four 4-ounce drinks

There are several stories regarding the origin of the sidecar, including my preferred explanation from David Embury, author of *The Fine Art of Mixing Drinks* (1948). Embury asserts that the drink was invented during the First World War by a friend of his who was driven to a Paris bistro in a motorcycle sidecar. This concoction helped him wind down from his exhilarating ride.

Pour the sugar onto a small plate. Cut a wedge from the reserved orange, then rub the juicy side of the wedge along the outer edge of the lip of each glass—not the inside of the rim. Holding each glass at an angle, roll the outer edge of the rim in the sugar until it is fully coated.

Fill a cocktail shaker with ice and add the brandy, Cointreau, and lemon juice. Shake vigorously until the outside of the shaker is beaded with sweat and frosty.

Strain into the cocktail glasses, garnish each with an orange twist, and serve.

Sugar for rimming the glasses

4 orange twists (see page 39) for garnish, the orange reserved for rimming the glasses

4 ounces brandy

4 ounces Cointreau

4 ounces fresh lemon juice (from approximately 3 lemons)

GLASSWARE Cocktail glasses (see page 24)

Rob Roy

Makes four 3½-ounce drinks

Original recipes for the Rob Roy, which date back to the early twentieth century, called for equal parts sweet vermouth and scotch. Over time it developed a ratio of 2½ times as much scotch as sweet vermouth. Most bars and restaurants make delicious Rob Roys with lighter blended scotches. For a more robust drink, try using a full-bodied scotch, such as Chivas Regal, or even a single malt, such as Glenlivet 10-year-old.

PLANNING AHEAD Place the cocktail glasses in the freezer or refrigerator 30 minutes before serving.

Fill a pitcher with ice and add the scotch, sweet vermouth, and bitters. Stir until the outside of the pitcher is thoroughly beaded with sweat and is extremely cold to the touch.

Strain into the cocktail glasses. Twist a lemon twist over each glass and float it on top of the drink.

ORANGE ROB ROY For a hint of orange, prepare the Rob Roy using orange bitters (see Mail-order Sources) in place of the Angostura bitters, and orange twists instead of lemon twists.

10 ounces scotch

4 ounces sweet vermouth

4 dashes Angostura bitters

4 lemon twists (see page 39) for garnish

GLASSWARE Cocktail glasses (see page 24)

The Bronx

Makes four 5-ounce drinks (photograph opposite)

Having spent many years in the Bronx, I have retained a fondness for the old neighborhood, and I was thrilled the first time a restaurant guest ordered a Bronx. This drink has an intriguing balance of aromatics from the gin and vermouth, citrus from the orange juice and bitters, and sweetness from the syrup.

Fill a cocktail shaker with ice and add all the ingredients. Shake just to blend.

Strain into cocktail glasses and serve.

6 ounces gin

6 ounces fresh orange juice (from approximately 2 oranges)

4 ounces dry vermouth

4 ounces sweet vermouth

1 teaspoon Simple Syrup (page 56) (optional)

2 to 4 dashes orange bitters (see Mail-order Sources) (optional)

GLASSWARE Cocktail glasses (see page 24)

Dark and Stormy

Makes two 6-ounce drinks

2 lime wedges

1 teaspoon sugar

4 ounces Gosling's Black Seal Rum

Ice for serving

8 ounces ginger beer

GLASSWARE Highball (see page 23) or beer glasses (see page 24)

This is the national drink of Bermuda, where both Gosling's Black Seal Rum and ginger beer are produced. Gosling's Black Seal Rum is one of the heaviest and darkest of all rums. It has a rich molasseslike flavor and color. The Dark and Stormy II (page 195) is the punch version of this drink.

Place 1 lime wedge and $1/2$ teaspoon sugar in each glass. Muddle them well (see page 22).

Add 2 ounces rum to each glass and stir. Fill the glasses with ice, top each with 4 ounces ginger beer, and serve.

Ramos Gin Fizz

Makes four 9-ounce drinks

Ice for serving

16 ounces Lemon Sour Mix (page 65)

8 ounces milk or cream

$3/4$ teaspoon orange flower water (see Straight Up)

12 ounces club soda

GLASSWARE Highball glasses (see page 23)

Created by Henry C. Ramos in 1888 at the Imperial Cabinet Saloon in New Orleans, the recipe for Ramos gin fizz may look heavy because of the cream, but it is an incredibly light and flavorful drink when measured and shaken just right.

Fill the highball glasses with ice.

Fill a cocktail shaker with ice and add the sour mix, milk, and orange flower water. Shake vigorously until the outside of the shaker is beaded with sweat and frosty.

Strain into the highball glasses, top off with soda, and serve.

STRAIGHT UP

Orange flower water is an aromatic liquid made from bitter Seville oranges. Its origins are Middle Eastern, and it has many uses in cooking, particularly in baking. Always use it sparingly, as it has a very pronounced perfume.

Negroni

Makes four 3-ounce drinks

One story has it that this drink was invented by Count Camillo Negroni in 1920s Florence. He apparently asked a bartender to add some gin to his favorite drink, the Americano. He then ordered this concoction so many times that the bartender dubbed it the Negroni. You can use vodka in place of the gin, but the gin lends the drink more depth and aroma.

Fill the rocks glasses with ice.

Fill a pitcher with ice and add the Campari, sweet vermouth, and gin. Stir just to blend.

Strain into the rocks glasses. Twist an orange twist over each drink, then rub the skin side on the rim of the glass, drop the twist in, and serve.

ORANGE NEGRONI To make a less potent yet still delicious drink, prepare the Negroni using half the listed amount of each liquor. Strain into four highball glasses, top each glass with fresh orange juice, and serve.

Ice for serving

4 ounces Campari

4 ounces sweet vermouth

4 ounces gin or vodka

4 orange twists (see page 39) for garnish

GLASSWARE Rocks glasses (see page 23)

Jack Rose

Makes four 4-ounce drinks

There are numerous theories about where this drink gets its name. Some believe that it was named after gangster Jack Rose in 1912. Others believe that it takes the Jack from applejack liquor and the Rose from the resulting color of the drink. Whatever its name's origins, the Jack Rose is a refreshingly sweet-tart cocktail, perfect before dinner or as a nightcap.

Use a vegetable peeler to cut around the circumference of the apple and remove 4 long strips of apple peel. Set aside.

Fill a cocktail shaker with ice and add the applejack, syrup, lemon juice, and grenadine. Shake vigorously until the outside of the shaker is beaded with sweat and frosty.

Strain into the cocktail glasses, float an apple twist on top of each, and serve.

1 apple

8 ounces applejack (see Straight Up, page 112)

4 ounces Simple Syrup (page 56)

4 ounces fresh lemon juice (from approximately 3 lemons)

2 teaspoons Grenadine (page 64) or use store-bought

GLASSWARE Cocktail glasses (see page 24)

Old-fashioned

Makes two 5-ounce drinks

1 orange round, cut in half
for muddling

2 Maraschino Cherries (page 53)
or use store-bought

1 teaspoon sugar

Ice for serving

6 ounces bourbon, rye, scotch,
or brandy

4 ounces club soda

GLASSWARE Rocks glasses
(see page 23)

The great thing about the old-fashioned is that it can
easily be made more or less sweet or more or less
diluted, as you prefer, without impinging on the integrity
of the drink.

Place 1 orange half slice, 1 cherry, and ½ teaspoon sugar in
each rocks glass. Muddle until the fruit is well mashed and
mixed with the sugar (see page 22).

Fill the glasses with ice, pour over the bourbon, and stir
well. Top off with soda, stir, and serve.

Mint Julep

Makes two 2½-ounce drinks

Early references to the mint julep, a drink that's been made for more than two hundred years, cite it as a strong drink taken by Virginians in the morning (what a way to start the day!). Juleps inspire many arguments on the *correct* way to make them and, of course, whether it was Virginians or Kentuckians who created them. Regardless of the answer to these worthy debates, the julep remains a lovely predinner spring- and summertime drink, served by the thousands on Kentucky Derby Day in May.

PLANNING AHEAD Place the glasses in the freezer or refrigerator 20 minutes before making the drinks.

Place 2 mint sprigs and ½ ounce syrup in the bottom of each glass. Muddle well (see page 22).

Fill the glasses with crushed ice and add the bourbon. Stir well, until the glasses are frosted. Garnish with the remaining mint and serve.

6 fresh mint sprigs

1 ounce Simple Syrup (page 56) or 2 teaspoons sugar

Crushed ice for serving

4 ounces bourbon

GLASSWARE Rocks glasses (see page 23) or silver julep cups, chilled

Mai Tai

Makes two 4-ounce drinks (photograph opposite)

Ice for serving

4 ounces dark rum

1½ ounces triple sec

1½ ounces fresh lime juice
(from 1 to 1½ limes)

½ ounce orgeat (see Straight Up)
or amaretto

2 fresh mint leaves for garnish

2 lime wedges for garnish

GLASSWARE Rocks glasses
(see page 23)

This was created by Victor Bergeron at his California restaurant, Trader Vic's, in the 1940s. Too often, mai tais are served in really large glasses and don't truly do service to the original drink. When made with premium ingredients and kept to a reasonable size, this drink will live up to its name, which means "out of this world" in Tahitian. If you cannot find orgeat, use amaretto in its place.

Fill the rocks glasses with ice.

Fill a cocktail shaker with ice and add the first 4 ingredients. Shake vigorously until the outside of the shaker is frosted and beaded with sweat.

Strain into the rocks glasses, top each glass with a mint leaf and a lime wedge, and serve.

STRAIGHT UP

Orgeat syrup is made from almonds and sugar. Very sweet, with a strong almond flavor, orgeat enhances many cocktails, most famously the mai tai. It is sometimes called almond syrup and is available online through sites that carry syrups (see Mail-order Sources).

Maiden's Prayer

Makes two 4¼-ounce drinks

3 ounces gin

3 ounces fresh orange juice
(from approximately 1 orange)

1½ ounces fresh lemon juice
(from approximately 1 lemon)

1 ounce triple sec

2 orange twists (see page 39)
for garnish

GLASSWARE Cocktail glasses
(see page 24)

This tasty, somewhat sour cocktail makes a refreshing, palate-opening preprandial.

Fill a cocktail shaker with ice and add all the ingredients except the orange twists. Shake vigorously until the outside of the shaker is frosted and beaded with sweat.

Strain in cocktail glasses, garnish with the orange twists, and serve.

Gin Rickey

Makes four 7½-ounce drinks

Ice for serving

8 ounces gin

2 ounces fresh lime juice
(from approximately 2 large limes)

20 ounces club soda

4 lime wedges for garnish

GLASSWARE Highball glasses
(see page 23)

Created in the late 1800s by a bartender at Shoemaker's Bar in Washington, D.C., the gin Rickey is named after Colonel Joseph Rickey. The addition of citrus and soda to gin makes this an extremely refreshing cocktail.

Fill the highball glasses with ice.

Fill a cocktail shaker with ice and add the gin and lime juice. Shake vigorously until the outside of the shaker is thoroughly beaded with sweat and is extremely cold to the touch.

Divide the cocktail among the 4 highball glasses. Top each with the club soda, garnish with a lime wedge, and serve.

RUM RICKEY Prepare the gin Rickey, replacing the gin with rum.

ORANGE RICKEY Prepare the gin Rickey, replacing 2 ounces of the gin with 2 ounces Cointreau to give a hint of sweetness.

PINEAPPLE RICKEY Prepare the gin Rickey, adding 4 ounces Pineapple Syrup (page 61) for a tropical touch.

Debonaire

Makes two 3¼-ounce drinks

5 ounces Highland malt scotch

1½ ounces Canton Ginger Liqueur
(see Straight Up)

GLASSWARE Cocktail glasses
(see page 24)

Their intense smokiness and pronounced iodinelike flavors make Highland scotches difficult to pair with other ingredients, so there are precious few cocktails that make great use of good Highland malt scotch. This cocktail, the creation of spirits writer Gary Regan, works perfectly and has inspired me to create other cocktails with whiskey and ginger as a base.

Fill a pitcher with ice and add both ingredients. Stir vigorously until the outside of the pitcher is frosted and beaded with sweat.

Strain into cocktail glasses and serve.

STRAIGHT UP

Canton Ginger Liqueur is a well-balanced ginger-based cordial with great spicy flavors and a hint of sweetness.

Bloodless Mary

Makes eight 4-ounce drinks

This drink was created by a fellow mixologist, Michael Waterhouse, of the New York restaurant Dylan Prime. He uses vodka infused with all but one of the flavors in a traditional Bloody Mary. The missing ingredient is, of course, the tomato juice. The bloodless Mary mix makes enough for eight full drinks, but it keeps indefinitely, so you can easily serve fewer than eight.

PLANNING AHEAD The bloodless Mary mix requires at least 2 days in the refrigerator. Once it has been strained, the mix will keep indefinitely in the refrigerator or freezer.

To prepare the mix, place the celery root and horseradish in a large pitcher or jar with a tight-fitting lid.

Place the peppercorns on a cutting board and, using the bottom of a heavy pan, coarsely crack the peppercorns. Alternatively, you may use a mortar and pestle. Add the cracked peppercorns to the pitcher.

Add the chipotle, Worcestershire sauce, Tabasco sauce, lemon zest, and vodka and stir to mix.

Allow the infusion to sit in the refrigerator for at least 2 days and up to 4 days. Strain the mix, discarding the solids, and store the infusion in the refrigerator or freezer until ready to serve.

When ready to serve, pour the celery salt onto a small plate. Rub the juicy side of the lemon wedge along the outer edge of the lip of each glass—not along the inside of the rim. Holding each glass at an angle, roll the outer edge of the rim in the celery salt until it is fully coated.

Using a vegetable peeler, cut thin slices of the celery stalk and place some into each glass. Fill a cocktail shaker or pitcher with ice. Add 4 ounces bloodless Mary mix per serving. Shake or stir vigorously until the outside of the shaker is thoroughly beaded with sweat and is extremely cold to the touch. Pour into the cocktail glasses and serve.

TRICK OF THE TRADE

Chipotles, which are dried, smoked jalapeño peppers, are fairly easy to find in major supermarkets, natural foods stores, or Latin markets. If you have trouble finding them, use any fresh, hot pepper: Simply split it lengthwise and add it to the bloodless Mary mix seeds and all. Celery root is also readily available, but you can substitute 6 to 8 ounces of diced rib celery. If you can't find fresh horseradish, use 2 heaping tablespoons prepared horseradish instead.

FOR THE BLOODLESS MARY MIX

1 small bulb celery root
(6 to 8 ounces), peeled
and cut into 1-inch cubes

6 to 8 ounces fresh horseradish
root, peeled and cut into
1-inch cubes

1 tablespoon black peppercorns

1 chipotle pepper
(see Trick of the Trade)

1 teaspoon Worcestershire sauce

1 teaspoon Tabasco sauce

Long zest of 1 lemon
(see page 39)

1 liter vodka

FOR THE COCKTAIL

2 tablespoons celery salt for
rimming the glass

1 lemon wedge for rimming
the glass

1 stalk celery for garnish

GLASSWARE Cocktail glasses
(see page 24)

Moscow Mule

Makes two 6-ounce drinks

Ice for serving

4 ounces Smirnoff vodka

8 ounces ginger beer

GLASSWARE Highball glasses
(see page 23)

The Smirnoff Vodka Company created this wonderfully simple drink in the 1940s to help promote its brand. Ginger beer is much drier and has a more pronounced ginger flavor than ginger ale. The better versions are actually brewed just like beer and are nonalcoholic.

Fill the highball glasses with ice.

Add 2 ounces vodka and 4 ounces ginger beer to each glass. Stir well and serve.

Americano

Makes two 7-ounce drinks

Ice for serving

3 ounces Campari

3 ounces sweet vermouth

8 ounces seltzer

GLASSWARE Highball glasses
(see page 23)

This drink was first produced in Milan, Italy, in the 1860s and called the Milan-Torino. During Prohibition, the Italian barmen noticed how much the American tourists enjoyed this drink and renamed it the Americano.

Fill the highball glasses with ice and add 1½ ounces Campari and 1½ ounces sweet vermouth to each glass.

Add 4 ounces seltzer to each glass. Stir well and serve.

Floridita

Makes two 6-ounce drinks

4 ounces white rum

3 ounces fresh grapefruit juice
(from approximately ½ grapefruit)

2 ounces fresh lime juice
(from approximately 2 limes)

1 ounce triple sec

1 ounce maraschino liqueur
(see Straight Up, page 74)

1 ounce Grenadine
(page 64) or use store-bought

2 fresh mint leaves for garnish

GLASSWARE Cocktail glasses
(see page 24)

This cocktail was created at the Floridita Hotel in Cuba sometime in the 1920s or 1930s. The addition of the grapefruit juice gives the Floridita a bit of tang.

Fill a cocktail shaker with ice and add all the ingredients except the mint. Shake vigorously until the outside of the shaker is beaded with sweat and frosty.

Strain into cocktail glasses, garnish with mint leaves, and serve.

Knickerbocker

Makes two 4-ounce drinks

Created by Jerry Thomas in 1862 when he was the bartender at the Occidental Hotel in San Francisco, this drink remains a classic more than 140 years later.

The soft, mellow rum and tart lemon are lightly sweetened by the raspberry syrup to make an eye-opening, refreshing drink that is perfect as an aperitif or to serve with brunch.

Fill a cocktail shaker with ice and add all the ingredients except the lemon wedges. Shake vigorously until the outside of the shaker is beaded with sweat and frosty.

Strain into cocktail glasses. Squeeze a lemon wedge over each drink, then drop the wedge in the glass and serve.

4 ounces dark rum

1 ounce triple sec

1 ounce Berry Syrup (page 62) or Grenadine (see page 64) or use store-bought

2 ounces fresh lemon juice (from approximately 2 lemons)

2 lemon wedges for garnish

GLASSWARE Cocktail glasses (see page 24)

Ward 8

Makes two 5-ounce drinks

There are various versions of this cocktail, but most agree that it was created in Boston in the 1890s and that its name is inspired by the city's being districted into eight wards.

Its smoky orange flavor makes it a great palate opener when served before dinner.

Fill the rocks glasses with ice.

Fill a cocktail shaker with ice and add the bourbon, syrup, citrus juices, and grenadine. Shake vigorously until the outside of the shaker is beaded with sweat and frosty.

Strain into the glasses. Garnish each with an orange slice and a cherry and serve.

Ice for serving

4 ounces bourbon

2 ounces Simple Syrup (page 56)

2 ounces fresh orange juice (from approximately ½ orange)

1½ ounces fresh lemon juice (from approximately 1 lemon)

½ ounce Grenadine (page 64) or use store-bought

2 orange slices for garnish

2 Maraschino Cherries (page 53) or use store-bought for garnish

GLASSWARE Rocks glasses (see page 23)

Valencia

Makes two 2½-ounce drinks

This drink dates back almost a hundred years and is named after Valencia oranges, once used to give this cocktail its juice. It is traditionally served in small portions and makes a quick and light preprandial.

Fill a cocktail shaker with ice. Shake vigorously until the outside of the shaker is beaded with sweat and frosty.

Strain into cocktail glasses and serve.

3 ounces apricot brandy

2 ounces fresh orange juice (from approximately ½ orange)

8 dashes orange bitters

GLASSWARE Cocktail glasses (see page 24)

Sours

Makes six 3-ounce drinks (left: Daisy; top right: Fix; bottom right: Sour)

Ice for serving

12 ounces whiskey, bourbon, vodka, gin, rum, or other spirit

6 ounces Lemon Sour Mix (page 65), or combine 5 ounces lemon juice (from approximately 4 lemons) with 2 tablespoons superfine sugar or 1 ounce Simple Syrup (page 56)

6 Maraschino Cherries (page 53) or use store-bought for garnish

GLASSWARE Wineglasses (see page 24)

Sweet and tangy sours are among the most popular of all cocktails. A sour is a combination of a base liquor—usually whiskey, bourbon, vodka, gin, or rum—made tart with lemon juice and balanced with a dash of syrup. Premade sour mix makes preparation a snap. With a few minor tweaks, the sour can be transformed into an equally delicious Daisy, Fix, Fizz, or Trina (see below).

Fill a cocktail shaker with ice and add the spirit and sour mix. Shake vigorously until the outside of the shaker is beaded with sweat and frosty.

Strain the cocktail into the wineglasses. Garnish each with a cherry and serve.

DAISY Prepare the Sour as above, using 5 ounces lemon juice and 1 ounce raspberry syrup (page 62) in place of the lemon sour mix. Garnish with pineapple wedges.

FIX Prepare the Sour as above, using 5 ounces lemon juice and 1 ounce Pineapple Syrup (page 61) in place of the lemon sour mix.

FIZZ To turn the Sour, Daisy, or Fix into a Fizz, strain the drink into a highball glass filled with ice and top off with club soda.

TRINA Prepare the Sour as above, replacing 2 ounces of lemon sour with 2 ounces blood orange juice (from approximately 1 blood orange). Serve in cocktail glasses garnished with a blood orange round.

Caipirinha

Makes two 3-ounce drinks

1 lime, cut into 8 wedges for muddling

2 teaspoons sugar

4 ounces cachaca

Ice for serving

GLASSWARE Rocks glasses (see page 23)

Caipirinha, which means "little countryside drink," is the national drink of Brazil. It is based on cachaca, a liquor distilled from sugarcane juice whose appealingly bitter bite is reminiscent of tequila.

Place 4 lime wedges and 1 teaspoon sugar in each rocks glass. Muddle the lime and sugar together to extract as much juice as possible (see page 22).

Divide the cachaca between the glasses and stir well. Fill each glass with ice, stir well again, and serve.

Rusty Nail

Makes two 3-ounce drinks

Ice for serving

4 ounces scotch

2 ounces Drambuie
(see Straight Up)

GLASSWARE Rocks glasses
(see page 23)

In this classic drink, the Drambuie softens the scotch while the scotch cuts right through the extreme sweetness of the Drambuie.

Fill the rocks glasses with ice.

Fill a cocktail pitcher with ice and add the scotch and Drambuie. Stir vigorously until the outside of the pitcher is beaded with sweat and frosty.

Strain into the glasses and serve.

STRAIGHT UP

Drambuie is a cordial that is a blend of scotch and honey. It tastes smoky, sweet, and herbal all at once. In Gaelic the name means "the drink that satisfies."

Swizzle

Makes two 4-ounce drinks

Crushed ice for serving

4 ounces Jamaican rum

2 ounces Simple Syrup (page 56)

1 ounce fresh lime juice
(from approximately 1 lime)

1 ounce fresh lemon juice
(from approximately 1 lemon)

2 dashes Angostura bitters

2 lime wedges for garnish

GLASSWARE Highball glasses
(see page 23)

This drink is named after the swizzle stick. The original swizzle sticks were created in Jamaica and were twelve or more inches long with spikes on the bottom that helped mix the drink.

Fill the highball glasses with crushed ice.

Fill a cocktail shaker with ice and add the rum, syrup, citrus juices, and bitters. Shake vigorously until the outside of the shaker is beaded with sweat and frosty.

Strain into the glasses, garnish with lime wedges, and serve.

Scarlett O'Hara

Makes two 5-ounce drinks

This drink and the one that follows were created after the release of *Gone With the Wind*. Southern Comfort is a sweetened, peach-flavored bourbon. It is great served on the rocks and is wonderful as a mixer.

Fill a cocktail shaker with ice and add all the ingredients except the cranberries. Shake vigorously until the outside of the shaker is beaded with sweat and frosty.

Strain into the cocktail glasses, garnish each glass with 3 cranberries, and serve.

4 ounces Southern Comfort

2 ounces fresh lime juice (from approximately 2 limes)

4 ounces cranberry juice

6 cranberries for garnish

GLASSWARE Cocktail glasses (see page 24)

Rhett Butler

Makes two 5-ounce drinks

Perhaps inspired by its namesake, who definitely didn't give a damn and likely preferred drinks with some kick, this one is a little more potent than the Scarlett O'Hara.

Fill a cocktail shaker with ice and add all the ingredients except the lime wedges. Shake vigorously until the outside of the shaker is beaded with sweat and frosty.

Strain into cocktail glasses, garnish with the lime wedges, and serve.

2 ounces Grand Marnier

2 ounces Southern Comfort

4 ounces cranberry juice

2 ounces fresh lime juice (from approximately 2 limes)

2 lime wedges for garnish

GLASSWARE Cocktail glasses (see page 24)

Between the Sheets

Makes two 3-ounce drinks

I can only imagine where this Prohibition-era cocktail got its name. The herbs from the Bénédictine, the orange from the Cointreau, and the kick from the brandy give this drink many layers of flavor that linger on the palate.

Fill a cocktail shaker with ice and add all the ingredients except the orange twists. Shake vigorously until the outside of the shaker is beaded with sweat and frosty.

Strain into cocktail glasses, garnish with the orange twists, and serve.

2 ounces brandy

1 ounce Bénédictine

1 ounce Cointreau

2 ounces fresh lemon juice (from approximately 2 lemons)

2 orange twists (see page 39) for garnish

GLASSWARE Cocktail glasses (see page 24)

111 APPLE CRISP

111 PEAR COBBLER

112 APPLE CRUSH

114 BLACKBERRY DAIQUIRI

116 CRANBERRY DAIQUIRI

117 BLACK CURRANT DAIQUIRI

118 SPARKLING CAMPARI
COCKTAIL

119 KAFFIR LIME KOCKTAIL

121 BANANA RUM FRAPPÉ

122 LEMON FRAPPÉ

122 GT BUCK

123 GREENMARKET GIBSON

123 SUMMER SUNSET

125 RASPBERRY TEN

126 BASIL MARTINI

129 ROSMARINO

130 GIN-GER & TONIC

130 CITRUS GIN

131 MARASCHINO
OLD-FASHIONED

131 POMPANO

132 TRIPLE RUM MARTINI

132 SALTY DOG

133 SHAGGY DOG

133 MONTECRISTO MUDDLE

134 GRAPE AND GRAIN

135 WHISKEY AND
GINGER MUDDLE

135 THE GRAND

136 SUNDAY HAM

136 POLARIS

136 CLOVE MARTINI

137 RUM AND MADEIRA COOLER

SPECIALTIES OF THE HOUSE

MOST ACCOMPLISHED CHEFS ARE WELL VERSED IN THE CLASSIC TECHNIQUES and dishes. They progress through their careers constantly influenced by their travels, experiences, and by fellow chefs. They in turn develop their own style based on these influences.

I too have been enormously influenced by the chefs I have worked with, from Alfred Portale at the Gotham Bar and Grill to Waldy Malouf at the Hudson River Club to Tom Colicchio and Claudia Fleming at Gramercy Tavern. Wherever I have worked, the food and the quality of the ingredients have inspired the drinks that I created. Over time, my personal style evolved into one that always considers cocktails in the context of the whole meal. During twenty years spent mixing drinks, I have developed a repertoire of recipes that complement how I like to eat and drink. In the last ten years or so, I stopped simply reinventing classics and began to create cocktails that fit within the context of a meal or a party. It was then that I began infusing herbs and fruits into my spirits and producing house-made cocktails. Just like a chef, I base my current recipes on my past experiences and, as I continue to experiment, I often find surprisingly good results in the unexpected.

Apple Crisp

Makes two 4½-ounce drinks (photograph on page 108, right)

This fall cocktail is perfect to drink before or with a dinner of pork loin roasted with apples or apricots. It is also good served after dinner, as the sharp bite and acidity of the calvados and the lemon make a refreshing digestif.

Fill a cocktail shaker with ice. Add the calvados, lemon juice, and Cointreau and shake vigorously until the outside of the shaker is thoroughly beaded with sweat and is extremely cold to the touch.

Fill the cocktail glasses ⅓ full of crushed ice and add the cocktail. Garnish each with a speared crab apple and serve.

4 ounces calvados or applejack (see Straight Up, page 112)

4 ounces fresh lemon juice (from approximately 3 lemons)

1 ounce Cointreau or triple sec

Crushed ice for serving

2 crab apples, each on a cocktail spear, for garnish

GLASSWARE Cocktail glasses (see page 24)

Pear Cobbler

Makes two 5-ounce drinks (photograph on page 108, center)

This drink is based on the classic Sidecar (page 91), a sublime mixture of fresh lemon, brandy, and Cointreau. The pear cobbler replaces the brandy with pear liqueur while the lemon and orange flavors remain the same, resulting in a delightfully crisp and fruity drink. If you can't find pear liqueur (Belle de Brillet is a good choice), replace it with 4 ounces brandy and 2 ounces pear nectar. This will yield two 6-ounce cocktails.

Try serving the Pear Cobbler with biscotti or shorbread cookies and dried fruit for a light dessert.

Fill the cocktail shaker or pitcher with ice. Add the sour mix and shake or stir vigorously.

Add the pear liqueur and triple sec. Shake or stir until the mix appears frothy on top.

Pour into two chilled cocktail glasses. Float a dried pear slice on top of each drink and serve immediately.

4 ounces Lemon Sour Mix (page 65)

4 ounces pear liqueur

2 ounces triple sec

2 dried pear slices for garnish

GLASSWARE Cocktail glasses, chilled (see page 24)

Apple Crush

Makes four 6-ounce drinks (photograph opposite and on page 108, left)

1 Rome apple

3 ounces fresh lemon juice (from approximately 2 lemons), lemon rinds reserved

2 tablespoons maple sugar or 2 teaspoons cinnamon mixed with 4 teaspoons sugar, for rimming the glass

10 ounces calvados or applejack (see Straight Up)

4 ounces vodka

4 ounces fresh-pressed apple cider

GLASSWARE Cocktail glasses (see page 23)

This drink was inspired by a holiday pie-making marathon. Rome apples' texture and acidity are perfectly balanced for cooking. They have a creamy feel in your mouth yet enough structure to stand up well to cooking. Use your own favorite here, and whether it is tart and very firm or sweet and slightly soft to the bite, make sure to buy fresh, local apples in season.

PLANNING AHEAD The apple must be chilled for at least 15 minutes and can be refrigerated for up to 1 hour.

Peel, core, and dice the apple into ½-inch cubes. Place the apple in a zippered plastic bag and add about 1 tablespoon of the lemon juice. Seal the bag and toss gently (this will help prevent discoloration). Chill thoroughly for 30 minutes in the refrigerator (the apple can stay for up to 1 hour in the refrigerator) or 15 minutes in the freezer.

When ready to serve, pour the maple sugar onto a small plate. Rub the juicy side of the reserved lemon rind (cut the rind if necessary to expose this side) along the outer edge of the lip of each glass—not along the inside of the rim. Holding each glass at an angle, roll the outer edge of the rim in the sugar until it is fully coated.

Fill a cocktail shaker with ice and add the calvados, vodka, cider, and remaining lemon juice. Shake vigorously until the outside of the shaker is thoroughly beaded with sweat and is extremely cold to the touch. Pour into the prepared glasses and serve.

STRAIGHT UP

Calvados is an apple brandy produced in the Normandy region of France. It's made from hard cider containing a combination of sweet and tart apples. The cider is double distilled in pot stills at a low temperature. After distillation, the calvados is aged in oak barrels for at least one year. The best versions are aged ten to fifteen years, and many are aged twenty-five years or longer. Applejack is the American version of calvados. While true aged calvados is generally better than most applejack, locally produced applejack offers better value at lower prices. I enjoy Laird's Applejack from New Jersey.

Blackberry Daiquiri

Makes two 5-ounce drinks and enough drunken blackberries for about 10 to 16 cocktails (photograph opposite, right)

FOR THE DRUNKEN BLACKBERRIES

2 pints blackberries, gently rinsed

¼ cup sugar

16 ounces dark rum

2 ounces Licor 43
(see Straight Up)

FOR THE COCKTAIL

4 ounces dark rum

4 ounces Lime Sour Mix
(page 65)

2 ounces Echte Kroatsbeere
Blackberry liqueur

Ice for serving

GLASSWARE Cocktail glasses
(see page 24)

The blackberry daiquiri, one of Gramercy Tavern's biggest sellers, was created to preserve an overabundance of fresh blackberries. They were cleaned, placed in a covered pitcher, sprinkled with sugar, and soaked with rum. Three days later, I was greeted by a fantastic concoction. Licor 43 is the perfect complement to the mellow sweetness of the rum and the tartness of the blackberries.

Echte Kroatsbeere Blackberry liqueur is preferable because it contains all-natural ingredients. If you cannot find it, use another high-quality blackberry brandy.

PLANNING AHEAD The drunken blackberries need at least 1 hour to soak, and are really best after 1 week. Leftover drunken blackberries can be refrigerated for up to 3 months.

To prepare the drunken blackberries, place the blackberries in a large canning jar or other container with a tight-fitting lid. Add the sugar, seal the container, and gently rotate the jar to mix the sugar and blackberries. Add the rum and the Licor 43 and again rotate the jar to mix. The blackberries will be ready to use after 1 hour, but are better after 24 hours and even better after a week.

When ready to serve, fill a cocktail shaker or pitcher with ice and add rum, sour mix, and blackberry liqueur. Shake or stir vigorously until the shaker is beaded with sweat and frosty and the mixture is frothy.

Place a few ice cubes in the two cocktail glasses and add 3 or 4 drunken blackberries to each. Pour the daiquiri over the ice and blackberries. Serve immediately.

STRAIGHT UP

Licor 43 is a Spanish liqueur made from 43 herbs and spices. The resulting liqueur is predominantly vanilla flavored and has a creamy texture. At 34 proof, it is a great cordial on its own or mixed with strong black coffee. More often than not, it is used as a mixer.

BONUS FROM THE BAR

Any remaining liquid from the drunken blackberries can be used as a mixer with seltzer for a refreshing summer highball. Or, for a topping for ice cream or pound cake, reduce the blackberries and their juice to a syrupy glaze over low heat for 5 to 10 minutes.

Cranberry Daiquiri

Makes six 6½-ounce drinks and enough cranberries for about 12 drinks

FOR THE CRANBERRIES

6 ounces fresh cranberries

4 ounces pure maple syrup

2 whole cloves

1 whole star anise

1 teaspoon grated orange zest (see page 39), orange flesh reserved

¼ teaspoon cinnamon

FOR THE COCKTAIL

3 tablespoons maple sugar for rimming the glass

Crushed ice or ice cubes for serving

18 ounces Lime Sour Mix (page 65)

15 ounces light rum

6 ounces cranberry liqueur (optional)

GLASSWARE Cocktail glasses (see page 24)

This recipe evolved from my annual Thanksgiving cranberry sauce (see Bonus from the Bar, below). The warm spices and maple syrup make it the quintessential autumn relish. Black Duck Cranberry Liqueur is not too difficult to find and is well worth the effort (see Mail-order Sources). If you can't find it, try making your own (see page 67) or substitute another red berry cordial, such as Chambord or Cherry Heering (see Straight Up, page 84).

PLANNING AHEAD The cranberries can be made as long as 2 weeks in advance and stored in the refrigerator.

Place all the ingredients for the cranberries in a deep saucepan and stir to combine thoroughly. Cook the mixture over medium heat, stirring frequently, just until you hear the berries begin to pop, about 5 minutes. Reduce the heat to low and simmer for 1 more minute. Transfer the cranberries to a bowl and let cool. Refrigerate until thoroughly chilled.

When ready to serve, pour the maple sugar onto a small plate. Slice a wedge from the reserved orange and rub the juicy side of the fruit along the outer edge of the lip of each glass—not along the inside of the rim. Holding each glass at an angle, roll the outer edge of the rim in the sugar until it is fully coated.

Add a tablespoon of crushed ice or several ice cubes to each glass. Put a heaping tablespoon of the cranberries with their juice into each glass.

Fill a large pitcher with a tight-fitting lid or an extra-large cocktail shaker with ice. Add the sour mix, rum, and cranberry liqueur. Shake or stir vigorously until the pitcher or shaker is thoroughly beaded with sweat and is extremely cold to the touch. Strain the cocktail mix into each glass and serve.

CRANBERRY DAIQUIRI PUNCH For a festive holiday punch, double or triple this recipe, then thoroughly chill all the ingredients before mixing in a punch bowl.

BONUS FROM THE BAR

MAPLE CRANBERRY SAUCE If you have any of the cooked cranberry mixture left over after serving a round of cranberry daiquiris, return it to the pot and simmer for 5 more minutes. Serve as a condiment at room temperature or cold. The cranberries will keep in the refrigerator for up to 2 weeks.

Black Currant Daiquiri

Makes six 4-ounce drinks and enough drunken currants
for 6 to 8 drinks

The sublime syrupy sweetness of the Pedro Ximenez
sherry and drunken currants is nicely balanced by the
mouth-puckering lime sour mix for a heavenly example
of the classic sweet-tart combination. Unlike the black
and red berries that are called currants, dried currants
are actually a type of raisin made from small Black Corinth
grapes. They are sometimes labeled zante currants.

PLANNING AHEAD The drunken currants can be made as little as
1 hour ahead, but they are really best after 48 hours. They last
for up to 4 weeks in the refrigerator.

To prepare the drunken currants, place the currants in a large
canning jar or other container with a tight-fitting lid. Add the
rum, Licor 43, and sherry. Seal the container and gently rotate
to mix. The currants will be ready to use in 1 hour, but the
longer they sit, the better they are.

When ready to serve, prepare the cocktail by filling a large
pitcher with ice and adding the rum, sour mix, and sherry.
Stir vigorously until the pitcher is beaded with sweat and the
mixture is well blended and frothy.

Place a few ice cubes in the rocks glasses and add a
teaspoon of drunken currants to each. Pour the daiquiri
over the ice and currants. Serve immediately.

STRAIGHT UP

Pedro Ximenez sherry is one of the world's greatest dessert
wines. Made from the Pedro Ximenez grape, it is thick, black,
syrupy, raisiny, and absolutely delicious. I use it for many recipes
both at the bar and in the kitchen. It is generally easy to find in
a well-stocked wine shop. Many large sherry producers in Spain
make Pedro Ximenez; two to look for are Alvear and Lustau.

BONUS FROM THE BAR

For a crêpe filling or to serve on French toast, simmer any
remaining drunken currants over low heat in a heavy-bottomed
pot until they reduce to a syrupy compote.

FOR THE DRUNKEN CURRANTS

2 ounces dried currants

1 ounce dark rum

1 ounce Licor 43
(see Straight Up, page 114)

1 ounce Pedro Ximenez sherry
(see Straight Up)

FOR THE COCKTAIL

12 ounces dark rum

8 ounces Lime Sour Mix
(page 65)

3 ounces Pedro Ximenez sherry

Ice for serving

GLASSWARE Rocks glasses
(see page 23)

FOR THE GRAPEFRUIT SYRUP

1 grapefruit

½ cup sugar

4 ounces water

FOR THE COCKTAIL

8 ounces vodka

8 ounces Campari

5½ ounces sweet vermouth

Ice cubes for serving

One 750-milliliter bottle sparkling Moscato

GLASSWARE Large wineglasses (see page 24)

Sparkling Campari Cocktail
Makes eight 6-ounce drinks

Not everyone appreciates the bitter taste of Campari; however, this cocktail's balanced and bubbly blend of sweet and tart makes it a superior aperitif.

PLANNING AHEAD The cocktail mix can be made as little as 1 hour ahead, but it is really best if made a full day in advance.

Cut the grapefruit in half and squeeze the juice from one half (you should have 3 to 4 ounces). Set the juice aside. Cut the grapefruit rind and the remaining half into wedges and set aside.

To prepare the grapefruit syrup, place the sugar and water in a medium nonreactive saucepan over medium heat and cook, stirring, until the sugar dissolves. Simmer until the syrup thickens slightly, about 2 minutes. Add the grapefruit wedges to the saucepan and cook until the grapefruit releases all of its juice, about 5 minutes. Remove the pan from the heat and let the syrup cool to room temperature.

To prepare the cocktail mix, add the vodka, Campari, sweet vermouth, and cooled grapefruit with syrup to a large canning jar or pitcher with a tight-fitting lid. Stir together thoroughly, cover, and let sit in the refrigerator for at least 1 hour or overnight (the longer the better).

To serve, add some ice to the wineglasses and strain the grapefruit mixture over the ice until the glasses are half full. Add a splash of the reserved grapefruit juice, top off with 3 ounces of Moscato per glass, and serve.

Kaffir Lime Kocktail

Makes enough Kaffir lime tequila for eighteen 3-ounce drinks

For years many people avoided tequila because there were few great-tasting ones on the market, and the only way anyone ever thought to serve or order them was as shots with salt and lime. Nowadays, there are wonderful high-quality brands widely available that make for great cocktails. The drink featured here is for the true tequila enthusiast who wants to taste the earthiness, complexity, and bite of great agave tequila. Kaffir lime leaves are available at Asian markets, spice emporiums, and online (see Mail-order Sources).

PLANNING AHEAD The Kaffir lime tequila can be made as few as 2 hours before serving, but it is really best after 2 days. It can be made ahead, and the strained tequila can be stored for up to 2 weeks in the refrigerator.

To prepare the Kaffir lime tequila, place the lime leaves in a 2-quart canning jar or other container with a tight-fitting lid. Add the honey and the boiling water, tightly close the jar, and shake vigorously. Let steep for 5 minutes.

Open the jar and add the tequila. Squeeze the juice from each lime half into the jar and then toss in the lime rinds themselves. Tightly close the jar and shake vigorously.

Allow to steep in the refrigerator for at least 2 hours and up to 2 days, gently shaking the jar occasionally to mix. The longer it sits, the richer the infusion will become. After 48 hours, strain the tequila and discard the lime leaves and limes. Transfer the infused tequila into a clean bottle or jar and store in the refrigerator for up to 2 weeks.

When ready to serve, fill each cocktail glass halfway with crushed ice.

Fill a cocktail shaker with ice, add 2 ounces Kaffir lime tequila for each serving, and shake vigorously until the outside of the shaker is thoroughly beaded with sweat and is extremely cold to the touch.

Pour the lime tequila into each cocktail glass, top with a Kaffir lime leaf and lime slice, and serve.

FOR THE KAFFIR LIME TEQUILA

10 to 20 Kaffir lime leaves, thoroughly rinsed, plus more for garnish

12 ounces honey

8 ounces boiling water

1 liter 100% agave tequila (see Straight Up, page 122)

4 limes, halved

FOR EACH COCKTAIL

Crushed ice for serving

1 Kaffir lime leaf for garnish

1 slice lime for garnish

GLASSWARE Cocktail glasses (see page 24)

Banana Rum Frappé

Makes fifteen 5½-ounce drinks

Even if you're sure you don't need to make the full fifteen servings this recipe allows for, go ahead and make the full recipe of banana rum. It has a number of good uses (see Bonus from the Bar) and keeps indefinitely once the bananas are strained.

PLANNING AHEAD The banana rum can be made as few as 4 hours in advance, but it is ideal after 48 hours.

To prepare the banana rum, cut the dried banana slices in half and place them in a large canning jar or pitcher with a tight-fitting lid. Add the water, molasses, and brown sugar, stir well, and let sit for 2 minutes.

Stir in the rum. Split the vanilla bean in half lengthwise and scrape out the seeds. Add the seeds and bean to the rum. Shake or stir vigorously to mix all ingredients. Refrigerate for up to 48 hours, stirring or shaking occasionally. After 48 hours at most, strain the rum, discarding the vanilla bean and reserving the bananas for another use (see Bonus from the Bar).

When ready to serve, pour the sugar and coconut into a small bowl and mix together thoroughly. Transfer the coconut sugar to a small plate. Rub the juicy side of the lemon or lime wedge along the outer edge of the lip of each glass—not along the inside of the rim. Holding each glass at an angle, roll the outer edge of the rim in the sugar until it is fully coated.

Fill a pitcher with ice, add the banana rum and pineapple juice, and stir briskly until the pitcher is beaded with sweat and frosty.

Add crushed ice to the prepared coupes. Pour the frappé over the ice, garnish with dried pineapple slices or banana chips, sprinkle with coconut, and serve.

BANANA RUM PUNCH Peel and freeze 4 large, ripe, fresh bananas until firm. Place them in a punch bowl and add the banana rum with the dried bananas, pineapple juice, and 1 liter of pear or apple cider or 1 liter of ginger beer. Sprinkle shredded coconut over the top and serve.

BONUS FROM THE BAR

The bananas that are strained out of the banana rum make a delicious topping for ice cream or cake. Also, once the pineapple juice is added, the cocktail mix itself (combined with some soy sauce) can be used as a marinade and base for grilled chicken or fish.

FOR THE BANANA RUM

12 dried banana slices or
2 cups dried banana chips

4 ounces boiling water

2 ounces unsulfured molasses

¼ cup packed brown sugar

1 liter dark rum

1 large vanilla bean

FOR THE COCKTAIL

4 tablespoons granulated sugar for rimming the glass

4 tablespoons shredded coconut, toasted, for rimming the glass, plus more for garnish

1 lemon or lime wedge for rimming the glass

16 ounces pineapple juice

Crushed ice for serving

Dried pineapple slices or banana chips for garnish

GLASSWARE Margarita coupes or large martini glasses (see page 24)

Lemon Frappé

Makes four 5-ounce drinks

Crushed ice for serving

1 lemon, quartered

Long zest of 1 orange or lime
(see page 39) for garnish

8 ounces vodka or gin

8 ounces Limoncello
(page 69) or use store-bought

GLASSWARE Wineglasses
(see page 24)

Limoncello is an Italian cordial made by macerating crushed lemons with sugar and then adding grappa or another clear distillate. The mixture sits until the flavors are blended according to the house style. It is relatively easy to find. Knapp Vineyards in New York's Finger Lakes wine region makes an excellent domestic version, or you can easily make your own.

Fill each wineglass with crushed ice. Squeeze a lemon wedge in each glass and then drop the lemon in. Using a zester, cut long strands from the orange or lime and lay them on top of the ice.

Pour 2 ounces each of the vodka or gin and limoncello into the glasses, stir until well blended, and serve.

GT Buck

Makes four 10-ounce drinks

Ice for serving

4 dashes orange bitters or
Angostura bitters or Peychaud's
bitters (see Mail-order Sources)

1 lemon, quartered

10 ounces 100% agave tequila
(see Straight Up)

30 ounces ginger ale

Long zest of 1 orange or lime
(see page 39) for garnish

GLASSWARE Highball glasses
(see page 23)

The classic gin buck is gin and ginger ale with a squeeze of lemon. It is simple and delicious. In my ceaseless quest for ways to enjoy tequila other than in a margarita, I adapted the gin buck's straightforward approach, adding orange bitters.

Fill each highball glass with ice. Add a dash of orange bitters to each glass. Squeeze a lemon wedge over each, then drop the wedge into the glass.

Divide the tequila among the glasses, add ginger ale to fill, and stir. Using a zester, cut long strands from the orange or lime and float the zest on top. Serve.

STRAIGHT UP

Tequila is made from the blue agave cactus. Look for a label that says "agave" or "100% agave"; otherwise the tequila probably has a percentage of sugarcane distillates blended in. Look for an aged, or *reposado,* tequila, as it has more pronounced, earthy, true tequila flavors. If you prefer a subtler taste, use silver tequila, which is unaged and has no color.

Greenmarket Gibson

Makes enough herb-infused vodka for fourteen 3-ounce drinks

This drink is inspired by the farmers at the Union Square Greenmarket in New York City, where walking among the rows of great produce is pure delight. The subtlety of the herb blend in this drink makes it a wonderful aperitif at any time of year. Add a peppery leaf such as arugula for even more zip.

PLANNING AHEAD The herb-infused vodka requires 3 days in the refrigerator. Once the herbs are removed from the infusion, it will keep indefinitely in the refrigerator.

To prepare the herb-infused vodka, place the herbs in a 2-quart canning jar or other container with a tight-fitting lid. Add the boiling water, close the jar tightly, and shake vigorously. Allow to steep until the herbs are bright green, about 10 minutes. Add the ice water, vodka, and dry vermouth. Close the jar tightly and shake vigorously. Allow to steep in a cool spot or the refrigerator for 3 days, until the liquid turns bright green. Remove and discard the herbs.

When ready to serve, fill a cocktail shaker with ice. Pour in 3 ounces herb-infused vodka per drink and shake vigorously until the outside of the shaker is thoroughly beaded with sweat and is extremely cold to the touch.

Strain the vodka into the cocktail glasses. Add an onion and carrot pickle to each and serve.

FOR THE HERB-INFUSED VODKA

1 small bunch or 1 dozen leaves fresh basil, rinsed

1 large branch rosemary

3 bay leaves

5 sprigs cilantro

5 sprigs parsley

2 ounces boiling water

2 ounces ice water

1 liter vodka

5½ ounces dry vermouth

FOR EACH COCKTAIL

1 Cocktail Onion (page 52) for garnish

1 Quick Carrot Pickle (page 50) for garnish

GLASSWARE Small cocktail glasses (see page 24)

Summer Sunset

Makes four 8-ounce drinks

In this drink, the richness of the rum and port is balanced by the acidity of the lemon juice. Serve this before a summer barbecue or even after the main meal is done.

Fill the rocks glasses with ice.

Fill a pitcher with ice and add the sour mix, rum, and port. Stir briskly until the mixture is frothy and the pitcher is beaded with sweat and frosty.

Strain the rum mixture into the glasses and lay an orange slice on top of each drink.

Gently pour 1 ounce cherry brandy over each orange slice and serve just before sunset.

Ice for serving

16 ounces Lemon Sour Mix (page 65)

8 ounces dark rum

4 ounces ruby port

Four ⅛-inch-thick round orange slices for garnish

4 ounces cherry brandy

GLASSWARE Rocks glasses (see page 23)

Raspberry Ten

Makes six 12-ounce drinks

Tanqueray No. Ten gin contains enhanced aromatics that make it seem naturally dry, with a hint of sweetness and herbaceousness that marry perfectly with the raspberries in this cocktail. Feel free to substitute your favorite berry in season for the raspberries.

PLANNING AHEAD The drunken raspberries can be used immediately after they are made, but they are best if allowed to sit at least 1 hour or even overnight.

To prepare the drunken raspberries, place them in a canning jar or other container with a tight-fitting lid. Add the confectioners' sugar, close the jar, and gently rotate it to combine the berries and sugar.

Add the crème de framboise, sweet vermouth, and lemon juice to the raspberries. Rotate the jar to mix. Use immediately or let it sit in the refrigerator overnight.

When ready to serve, fill the highball glasses with ice. Spoon 2 to 3 tablespoons drunken raspberries with their juice over the ice. Add 2 ounces gin to each highball glass, top off with tonic water, and serve.

STRAIGHT UP

Crème de framboise is a raspberry cordial originally from France, though nowadays it is made all over the world. Crème de framboise has incredible depth of flavor, great acidity, and a creamy sweetness; it makes a heavenly after-dinner drink served on its own. If you are not able to find it, substitute crème de cassis (black currant liqueur) or cherry brandy.

FOR THE DRUNKEN RASPBERRIES

½ pint raspberries, rinsed if necessary

3 tablespoons confectioners' sugar

3 ounces crème de framboise (see Straight Up)

3 ounces sweet vermouth

1½ ounces fresh lemon juice (from approximately 1 lemon)

FOR THE COCKTAIL

Ice for serving

12 ounces Tanqueray No. Ten gin

48 ounces tonic water

GLASSWARE Highball glasses (see page 23)

Basil Martini

Makes enough basil-infused vodka for twelve 3-ounce drinks

FOR THE BASIL-INFUSED VODKA

1 full bunch fresh basil

2 ounces boiling water

2 ounces ice-cold water

1 liter vodka

5½ ounces dry vermouth

FOR EACH 3-OUNCE COCKTAIL

½ ounce Bloody Mary mix
(page 215) or tomato juice

Crushed ice for serving

3 ounces basil-infused vodka

1 Oven-Dried Tomato Chip
(page 49) for garnish

or

1 sun-dried tomato
(not packed in oil)
cut in julienne for garnish

or

Fresh basil leaves cut into
chiffonade or a few fresh
baby basil leaves for garnish

GLASSWARE Cocktail glasses
(see page 24)

Basil, with its peppery heat and aromatic sweetness, lends itself to many uses, including cocktails. I originally created this drink as a savory preprandial with a vodka infusion, but I felt the cocktail needed more zip. I entered the kitchen at Gramercy Tavern one morning and found our chef about to toss out the remaining bits of oven-dried tomato chips. I quickly rescued them, and that night, they floated atop the basil martini. The addition of a drop of Bloody Mary mix gives both color and delicate flavor to this distinctive specialty drink.

PLANNING AHEAD The basil-infused vodka requires 3 days in the refrigerator. Once the basil is removed, the infusion will keep indefinitely in the refrigerator.

To prepare the basil-infused vodka, thoroughly rinse the basil under cold running water and place it in a 2-quart canning jar or other container with a tight-fitting lid. Add the boiling water, close the jar tightly, and shake vigorously. Allow to steep until the basil is bright green, about 10 minutes.

Open the jar and add the ice water, vodka, and vermouth. Close the jar tightly and shake vigorously. Allow to steep in a cool spot or in the refrigerator for 3 days, until the liquid turns bright green. Remove and discard the basil.

When ready to serve, pour ½ ounce Bloody Mary mix or tomato juice into each cocktail glass. Fill each glass by ⅓ with crushed ice.

Fill a cocktail shaker with ice, add 3 ounces of basil-infused vodka per serving, and shake vigorously until the outside of the shaker is thoroughly beaded with sweat and is extremely cold to the touch.

Divide the vodka among the cocktail glasses and top each drink with a tomato chip or a little julienned sun-dried tomato or a few strips or baby leaves of basil and serve.

TRICK OF THE TRADE

If the basil stays in the vodka too long, it will take on a brown-green color and the infusion will lose its fresh taste and appearance. If this happens, strain the infusion and discard the old basil. Add 1½ ounces vermouth and a few sprigs of fresh basil to the mixture. Cover the jar and chill in the refrigerator for 24 hours before using.

Rosmarino

Makes enough rosemary-infused vodka for sixteen 3-ounce drinks

This savory cocktail's unique and spirited taste comes from rosemary-infused vodka. The addition of vermouth and Pernod, an anise-based liqueur, makes this a potent and powerfully flavored cocktail, perfect to serve as an aperitif before a hearty meal.

PLANNING AHEAD The rosemary-infused vodka requires 2 days in the refrigerator. Once the rosemary is removed, the infusion will keep indefinitely in the refrigerator.

To prepare the rosemary-infused vodka, place the rosemary in a 2-quart canning jar or other container with a tight-fitting lid. Add the boiling water, close the jar tightly, and shake vigorously. Allow to steep until the rosemary is bright green, about 10 minutes.

Open the jar and add the ice water, vodka, vermouth, and Pernod. Close the jar tightly and shake vigorously. Allow to steep in a cool spot or the refrigerator for 2 days, until the liquid turns bright green. Remove and discard the rosemary.

When ready to serve, place two caper berries in the bottom of each cocktail glass.

Fill a cocktail shaker with ice, add 3 ounces of rosemary-infused vodka per serving, and shake vigorously until the outside of the shaker is thoroughly beaded with sweat and is extremely cold to the touch.

Pour the vodka over the caper berries and serve.

STRAIGHT UP

Caper berries are the fruits produced by the caper bush. The small caper that you generally see is the flower bud of the same plant. The caper grows all over the Mediterranean and is used extensively in many French, Italian, and Spanish dishes. The caper berry is larger and more bulbous than the caper and has a more pronounced bite and crunch. Try to use brined caper berries, not the salted kind, which taste so salty they overpower the drink. If you cannot find caper berries, you can substitute olives, pearl onions, or any other brined or pickled vegetable you like.

FOR THE ROSEMARY-INFUSED VODKA

Four 8-inch branches of rosemary, rinsed

2 ounces boiling water

8 ounces ice-cold water

1 liter vodka

4 ounces dry vermouth

2 ounces Pernod
(see Straight Up, page 221)

FOR EACH 3-OUNCE COCKTAIL

2 caper berries for garnish
(see Straight Up)

GLASSWARE Cocktail glasses
(see page 24)

Gin-ger & Tonic
Makes ten 10-ounce drinks

8 ounces Ginger Syrup (page 59)

1 liter Tanqueray No. Ten gin or another dry gin

One 1- to 1½-inch length of ginger, peeled and halved

2 limes, cut into wedges

Ice cubes for serving

About 2 liters tonic water

2 limes, each cut crosswise into 5 rounds, for garnish

GLASSWARE Large wineglasses (see page 24)

The gin-ger & tonic is best in the summer months, when the temperature is high and guests need to slake their thirst. It is a perfect barbecue cocktail, enhancing the smoky and salty flavors of the grill with its combination of sweet tang and mild bitterness. The gin-ger & tonic also stands well on its own at a cocktail party, since it is neither too sweet nor too tart and can therefore go with almost any type of hors d'oeuvre. It is very easy to adapt this recipe for either a smaller or bigger crowd. However many gin-ger & tonics you prepare for your crowd, remember that the final drinks should be equal parts cocktail mix and tonic.

PLANNING AHEAD The cocktail mix requires at least 24 hours in the refrigerator and will keep for 1 month.

Pour the ginger syrup into a 2-quart canning jar or other container with a tight-fitting lid and add the gin, ginger, and lime wedges. Stir, cover, and refrigerate for at least 24 hours. The cocktail mix will last one month in the refrigerator; it is not necessary to remove the ginger or lime wedges, but make sure to stir well before using.

To serve, fill the wineglasses with ice. Divide the gin mixture among the glasses (each should be about half full) and top off with tonic water. Float a fresh lime slice on each cocktail and serve.

Citrus Gin
Makes two 3-ounce drinks

4 ounces gin

1 ounce dry vermouth

1 ounce Limoncello (page 69) or use store-bought

4 dashes orange bitters

GLASSWARE Cocktail glasses (see page 24)

This is a particular favorite in the hottest months—a gin martini with a summery edge. Angostura bitters can be used in place of the orange bitters; they will change the color of the drink from yellow to pink.

Fill a cocktail pitcher with ice and add all the ingredients. Stir vigorously until the outside of the pitcher is beaded with sweat and frosty.

Strain into cocktail glasses and serve.

Maraschino Old-fashioned

Makes four 5½-ounce drinks

The classic Old-fashioned (page 96) is made with bourbon, sugar, orange, and a cherry muddled together. Using an extra cherry and cherry syrup makes the drink a little more fruit-forward and refreshing. It's especially sublime when made with homemade maraschino cherries.

Into each rocks glass, place 2 maraschino cherries with a healthy dose of their syrup, ½ teaspoon sugar, ½ teaspoon bitters, and an orange slice. Thoroughly muddle the ingredients (see page 22).

Fill each rocks glass with ice and pour in 3 ounces bourbon. Stir vigorously until well blended. Top off with club soda and serve.

8 Maraschino Cherries (page 53) or use store-bought for garnish

2 ounces maraschino cherry syrup

2 teaspoons sugar

2 teaspoons Angostura bitters

4 half slices of orange

Ice for serving

12 ounces bourbon

8 ounces club soda

GLASSWARE Rocks glasses (see page 23)

Pompano

Makes two 5-ounce drinks

I like an aromatic gin such as Tanqueray No. Ten in this drink, but if you prefer a mellower taste, use vodka instead. The bitters are optional, but they do make the drink more complex. To serve this drink to a group, mix a larger batch in a pitcher instead of a cocktail shaker.

Pour the turbinado sugar onto a small plate. Rub the juicy side of the grapefruit along the outer edge of the lip of each glass—not along the inside of the rim. Holding each glass at an angle, roll the outer edge of the rim in the sugar until it is fully coated. Add some crushed ice to each glass.

Squeeze the juice from the grapefruit (you should have 3 to 4 ounces). Fill a cocktail shaker or pitcher with ice, and add the grapefruit juice and the superfine sugar. Stir until the sugar has dissolved.

Add the gin, dry vermouth, and bitters to the cocktail shaker. Stir briskly until the shaker or pitcher is beaded with sweat and frosty.

Strain into the cocktail glasses, add a lemon twist to each, and serve.

2 teaspoons turbinado sugar (see page 41) or granulated sugar, for rimming the glasses

½ grapefruit

Crushed ice for serving

½ teaspoon superfine sugar

4 ounces gin or vodka

1½ ounces dry vermouth

2 dashes orange bitters (see Mail-order Sources) or Angostura bitters

2 large lemon twists (see page 39) for garnish

GLASSWARE Cocktail glasses (see page 24)

Triple Rum Martini

Makes two 4-ounce drinks

2 ounces Gosling's Black Seal Rum

2 ounces Bacardi Limón

2 ounces Rum Syrup (page 59)

2 ounces fresh lemon juice
(from approximately 2 lemons)

2 lemon twists (see page 39)
for garnish

GLASSWARE Cocktail glasses
(see page 24)

Mixing rums of different flavors and styles makes this multilayered cocktail a favorite among rum lovers. A dark rum such as Gosling's Black Seal has loads of rum flavor and lots of weight. Bacardi Limón is a lemon-flavored rum and is one of the greatest mixers.

Fill a cocktail pitcher with ice and add all the ingredients except the lemon twists. Stir vigorously until the outside of the pitcher is beaded with sweat and frosty.

Strain into cocktail glasses, garnish with the lemon twists, and serve.

Salty Dog

Makes four 5-ounce drinks

1 to 1½ grapefruits

2 tablespoons Hawaiian Alaea sea salt (see Mail-order Sources) or kosher salt for rimming the glass

8 ounces vodka or gin

2 ounces sweet vermouth

2 ounces Cointreau

GLASSWARE Cocktail glasses
(see page 24)

Try using Hawaiian Alaea sea salt to rim the glass for this drink. Mixed with powdered Hawaiian red clay, the salt's brick-orange color and robust salinity beautifully complement the rosy hue and refreshingly tart and citrusy flavor of the salty dog.

Remove four long strips (twists) of rind from the grapefruit, being careful not to remove very much of the white pith (see page 39). Cut the grapefruit in half and squeeze the juice from each half (you should have about 8 ounces) and set aside. Reserve one grapefruit rind.

Pour the salt onto a small plate. Cut the reserved grapefruit rind in half, then rub the juicy side of the fruit along the outer edge of the lip of each glass—not along the inside of the rim. Holding each glass at an angle, roll the outer edge of the rim in the salt until it is fully coated.

Fill a cocktail shaker with ice and add the vodka, vermouth, Cointreau, and grapefruit juice. Shake vigorously until the outside of the shaker is thoroughly beaded with sweat and is extremely cold to the touch.

Strain into the cocktail glasses, add a grapefruit twist to each, and serve.

Shaggy Dog

Makes two 4-ounce drinks

The first time I made dinner for my girlfriend, Terri Ludwig, I pulled out all the stops. I bought bags and bags of groceries plus vodka and vermouth for dirty martinis. Terri adores olives, and I thought dirty martinis, which include briny olive juice, would be a perfect start to the evening. Just as I was mixing the martinis I realized I had completely forgotten the olives. Luckily I had a jar of caper berries in the fridge and made a quick substitution. The improvisation must have worked—she is now Terri Mautone. As for how the drink got its name, now that's another story. . . .

Fill a cocktail shaker or pitcher with ice and add the vodka, dry vermouth, and brine.

Stir briskly until the shaker or pitcher is beaded with sweat and frosty.

Put a caper berry into each cocktail glass, strain the vodka into the glass, and serve.

5 ounces vodka

2 ounces dry vermouth

1 ounce brine from the jar of caper berries

2 large caper berries for garnish (see Straight Up, page 129)

GLASSWARE Cocktail glasses (see page 24)

Montecristo Muddle

Makes two 6-ounce drinks

This variation of the classic Old-fashioned (page 96) replaces bourbon with smoother, suppler rum. Its fruitiness and strength make it a good accompaniment to a cheese course. Turbinado sugar is especially welcome in this drink, where its caramel flavors complement the Montecristo rum's subtle smokiness.

PLANNING AHEAD The cherries can be made up to 2 weeks in advance and stored in the refrigerator.

Place 1 orange slice, 1 teaspoon sugar, and 3 cherries along with some of their syrup in each of the rocks glasses.

Muddle the ingredients together (see page 22). Add ice and 3 ounces rum to each glass and stir thoroughly.

Top off each glass with water, stir again, and serve.

2 round orange slices

2 teaspoons turbinado (see page 41) or granulated sugar

6 Maraschino Cherries (page 53) or use store-bought

Ice for serving

6 ounces Montecristo rum

2 ounces water

GLASSWARE Rocks glasses (see page 23)

STRAIGHT UP

Montecristo rum is fairly new to the market. It is made in Guatemala and is aged for twelve years in oak barrels previously used to age bourbon. This gives it a slightly smoky, robust, and unique flavor.

Grape and Grain

Makes four 6-ounce drinks

16 black grapes

4 half rounds of orange

4 teaspoons sugar

8 dashes Angostura bitters

Ice for serving

12 ounces bourbon

12 ounces seltzer

GLASSWARE Rocks glasses
(see page 23)

I first made this straightforward variation of the Old-fashioned (page 96) one autumn when cherries were out of season but fat, ripe grapes were just coming in. Use the darkest grapes you can find, as they generally have the richest flavor. Don't worry about seeds, they won't hurt the drink. For a stronger bourbon taste, use less seltzer.

Place 4 grapes in each rocks glass along with 1 orange half round, 1 teaspoon sugar, and 2 dashes bitters. Muddle the ingredients together (see page 22).

Fill the glasses with ice. Add 3 ounces bourbon to each and stir well. Top off each glass with seltzer and serve.

Whiskey and Ginger Muddle

Makes four 5-ounce drinks

I like to serve this to my friends who tell me they do not like bourbon, for the blend of smoky bourbon, ginger, and apricot is sublime and will turn anyone into a convert. For guests who don't care for mint, serve this as an alternative to the Mint Julep (page 97) on Kentucky Derby Day.

With a mortar and pestle or in a large bowl, muddle the ginger, apricots, and sugar together well (see page 22).

Divide the mixture between the rocks glasses. Add 2 ounces bourbon and 1 ounce apricot brandy to each glass and stir well to mix.

Fill each glass with crushed ice, top with 2 ounces water, and stir well. Serve.

One 2-inch knob fresh ginger, cut into 8 pieces

4 dried apricots

4 teaspoons sugar

8 ounces bourbon

4 ounces apricot brandy

Crushed ice for serving

8 ounces water

GLASSWARE Rocks glasses (see page 23)

The Grand

Makes four 3-ounce drinks

Although the Grand Marnier and sugar suggest a sweet cocktail, the grand is actually quite balanced and even a bit dry—it makes a wonderful aperitif.

To prepare the cocktail mix, place the orange slices, sugar, bitters, star anise, and boiling water in a heavy pitcher. Muddle together until the flesh of the orange is broken up (see page 22). Add the Grand Marnier, amontillado sherry, and orange juice and stir well. Add ice to the pitcher and stir briskly until the pitcher is beaded with sweat and frosty and the mixture is very cold.

Add a couple of ice cubes, 1 orange slice, and 1 whole star anise to each cocktail glass. Strain the cocktail mix into each glass and serve.

4 orange slices

1 tablespoon sugar

1/2 teaspoon Angostura bitters

4 whole star anise

2 ounces boiling water

4 ounces Grand Marnier

4 ounces amontillado sherry

2 ounces orange juice

Ice for serving

4 orange slices for garnish

4 whole star anise for garnish

GLASSWARE Cocktail glasses (see page 24)

Sunday Ham

Makes six 6-ounce drinks

Ice for serving

18 ounces pineapple juice

12 ounces bourbon

6 ounces Spiced Syrup (page 62)

6 pineapple wedges (see page 39) for garnish

6 fresh mint leaves for garnish

GLASSWARE Highball glasses (see page 23)

This blend of clove, pineapple, and bourbon is reminiscent of baked ham, only in a glass! Serve this drink before a hearty meal of savory, rich roasted meat.

Fill the highball glasses with ice. Fill a large pitcher with ice and add the pineapple juice, bourbon, and syrup. Stir vigorously until well blended.

Strain into the highball glasses. Garnish each with a pineapple wedge and a mint leaf and serve.

Polaris

Makes two 4-ounce drinks

6 ounces brandy

1 ounce sweet vermouth

1 ounce Cherry Heering (see Straight Up, page 84)

4 dashes bitters

2 orange twists (see page 39) for garnish

GLASSWARE Cocktail glasses (see page 24)

While stargazing on several cold nights last winter, I tried to warm my bones with a therapeutic shot of brandy. Over the course of the winter, I concocted this cocktail to keep me warm and aligned with my telescope as I searched for Polaris, the North Star.

Fill a cocktail shaker with ice and add all the ingredients except the orange twists. Stir vigorously until the outside of the shaker is beaded with sweat and frosty.

Strain into cocktail glasses, garnish with the orange twists, and serve.

Clove Martini

Makes two 3-ounce drinks

2 ounces Grey Goose La Vanille

2½ ounces Grey Goose Vodka

1½ ounces Spiced Syrup (page 62)

6 whole cloves for garnish

GLASSWARE Cocktail glasses (see page 24)

When I first tasted Grey Goose La Vanille, a vanilla-flavored vodka, I flipped for it. Mixed with regular vodka and clove syrup, it has become a staple for my friends who have a sweet tooth but do not want a heavy drink. It makes an equally great aperitif and after-dinner drink or nightcap.

Fill a cocktail shaker with ice and add all the ingredients except the cloves. Stir vigorously until the outside of the shaker is beaded with sweat and frosty.

Strain into cocktail glasses, add 3 cloves to each glass, and serve.

Rum and Madeira Cooler

Makes four 10-ounce drinks

Each sip of this drink is a surprising and delicious mix of flavors, starting with the fresh aroma of mint followed by a warm and spicy hint of nutmeg and amaretto, and ending with a tropical blast from the cooler. For a refreshing punch, triple the recipe and mix all ingredients except the nutmeg in a punch bowl. Keep the nutmeg grater next to your punch bowl and let your guests serve themselves.

Fill each collins glass halfway with ice. Squeeze 2 lemon and 2 lime wedges into each glass, then drop the wedges into the glass. Fill the glasses the rest of the way with ice.

Fill a large pitcher with ice. Add the pineapple juice, rum, and Madeira and stir briskly until well mixed. Divide evenly among the glasses.

Gently pour 1 teaspoon of amaretto into each glass. Do not stir. Grate a little nutmeg on top, garnish with a mint leaf, and serve.

RUM AND MADEIRA COCKTAIL Omit the pineapple juice in the Rum and Madeira Cooler and mix the lemon and lime juice, rum, and Madeira in a shaker. Shake vigorously and pour into four cocktail glasses. Gently pour 1 teaspoon amaretto over each drink, grate some nutmeg on top, and serve.

STRAIGHT UP

Madeira is a fortified wine produced on the island of Madeira in the Atlantic. It is in essence "baked" to concentrate its flavors or aged at great length in barrels at much higher temperatures than dry wine. Madeira is made from several grapes: Sercial, Verdelho, Bual, and Malmsey. It is among the hardiest and most full-bodied wines in the world. For this recipe, try to find a medium-sweet, inexpensive blend such as Blandy's 5-year-old Bual.

Ice for serving

2 lemons, quartered (8 pieces total)

2 limes, quartered (8 pieces total)

20 ounces pineapple juice

8 ounces dark rum

8 ounces Madeira (see Straight Up)

4 teaspoons amaretto or other nut-flavored cordial for garnish

Fresh grated nutmeg for garnish

4 mint leaves for garnish

GLASSWARE Collins glasses (see page 23)

141 CHERRY SUGAR FIZZ

142 MAGNIFICENT MIMOSA

142 GRAND MIMOSA

143 THE NORMANDY

143 SPARKLING RUM RUNNER

144 APRICOT SUNDAY

145 FRENCH 75

145 KIR ROYALE

146 PARK AVENUE

146 BLOOD ORANGE SPARKLER

149 AUTUMN PUNCH

150 ADELINA

150 THANKSGIVING SPARKLER

151 PEAR, POIRE

151 BRANDYWINE SOUR

BUBBLIES AND A BIT OF DECADENCE

FROM THE LOUD POP OF THE CORK TO THE GUSH OF THE FIRST POUR INTO THE glass, sparkling wines and Champagnes always have a festive and celebratory feel to them. While most people think about serving sparkling wines for a special occasion, they are actually great food wines, perfect for brunch, lunch, or a dinner party. Their acidity and effervescence cut through rich foods and are a refreshing counterbalance to hot, spicy dishes.

Unless otherwise specified, all the recipes in this book use a brut-style sparkling wine. Brut is one of the driest styles of sparkling wines and also the most widely available. All Champagnes are sparkling wines; not all sparkling wines, however, are Champagnes. Champagne is made only in the Champagne region of France, about sixty miles east of Paris. Any sparkling wine that does not come from this region is not true Champagne.

Aside from French Champagne, wonderful sparkling wines are being produced all over the world. Almost every grape-growing country produces some form of bubbly. One of my favorites is Prosecco, which is both the name of a grape and a style of sparkling wine from the Friuli region of Italy. It is light, crisp, refreshing, and moderately priced. Another option is Cava from Spain. *Cava* is the Spanish term for sparkling wines made by the French Champagne method. They are generally full flavored, ripe with crisp acidity, and some of the best values in the wine world today. California produces many sparkling wines, most of which are full of fruit and have deep layers of flavors. New York State produces some of the richest and most vibrant domestic sparkling wines. They are very affordable and quite similar in style to the French versions.

Cherry Sugar Fizz

Makes four 5½-ounce drinks

With its sugar-rimmed glass and brown sugar cubes, this cocktail may look as if it will be overly sweet, but it is well balanced by the bitters and the natural acidity of the sparkling wine. Try serving this with a meal of Chinese takeout or your own Asian-inspired cooking. Contrary to my usual instructions for rimming a glass, this glass is dipped in syrup so that the sugar coating covers both the inside and outside of the rim, ensuring that with every sip you get just enough cherry sugar flavor to balance the drink.

PLANNING AHEAD Chill the sparkling wine for at least 30 minutes before preparing cocktails.

Pour the cherry syrup on a small plate and place the sugar on another. Working with one champagne glass at a time, invert it and dip the rim in the syrup, allowing any excess to drip off, then immediately dip lightly in the sugar. The sugar rim should be a light pink color.

Place 3 maraschino cherries, a brown sugar cube, and 2 dashes of bitters into each champagne glass. Fill the glasses with the sparkling wine and serve immediately.

5 teaspoons syrup from maraschino cherries, for rimming the glasses

¼ cup granulated sugar, for rimming the glasses

12 Maraschino Cherries (page 53) or use store-bought

4 brown sugar cubes

8 dashes Angostura bitters

One 750-milliliter bottle sparkling wine, chilled

GLASSWARE Champagne glasses (see page 24)

Magnificent Mimosa

Makes six 6-ounce drinks

One 750-milliliter bottle sparkling wine, chilled

12 ounces fresh orange juice (from approximately 4 oranges)

3 ounces Cointreau

GLASSWARE Champagne glasses (see page 24)

The mimosa gets a bum rap and is too often served as a cheap add-on during a price-fixed brunch. These concoctions of not-so-great Champagne and too much orange juice have decimated the image of the mimosa. Using fresh-squeezed juice and Cointreau will give you a delightful beverage worthy of your dinner table. It makes a wonderful aperitif, or try serving it with a first course of smoked salmon or seared scallops. And unlike most still, dry wines, the mimosa will stand up to a strong vinaigrette in a salad course.

PLANNING AHEAD Chill the sparkling wine for at least 30 minutes before making the cocktails.

Divide the sparkling wine among the 6 champagne glasses. This will work out to approximately 4 ounces per glass.

Top each glass with 2 ounces of orange juice, then float 1/2 ounce of Cointreau on top of each. Serve and sip slowly.

Grand Mimosa

Makes five 5-ounce drinks

10 orange slices

5 fresh strawberries

2½ teaspoons sugar

2½ ounces Grand Marnier

One 750-milliliter bottle sparkling wine, chilled

GLASSWARE Champagne glasses (see page 24)

The *grand* in the name of this drink stands for Grand Marnier, which is a blend of curaçao oranges and brandy. It is widely available and wonderful on its own or as a mixer. Grand Marnier is heavier than Cointreau, so this drink has more weight than a straight mimosa. It makes a wonderful aperitif and will even stand up to a rich entrée such as roast duck or chicken.

PLANNING AHEAD Chill the sparkling wine for at least 30 minutes before making the cocktails.

In each of the champagne glasses, place 2 orange slices, 1 strawberry, and 1/2 teaspoon sugar. Gently muddle the ingredients together (see page 22).

Add 1/2 ounce of the Grand Marnier to each glass, then divide the sparkling wine evenly among the glasses. Serve.

The Normandy

Makes six 6-ounce drinks (photograph on page 138)

Choose a young, light calvados for this drink, such as Giard five-year-old. Even though there is sugar, cinnamon, and apple in the drink, it is more of a savory cocktail, perfect as an aperitif and yet mealworthy as well.

PLANNING AHEAD You can prepare the diced apples up to 8 hours in advance and refrigerate them. Chill the sparkling wine for at least 30 minutes before making the cocktails.

Place the lemon juice and 2 teaspoons sugar in a bowl and mix. Add the apple and calvados and stir well.

    Mix the sugar and cinnamon on a small plate. Rub the juicy side of the reserved lemon rind along the outer edge of the lip of each champagne glass—not along the inside of the rim. Holding each glass at an angle, roll the outer edge of the rim in the cinnamon sugar until it is fully coated.

    Divide the apple mixture evenly among the glasses. Fill each glass with the sparkling wine and serve.

1 ounce fresh lemon juice
(from approximately 1 lemon),
rind reserved for rimming the glass

2 teaspoons sugar

1 small McIntosh apple, peeled, cored, and cut into 1/4-inch dice

6 ounces calvados
(see Straight Up, page 112)

1 tablespoon sugar for rimming the glass

1/2 teaspoon cinnamon

One 750-milliliter bottle sparkling wine, chilled

GLASSWARE Champagne glasses
(see page 24)

Sparkling Rum Runner

Makes five 8-ounce drinks

This sparkling version of the classic Rum Runner can be served both as an aperitif and with dinner.

Fill a cocktail pitcher with ice and add the rum, syrup, pineapple juice, and bitters. Stir until well blended.

    Divide the rum mixture, then the sparkling wine, among the glasses. Squeeze a lime wedge into each drink, then drop the wedge into the glass and serve.

5 ounces white rum

5 ounces Rum Syrup (page 59)

5 ounces pineapple juice

10 dashes Angostura bitters

One 750-milliliter bottle sparkling wine, chilled

5 lime wedges for garnish

GLASSWARE Champagne glasses
(see page 24)

Apricot Sunday

Makes six 7-ounce drinks

FOR THE APRICOT PUREE

6 ounces dried apricots
(6 to 8) or peeled fresh apricots
(approximately 3)

8 ounces boiling water

1 teaspoon sugar

3 ounces apricot brandy

FOR THE COCKTAIL

One 750-milliliter bottle sparkling
wine, chilled

6 dried apricots or fresh apricot
slices for garnish

GLASSWARE Champagne glasses
(see page 24)

The creamy texture and succulence of apricot puree make this subtly bubbly cocktail richer than a mimosa. Serve it as an after-dinner drink with biscotti, or even on its own as a refreshing late-night cocktail. The apricot puree can easily be doubled if you are serving a larger group.

PLANNING AHEAD The apricot puree requires 5 minutes' resting time and at least 20 minutes in the refrigerator. It can be made up to 1 day in advance and stored in the refrigerator or up to 1 month in advance and frozen. If it's frozen, defrost overnight in the refrigerator before using. Chill the sparkling wine at least 30 minutes before making the cocktails.

To prepare the apricot puree, place the 6 ounces apricots in a blender, add the boiling water, and let stand for 5 minutes to soften. Add the sugar and apricot brandy and puree until smooth. The mixture should have the consistency of heavy cream. If it is too thick, add more water or apricot brandy (or both) to thin it out. Place in the refrigerator until cool, at least 20 minutes.

When ready to serve, fill each champagne glass halfway with sparkling wine. Divide the puree among the glasses, then fill them the rest of the way with the sparkling wine. Stir gently.

If garnishing with dried apricots, float one on each drink. If garnishing with fresh apricot slices, float one on each drink or place a few slices on cocktail spears and add a spear to each drink, and serve.

PEACH SUNDAY Prepare the apricot Sunday using peaches (6 ounces or about 2, plus 6 slices for garnish) instead of apricots and peach brandy in place of the apricot brandy.

PEAR SUNDAY Prepare the apricot Sunday using pears (6 ounces or about 2, plus 6 slices for garnish) instead of apricots and pear eau-de-vie in place of the apricot brandy.

French 75

Makes six 6-ounce drinks (photograph on page 148, right)

Named after a piece of French artillery used during World War I, this drink was originally made with gin. Over time it became more popular made with brandy. Try experimenting with both versions.

PLANNING AHEAD Chill the sparkling wine at least 30 minutes before making the cocktails.

In each of the 6 champagne glasses, place 1 sugar cube or ½ teaspoon sugar, 2 dashes orange bitters, and 1 ounce gin.

Squeeze a lemon wedge into each glass and discard the wedge. Stir.

Divide the sparkling wine evenly among the glasses, garnish each with an orange twist, and serve.

6 brown or white sugar cubes or 3 teaspoons granulated brown or white sugar

12 dashes orange bitters

6 ounces gin or brandy

6 lemon wedges

One 750-milliliter bottle sparkling wine, chilled

6 orange twists (see page 39) for garnish (optional)

GLASSWARE Champagne glasses (see page 24)

Kir Royale

Makes five 6-ounce drinks

Kir is a classic French aperitif that combines crème de cassis, a liqueur made from black currants, with dry white wine. The kir royale is made with sparkling wine. Many cheap versions of crème de cassis are, unfortunately, light and artificial tasting. The better versions are very dark in color and richly flavored. It is worth paying more for a better brand, as it makes an eminently better drink. Consider trying the delicious cassis made by Clinton Vineyards, in New York State. Garnish this cocktail with long lemon swirls made using a channel knife (see page 39), which not only look nice but add an appealing flavor.

Divide the sparkling wine among the glasses and add 1 ounce cassis to each glass.

Garnish each glass with a lemon swirl, placing one end inside the drink and hanging the other end over the edge of the glass. Serve.

One 750-milliliter bottle sparkling wine, chilled

5 ounces crème de cassis

5 long lemon swirls from approximately 2 lemons (see page 39) for garnish

GLASSWARE Champagne glasses (see page 24)

Park Avenue

Makes six 6-ounce drinks

Sugar for rimming the glasses

1 lemon wedge for rimming the glasses

6 teaspoons Red Wine Syrup (page 60) or Grenadine (page 64) or use store-bought or Berry Syrup (page 62) or Simple Syrup (page 56)

6 ounces brandy

One 750-milliliter bottle sparkling wine, chilled

3 ounces Grand Marnier

GLASSWARE Champagne glasses (see page 24)

This intriguing blend of ingredients forms a unique cocktail that is perfect as a dinner preprandial. Perhaps like a Manhattan (page 77) or Rob Roy (page 93), the Park Avenue is an acquired taste, but once it is acquired, one's taste for it never wanes. If you do not have leftover red wine to make the syrup, you can substitute grenadine, berry syrup, or simple syrup.

PLANNING AHEAD Chill the sparkling wine for at least 30 minutes before making the cocktails.

Pour the sugar onto a small plate. Rub the juicy side of the lemon wedge along the outer edge of the lip of each champagne glass—not along the inside of the rim. Holding each glass at an angle, roll the outer edge of the rim in the sugar until it is fully coated.

Into each glass, place 1 teaspoon red wine syrup and 1 ounce brandy. Stir well.

Divide the sparkling wine evenly among the glasses. Float ½ ounce Grand Marnier on each drink and serve.

Blood Orange Sparkler

Makes six 5-ounce drinks (photograph opposite)

1 blood orange

3 teaspoons sugar

3 teaspoons sweet vermouth

One 750-milliliter bottle sparkling wine, chilled

Blood orange slices for garnish

GLASSWARE Wineglasses (see page 24)

Blood oranges are a seasonal treat; look for them from December to May. They are grown throughout the Mediterranean as well as in California.

PLANNING AHEAD Chill the sparkling wine for at least 30 minutes before making the cocktails.

Using a sharp knife, cut off and discard the ends of the blood orange. Stand it upright on a cutting board and slice the rind and white pith off the fruit using a gentle downward sawing motion, cutting away as little of the flesh as possible. Discard the rinds.

Cut the fruit crosswise into ½-inch slices. Divide the slices evenly among the 6 wineglasses.

Sprinkle ½ teaspoon sugar into each glass and muddle to extract the orange juice (see page 22). Add ½ teaspoon vermouth to each glass and stir.

Divide the sparkling wine among the glasses, stir, garnish with blood orange slices, and serve.

Autumn Punch

Makes twelve 7½-ounce servings (photograph opposite, left)

This cocktail is rich and weighty enough to stand up to a range of foods while still being effervescent and refreshing.

PLANNING AHEAD The candied chilled grapefruit peel must be simmered for about 3 hours, blanched three times, and chilled at least 30 minutes. The candied peel can be stored with its syrup in an airtight container for up to 2 weeks in the refrigerator. Chill the sparkling wine and sherry for at least 30 minutes before finishing the punch.

To prepare the candied grapefruit peel, juice the grapefruits and set the juice aside in the refrigerator. Pull or cut away the fruit from the peel, taking care to keep the pieces of peel as big as possible and retaining the white pith. Discard the fruit.

Bring a pot of water to a boil and fill a large bowl with ice water. Blanch the peel in the boiling water for 30 seconds, then shock it in the cold water. Repeat two times, using fresh boiling water and ice water each time to remove any bitterness.

Meanwhile, place the water, sugar, and 2 star anise in a medium-large nonreactive saucepan and stir to moisten the sugar. Bring to a gentle boil over medium-high heat. Reduce the heat and simmer until the sugar is completely dissolved and the syrup is slightly thickened, 3 to 5 minutes. Add the blanched rinds to the syrup and simmer over low heat for about 3 hours, until the syrup and rind are both a dark caramel pink color and the rinds are easily pierced with a knife and have a sweet-tart flavor.

Let the syrup and grapefruit cool at room temperature and then chill thoroughly before proceeding.

To prepare the punch, remove the candied peel from the syrup and cut it into long, thin strips. Set aside 2 to 3 dozen strips. Transfer the remaining peel and 8 ounces syrup to a punch bowl. Pour in the sparkling wine, reserved grapefruit juice, and sherry and stir gently until mixed. Taste and add more sherry if you prefer it sweeter.

To serve, place several of the reserved grapefruit strips in the bottom of the champagne glasses and ladle the punch over them. Place the star anise on top.

TRICK OF THE TRADE

Instead of candying the grapefruit peel yourself, make the syrup as above, replacing 8 ounces of the water with 8 ounces grapefruit juice. Add 1 or 2 pounds of store-bought candied grapefruit to the syrup and simmer on low until the grapefruit is warmed through and softened, 5 to 10 minutes.

FOR THE CANDIED GRAPEFRUIT PEEL

2 grapefruits

24 ounces water

2 cups sugar

2 whole star anise (optional)

FOR THE PUNCH

Two 750-milliliter bottles sparkling wine, chilled

8 ounces Pedro Ximenez sherry (see Straight Up, page 117), or more to taste, chilled

12 whole star anise for garnish (optional)

GLASSWARE Champagne glasses (see page 24)

Adelina

Makes six 5-ounce drinks

12 fresh strawberries, rinsed

6 teaspoons Berry Syrup prepared with strawberries (page 62) or Simple Syrup (page 56) or sugar

6 ounces strawberry liqueur

One 750-milliliter bottle sparkling wine, chilled

GLASSWARE Champagne glasses (see page 24)

My mom, Adelina, has always loved sweet sparkling wines such as spumante. I created this drink in her honor.

PLANNING AHEAD Chill the sparkling wine for at least 30 minutes before making the cocktails.

Hull 6 of the strawberries and cut them into ¼-inch cubes. Divide them evenly among the 6 glasses. Cut a ½-inch-deep slit into the bottom of the remaining 6 strawberries. Set aside.

Place 1 teaspoon syrup and 1 ounce strawberry liqueur into each champagne glass.

Divide the sparkling wine evenly among the glasses, perch a reserved strawberry on the edge of each glass, and serve.

Thanksgiving Sparkler

Makes five 5-ounce drinks

Granulated brown sugar for rimming the glasses

Lemon wedge for rimming the glasses

Scant ⅛ teaspoon cinnamon

Scant ⅛ teaspoon ground cloves

Scant ⅛ teaspoon ground allspice

Scant ⅛ teaspoon ground ginger

5 brown sugar cubes

5 ounces brandy

One 750-milliliter bottle sparkling wine, chilled

Freshly grated nutmeg for garnish

GLASSWARE Champagne glasses (see page 24)

One Thanksgiving I went looking for a little something more to sip as the pumpkin pie was being served. I spied a half-filled bottle of Champagne and inspiration struck. Sparkling wine combines here with traditional Thanksgiving flavors for a festive drink that is a perfect accompaniment to hors d'oeuvres or dessert.

PLANNING AHEAD Chill the sparkling wine for at least 30 minutes before preparing the cocktails.

Pour the sugar onto a small plate. Rub the juicy side of the lemon wedge along the outer edge of the lip of each glass— not along the inside of the rim. Holding each glass at an angle, roll the outer edge of the rim in the sugar until it is fully coated.

In a small bowl or ramekin, mix together the cinnamon, cloves, allspice, and ginger, then divide the mixture evenly among the champagne glasses.

Add 1 sugar cube and 1 ounce brandy to each glass. Stir well until the spices are well blended into the brandy.

Divide the sparkling wine evenly among the glasses, grate fresh nutmeg over the tops, and serve.

Pear, Poire

Makes six 6-ounce drinks

Many domestic and imported pear liqueurs and pear brandies are available. Choose one that is rich and a little sweet as opposed to one that is sharp, such as a grappa. One recommended brand is Belle de Brillet from France.

PLANNING AHEAD You can prepare the diced pears up to 8 hours in advance and store them in the refrigerator. Chill the sparkling wine for at least 30 minutes before making the cocktails.

Place the lemon juice and sugar in a bowl and stir to combine.

Peel, core, and chop the pear into ¼-inch dice and add it to the bowl. Add the pear liqueur and stir well.

Divide the pear mixture evenly among the champagne glasses. Fill each glass with the sparkling wine and serve.

1 ounce fresh lemon juice (from approximately 1 lemon)

2 teaspoons sugar

1 small ripe Bartlett pear

6 ounces pear liqueur

One 750-milliliter bottle sparkling wine, chilled

GLASSWARE Champagne glasses (see page 24)

Brandywine Sour

Makes four 5-ounce drinks

The flavor of the finished drink can vary quite dramatically—with undertones of almonds or orange blossoms or the predominant flavor of the dessert wine used.

PLANNING AHEAD Chill the wine for at least 30 minutes before making the cocktails.

Fill the rocks glasses with ice.

Fill a large pitcher with ice and add the sour mix, dessert wine, and brandy. Stir briskly until the mixture is frothy.

Strain the sour into the glasses. Float 1 teaspoon syrup over each cocktail and serve.

Ice for serving

8 ounces Lemon Sour Mix (page 65)

4 ounces dessert wine, chilled

8 ounces brandy

4 teaspoons Red Wine Syrup (page 60) or Grenadine (page 64) or use store-bought, or port

GLASSWARE Rocks glasses (see page 23)

155   HOLIDAY EGGNOG

156   THANKSGIVING NOG

156   PINEAPPLE NOG

157   IRIS'S COFFEE NOG

158   GENERAL WASHINGTON'S GROG

158   HOT SPIKED CIDER

159   PUMPKIN CIDER

159   RUM RAISIN CIDER

160   APRICOT MULLED WINE

162   FIG MULLED WINE

163   HOT CHOCOLATE CHOCOLATE

163   CHRISTMAS EVE CHOCOLATE

164   VANILLA "COCOA"

164   CHESTNUT HOT CHOCOLATE

166   BANANA BUTTERED RUM

NOGS, GROGS, AND OTHER HOLIDAY WARMERS

NOTHING BEATS THE COLD LIKE A PIPING HOT DRINK, NO MATTER HOW OLD YOU are. Growing up in the Northeast meant spending wintertime enduring many a snowball fight, being buried in snow forts for what seemed like hours, and dozens of spills off my Flexible Flyer sled. Walking into the house beaten, battered, and soaking wet after hours of play, my siblings and I would be greeted with steaming mugs of hot chocolate topped with as many marshmallows as the mug would hold. Now that I'm older, I still love playing in the snow, only now I've traded my sled for skis and hot chocolate for spiked hot nog.

Nogs are hot drinks made with a base of cream or eggs. They are always rich, thick, and decadent. Grogs were originally made from rum, sugar, molasses, lemon, and water and could be served either hot or cold. Over time, the term *grog* has come to refer to a hot beverage with rum.

The following recipes are hearty mugs of potent potables—nogs and grogs meant to warm both body and spirit and maybe even rekindle our youth for a few moments. Serve these winter warmers right after a day of cold-weather play, for dessert, or as a nightcap.

If you're looking for other favorite hot drinks such as toddies, tea tonics, and spiced coffee, you'll find them later in the book in "Java Heaven and Spiked Tea Time"—they're so good they deserve their own chapter.

Holiday Eggnog

Makes sixteen 4-ounce servings (photograph on page 152)

Though many eggnogs use raw eggs, this one is based on classic crème anglaise, so the eggs are cooked. After you make this base, the variety of liquor, the spices, and the consistency are up to you. I like mine rich, thick, and spicy. For a nonalcoholic version, simply eliminate the liquor and add a little more milk or cream to get the desired consistency.

PLANNING AHEAD The whole nog can be made up to 12 hours in advance and stored in the refrigerator. Just give it a good whisking before serving.

To prepare the crème anglaise, have ready a large bowl full of ice. You'll also need a double boiler. (Instead, you can use a medium-large saucepan and a heatproof bowl that fits in the saucepan without touching the bottom and whose edges hang over the edges of the saucepan.)

Place the milk in a saucepan over high heat. As soon as it begins to boil, stir briskly and remove from the heat. Meanwhile, in the bottom of the double boiler, add just enough water so that the top part of the double boiler or the bowl remains above the water. Bring to a boil, then reduce to a low simmer.

In the top of the double boiler, whisk together the egg yolks, sugar, flour, and salt. Whisking constantly, slowly pour in the hot milk.

Cook the mixture over, not in, the simmering water, stirring constantly until the mixture is thickened and coats the back of a spoon.

Remove the double boiler top from the heat and set it in the bowl of ice for 5 minutes, stirring occasionally. Add the vanilla extract and stir.

To prepare the eggnog, mix the crème anglaise and all remaining ingredients except the nutmeg and confectioners' sugar in a bowl. Taste, adding as much confectioners' sugar as you wish for a sweeter nog.

Transfer the eggnog to the punch bowl and grate the nutmeg and orange zest over it, if desired. Chill for an hour or serve at room temperature.

FOR THE CRÈME ANGLAISE

16 ounces milk

4 large egg yolks

3 tablespoons sugar

2 tablespoons flour

Pinch of salt

1 teaspoon vanilla extract

FOR THE NOG

16 ounces milk

16 ounces heavy cream

¼ teaspoon cinnamon

⅛ teaspoon ground cloves

6 ounces dark rum

3 ounces bourbon

3 ounces brandy

½ cup confectioners' sugar (optional)

Freshly grated nutmeg for garnish

Grated orange zest (see page 39) for garnish (optional)

GLASSWARE Punch cups and punch bowl (see page 25)

Thanksgiving Nog

Makes six 7½-ounce servings

8 ounces water

8 ounces milk or cream

½ cup dark brown sugar

1 tablespoon molasses

1 teaspoon vanilla

¼ teaspoon cinnamon, plus more for garnish

⅛ teaspoon ground cloves

⅛ teaspoon ground allspice

⅛ teaspoon ground nutmeg

⅛ teaspoon ground mace

One 15-ounce can (about 2 cups) pumpkin puree

10 ounces dark rum, brandy, or bourbon

Spiced Whipped Cream (page 54)

6 cinnamon sticks for garnish

GLASSWARE Mugs (see page 25; see Trick of the Trade)

The inspiration for this nog was the roasted pumpkin left over from pumpkin soup. Serve this drink warm after dinner with a big plate of cookies.

PLANNING AHEAD The whole nog can be made a day or two in advance and refrigerated, then warmed on the stove or in the microwave when ready to serve. It can also be frozen for several weeks.

Stir together the water, milk, sugar, molasses, vanilla, and spices in a medium-large saucepan. Simmer on low heat, stirring regularly, until the sugar has dissolved and the spices are incorporated, about 5 minutes.

Stir in the pumpkin and continue simmering until the nog is hot, about 15 minutes. It should be the consistency of very thick cream. If it seems too thick or pasty, add more water or milk. Bear in mind that the rum will thin the mixture further.

Remove the nog from the heat and stir in the rum. Ladle into mugs, garnish with whipped cream, cinnamon sticks, and cinnamon, and serve.

TRICK OF THE TRADE

For an impressive holiday presentation, hollow out a large pumpkin and serve this drink in a pumpkin terrine. Or hollow out several small pumpkins and serve the nog in pumpkin "mugs."

Pineapple Nog

Makes eight 7-ounce servings

24 ounces water

16 ounces Pineapple Syrup (page 61), some pineapple chunks reserved for garnish

8 ounces light rum

8 ounces Madeira (see Straight Up, page 137)

8 tablespoons butter (optional)

Freshly grated nutmeg for garnish

GLASSWARE Mugs (see page 25)

The *idea* of hot buttered rum is often more desirable than the drink itself. This variation of the classic, with its addition of pineapple and Madeira, makes a much more flavorful beverage. Try serving it instead of coffee for or with dessert, or as a nightcap.

Bring the water to a boil in a large saucepan. Add the pineapple syrup, rum, and Madeira and simmer until hot.

Ladle into mugs. Add a few chunks of pineapple to each mug and, if desired, float a tablespoon of butter on each. Grate fresh nutmeg on top and serve.

Iris's Coffee Nog

Makes sixteen 4-ounce servings

Modesto Battista, the steward of Gramercy Tavern, oversees anything and everything. His wife, Iris, handles much of the prep work for the kitchens. A few cold and lucky Saturday mornings, Iris made us a nonalcoholic version of this nog. Modesto would thump his chest and say that it makes you strong, and I believe him. Here is the spiked version. Try serving this as dessert at Sunday brunch. For a thicker nog, simmer it longer. If you prefer it thinner, add more coffee or milk.

PLANNING AHEAD The whole nog can be made up to 12 hours in advance and stored in the refrigerator. Just give it a good whisking before serving.

To prepare the crème anglaise, have ready a large bowl full of ice and a double boiler. (Instead, you can use a medium-large saucepan with a heatproof bowl that fits in the saucepan without touching the bottom and whose edges hang over the edges of the saucepan.)

Place the milk in a saucepan over high heat. As soon as it begins to boil, stir briskly and remove from the heat. Meanwhile, in the bottom of the double boiler, add enough water so that the top half of the double boiler does not touch the water. Bring to a boil, then reduce to a low simmer.

In the top of the double boiler, whisk together the egg yolks, sugar, flour, and salt. Whisking constantly, slowly pour in the hot milk.

Cook the mixture over, not in, the simmering water, stirring constantly until the mixture is thickened and coats the back of a spoon.

Remove the double boiler top from the heat and set in the bowl of ice for 5 minutes, stirring occasionally. Add the vanilla extract and stir.

To prepare the nog, place all the ingredients for the nog except the nutmeg in a large saucepan over low heat. Heat just until the mixture is well blended and warm.

Add the crème anglaise and stir well to blend. Heat to the desired temperature.

Ladle into mugs, grate fresh nutmeg on top, and serve.

FOR THE CRÈME ANGLAISE

16 ounces milk

4 large egg yolks

3 tablespoons sugar

2 tablespoons flour

Pinch of salt

1 teaspoon vanilla extract

FOR THE NOG

16 ounces strong black coffee

8 ounces milk

8 ounces heavy cream

6 ounces dark rum

3 ounces Kahlúa

½ cup sugar

¼ teaspoon cinnamon

⅛ teaspoon ground cloves

Freshly grated nutmeg for garnish

GLASSWARE Mugs (see page 25)

General Washington's Grog
Makes four 8-ounce servings

20 ounces boiling water

4 ounces Madeira
(see Straight Up, page 137)

4 ounces rum

4 ounces bourbon

4 teaspoons brown sugar

4 whole cloves

4 cinnamon sticks

4 tablespoons butter (optional)

GLASSWARE Mugs (see page 25)

Many historical accounts reveal that General Washington loved to imbibe and even made his own whiskey at Mount Vernon. How else could you get through winters in Valley Forge? Rich and aromatic with warm spices, this grog is my ode to George. It is likely very similar to what the great general himself drank.

Bring the water to a boil. Reduce the heat to a simmer and stir in all the remaining ingredients except the butter.

When the grog is hot, remove it from the heat. Using a slotted spoon, remove the cinammon sticks and reserve. Ladle the grog into the mugs, adding 1 reserved cinnamon stick to each. Float a tablespoon of butter on top of each, if desired, and serve.

Hot Spiked Cider
Makes eight 11-ounce servings

FOR THE DRUNKEN FRUIT

8 large dried apple rings

Small handful dried currants (optional)

4 ounces calvados or applejack
(see Straight Up, page 112)

FOR THE DRINK

64 ounces fresh apple cider

12 whole cloves

6 whole star anise

3 cinnamon sticks

½ teaspoon freshly grated nutmeg

2 tablespoons brown sugar for dredging the apple slices

24 ounces dark rum

8 extra-long cinnamon sticks

GLASSWARE Mugs (see page 25)

Soaking the dried apples in calvados or applejack adds a kick to this smooth, mellow rum drink.

PLANNING AHEAD The drunken fruit must sit in the refrigerator overnight.

Place the dried apples and currants in a large plastic zippered bag, add the calvados, and seal the bag. Allow to steep in the refrigerator overnight.

When ready to serve, gently warm the cider and spices in a pot—do not allow the mixture to boil. Meanwhile, remove the apple slices from the plastic bag and dredge each in the brown sugar.

Pour a healthy shot of rum into each mug and add the cider. I do not mind if the mulling spices get into the finished drink, but if you prefer your drink without the spices, you may pour the cider through a fine-mesh strainer into the mugs. Float one or two sugared apple slices on each drink, spoon the currants over the apples, add a long cinnamon stick, and serve.

SPIKED PEAR CIDER Prepare the hot spiked cider using pear cider in place of the apple cider, Poire William (a pear eau-de-vie) instead of the calvados, and dried pears instead of the dried apples.

Pumpkin Cider

Makes twelve 7-ounce servings

Many chefs add apples to their pumpkin soup to give it a hint of natural sweetness and complexity. Here I have reversed the technique—the pumpkin lends a savory note to the sweet cider.

Preheat a medium saucepan over medium heat. Add the butter, sugar, and pumpkin. Sauté the pumpkin, turning regularly, until the sides have become slightly caramelized, about 8 minutes. If you feel the pumpkin becoming soft, remove the pan from the heat to avoid overcooking.

Stir in all the remaining ingredients except the rum, calvados, and nutmeg. Reduce the heat to simmer and cook, stirring regularly, until hot.

Stir in the rum and calvados. Ladle into mugs, grate fresh nutmeg on top, and serve.

1 tablespoon butter

1 tablespoon sugar

Twelve 1-inch cubes pumpkin or butternut squash

64 ounces fresh apple cider

12 whole cloves

6 whole star anise

3 cinnamon sticks

12 ounces dark rum

12 ounces calvados or applejack (see Straight Up, page 112)

Freshly grated nutmeg for garnish

GLASSWARE Mugs (see page 25)

BONUS FROM THE BAR

CIDER SYRUP For a unique and heavenly apple syrup to enjoy with your Sunday-morning pancakes, simmer any leftover hot spiked cider in a heavy-bottomed pot over low heat until it reduces to a syrup, about 15 minutes, depending on the amount of liquid to be reduced. The pancakes will be especially delicious if you serve them topped with leftover drunken fruit.

Rum Raisin Cider

Makes twelve 7-ounce servings

Cooking the raisins and spices in butter brings out their pungency, which makes for a less cloying drink with more intense flavors.

Preheat a large saucepan over medium heat. Add the butter, sugar, raisins, cloves, cinnamon sticks, and star anise. Sauté, stirring constantly, until the sugar has caramelized and the spices have released their aromas, about 5 minutes.

Add the calvados and simmer until the raisins have plumped up, about 3 minutes more.

Add the cider and heat, stirring regularly, until hot.

Stir in the rum, ladle into mugs, and serve.

1 tablespoon butter

1 tablespoon sugar

1 cup raisins

12 whole cloves

3 cinnamon sticks

1 whole star anise

4 ounces calvados or applejack (see Straight Up, page 112)

64 ounces fresh apple cider

24 ounces dark rum

GLASSWARE Mugs (see page 25)

Apricot Mulled Wine

Makes 8 servings

FOR THE APRICOT BASE

1 orange or blood orange

24 dried apricots, finely diced

16 ounces apricot or peach brandy

½ cup sugar

6 whole cloves

4 to 6 whole star anise

3 cinnamon sticks

½ teaspoon freshly grated nutmeg

FOR THE MULLED WINE

One 750-milliliter bottle Riesling

8 ounces apricot or peach brandy

8 cinnamon sticks

GLASSWARE Mugs (see page 25)

Though mulled wines are typically red, the urge to tinker with the classic led to this delicious variation. Riesling, with its peach and apricot notes, is a favorite wine variety because of its versatility, food friendliness, and incredible fruit flavors. You can substitute 12 dried peaches for the 24 dried apricots if desired. If you want to make this recipe in advance, see the Trick of the Trade in Fig Mulled Wine (page 162) for heating and serving instructions.

A fun way to serve this is in a punch bowl—just be sure the bowl is heatproof. Add the cinnamon stick and orange rind garnishes directly to the punch bowl and, for an extra festive touch, peel and slice 1 or 2 oranges or blood oranges as for the Blood Orange Sparkler (page 146) and float the fruit slices on top.

To prepare the apricot base, peel the rind from the orange and set it aside. Cut the orange lengthwise into 8 segments, trimming and discarding any white pith.

Place the fruit and all the ingredients for the base in a large heavy-bottomed pot. Set over medium heat and bring the mixture just to a boil. Immediately reduce the heat to medium low and simmer, stirring often, until the apricots are extremely soft and the mixture is reduced almost to a glaze, 20 to 30 minutes.

Meanwhile, trim and discard the white pith from the reserved orange rind. Very thinly slice the rind and set aside.

When the base is reduced, add the wine and brandy and simmer just until hot. Do not allow the mixture to boil.

To serve, ladle the mulled wine into mugs. Add a cinnamon stick and a bit of sliced orange rind to each mug and serve.

Fig Mulled Wine

Makes 8 servings

FOR THE FIG BASE

2 dozen dried black mission figs

1 orange

16 ounces port

½ cup brown sugar

6 whole cloves

4 to 6 whole star anise

3 cinnamon sticks

½ teaspoon freshly grated nutmeg

FOR THE MULLED WINE

One 750-milliliter bottle pinot noir

8 ounces cherry brandy or any dark fruit brandy or Grand Marnier

8 cinnamon sticks for garnish

GLASSWARE Mugs (see page 25) and a soup terrine, if desired

This recipe is extremely versatile and can easily be doubled. Any leftover mulled wine can be kept in the refrigerator for up to four days. If you are not a fan of figs, use your favorite dried fruit, such as plums or cherries, instead. I often serve mulled wine in a soup terrine and allow my guests to serve themselves.

I usually use a California pinot noir because of its bright fruit, but any hearty wine with good fruit and low acid will be fine.

To prepare the fruit, trim the stems from the dried figs and discard. Cut the figs into small dice. Peel the rind from the orange and set aside. Cut the orange lengthwise into 8 segments, trimming and discarding any white pith.

To prepare the fig base, place all the ingredients for the base in a large heavy-bottomed pot. Bring the mixture just to a boil over medium heat. Immediately reduce the heat to medium-low and simmer until the figs are extremely soft and the mixture is reduced almost to a glaze, 20 to 30 minutes.

Meanwhile, trim and discard the white pith from the reserved orange rind. Very thinly slice the rind and set it aside.

When the base is reduced, add the wine and brandy and simmer just until hot. Do not allow the mixture to boil.

Ladle the mulled wine into mugs. Add a cinnamon stick and a bit of sliced orange rind to each mug and serve. Alternatively, pour all the mulled wine into a soup terrine, arrange the garnishes in the mugs, and let your guests serve themselves.

TRICK OF THE TRADE

For a steeped version of this drink, make the fig base and let it cool completely. Add the wine and brandy and refrigerate for up to 2 weeks, allowing the flavors to blend. When you're ready to serve, heat the mixture on the stovetop over low heat or "steam" individual servings in the microwave or with a cappuccino maker.

BONUS FROM THE BAR

FIG WINE TOPPING For a heavenly topping for ice cream or pound cake, simmer any remaining mulled wine over low heat in a heavy-bottomed pot until it reduces to a syrupy glaze, about 15 minutes, depending on the amount of liquid to be reduced. Let cool slightly before using as a topping.

Hot Chocolate Chocolate

Makes six 10-ounce servings

This favorite recipe is named chocolate twice because it uses both cocoa powder and whole chocolate. Don't think this recipe is for kids only—end a winter dinner party with mugs full of hot chocolate and a plate of biscotti. Marshmallow Fluff makes a great and unexpectedly smooth topping. The molasses adds a slightly smoky, spicy richness.

Place the milk, cocoa powder, confectioners' sugar, vanilla, molasses, and salt in a large saucepan over medium heat. Cook, whisking constantly, until the mixture is hot, about 5 minutes.

Add the chocolate and cook, stirring constantly, until the chocolate has melted completely.

Remove from the heat and pour into mugs. Top with a generous helping of Fluff, stir with a cinnamon stick, and serve.

48 ounces milk

6 tablespoons cocoa powder

3 tablespoons confectioners' sugar

1 teaspoon vanilla extract

1 teaspoon molasses (optional)

Scant 1/8 teaspoon salt

9 ounces dark or milk chocolate, chopped into small pieces

6 super-heaping tablespoons Marshmallow Fluff or Tangy Whipped Cream (page 54) for garnish

6 cinnamon sticks for garnish

GLASSWARE Mugs (see page 25)

Christmas Eve Chocolate

Makes sixteen 2-ounce servings

When I was growing up, my friend Steve Santaniello's mother threw the best Christmas Eve parties in the neighborhood. This high-octane drink, a cross between hot chocolate and coffee, was always served around ten o'clock so we would be sure to be awake at midnight to ring in Christmas Day.

In a saucepan over medium heat, combine the coffee, chocolate, and sugar. Cook, stirring constantly, until the chocolate has completely melted and the mixture is steaming hot.

Add the liquors and continue to heat, stirring well, for 1 minute.

Serve in tiny espresso cups, topped, if desired, with a dollop of whipped cream.

12 ounces strong black coffee or espresso

8 ounces dark chocolate, chopped into small pieces

1/4 cup sugar

3 ounces Kahlúa

3 ounces dark crème de cacao

2 ounces grappa or brandy

Whipped Cream (page 54) for garnish (optional)

GLASSWARE Espresso or small coffee cups

Vanilla "Cocoa"

Makes eight 6-ounce servings (photograph opposite, top)

24 ounces milk

8 ounces Vanilla Vodka Syrup (page 60) or Vanilla Syrup (page 58) or Simple Syrup (page 56)

Pinch of salt

1 vanilla bean

12 ounces white chocolate, chopped into small pieces, plus extra for garnish

4 ounces Licor 43 (see Straight Up, page 114) (optional)

4 ounces Godiva White Chocolate Liqueur (optional)

Whipped Cream (page 54) or Marshmallow Fluff for garnish

Cocoa powder for garnish

GLASSWARE Mugs (see page 25)

The pleasure of this warming drink comes as much from its creamy, smooth texture as its sweet, vanilla flavor. White chocolate gives a silken feel to the drink, so use the highest quality you can find. To prepare the white chocolate shavings for garnish, follow the first step in the recipe for the White Chocolate Martini (page 204).

Place the milk, syrup, and salt in a medium saucepan over medium heat. Cook, stirring regularly, until the mixture is hot, about 5 minutes.

Split the vanilla bean lengthwise, scrape out the seeds, and add them to the pot. Save the leftover bean for another use.

Add the white chocolate and cook, stirring constantly, until the chocolate has melted completely.

Stir in the liquors, if desired, and ladle into mugs. Top with whipped cream, sprinkle with cocoa powder, and serve.

Chestnut Hot Chocolate

Makes eight 6-ounce servings (photograph opposite, bottom)

24 ounces milk

½ cup sugar

Pinch of cinnamon

Pinch of salt

12 ounces dark chocolate, chopped into small pieces

12 ounces chestnut puree (see Trick of the Trade)

4 ounces Frangelico (optional)

4 ounces brandy (optional)

Whipped Cream or Chocolaty Whipped Cream (page 54) for garnish

8 chestnut pieces for garnish (optional)

GLASSWARE Mugs (see page 25)

There used to be a store in Manhattan called Paprika Weiss that sold amazing chestnut puree dipped in chocolate—here it is in a mug.

Place the milk, sugar, cinnamon, and salt in a large saucepan over medium heat. Cook, stirring regularly, until the mixture is hot, about 5 minutes.

Add the chocolate and cook, stirring constantly, until the chocolate has melted completely.

Add the chestnut puree and cook, stirring constantly, until the puree is completely incorporated.

Stir in the liquors, if desired. Ladle into mugs, top with whipped cream, and a chestnut piece, if desired, and serve.

TRICK OF THE TRADE

Chestnut puree is easy to find in most grocery stores. If unavailable, process 8 ounces packaged chestnut pieces with 4 ounces water and 1 tablespoon sugar in a food processor.

Banana Buttered Rum

Makes ten 8-ounce servings and enough banana butter for
16 servings

FOR THE BANANA BUTTER

1 pound unsalted butter, softened

1 ripe banana, mashed

½ pound brown sugar

½ tablespoon cinnamon

¼ teaspoon grated nutmeg

¼ teaspoon ground cloves

FOR EACH SERVING

2 heaping tablespoons banana
butter

2 ounces dark rum

Boiling water

1 or 2 whole star anise for garnish

1 cinnamon stick for garnish

GLASSWARE Mugs (see page 25)

Hot buttered rum is the quintessential winter drink,
served in ski lodges across the world, where chilly skiers
gladly warm their hands around steaming mugs. I often
serve this banana-flavored toddy for dessert with a plate
of butter cookies. I urge you to make the full batch of
banana butter, for whatever you do not use will last for
several months and can be spread on warm pancakes
or French toast. It even makes toasted store-bought
raisin bread an especially yummy treat.

PLANNING AHEAD The banana butter can be refrigerated for
up to 1 week or frozen for up to 3 months. Let it come to
room temperature before using. If it's frozen, thaw at room
temperature or slice the frozen butter into 1-inch-thick
pieces, arrange on a plate, and soften in the microwave for
10 seconds.

To make the banana butter, place all of the ingredients for the
banana butter in the bowl of a food processor and process
until well combined. Roll the mixture into a cylinder in a piece
of plastic wrap and refrigerate until ready to use. Let the butter
come to room temperature before serving.

When ready to serve, add 2 heaping tablespoons of
banana butter to each mug. Top with 2 ounces rum and fill
the glass ⅔ full with boiling water.

Float a star anise or two on top of the butter. Add a
cinnamon stick and stir the mixture using the stick. Serve
immediately.

BUTTERED RUM Prepare the banana butter, above, omitting the
banana and keeping all other ingredients as specified.

171	CLASSIC SANGRIA		183	BITTER PILL
171	CHAMPAGNE SANGRIA		184	WATERMELON COOLER
172	PINEAPPLE SANGRIA		184	PEAR CIDER COOLER
173	FRESH MINT SANGRIA		185	MOSCATO COOLER
174	PEACH SANGRIA		185	BLACKBERRY COOLER
175	STRAWBERRY KIWI SANGRIA		186	PLUM SAKE
176	PRICKLY PEAR SANGRIA		187	NEVISIAN SMILE
176	LEMON JULEP		187	FROZEN RASPBERRY DAIQUIRI
177	MOCHA RUM COOLER		188	LAVA FLOW
177	LIME TEQUILA FRAPPÉ		189	THE NICK-O-CINO
178	COCONUT RUM FRAPPÉ		189	FROZEN MANGO SMASH
179	PINEAPPLE SLING			
179	RUM SLING			
180	TEA & WHISKEY HIGHBALL			
180	TENBERRY HIGHBALL			
182	CIDER HIGHBALL			
182	MARASCHINO HIGHBALL			
183	SUMMER BUCK			

SUMMER SPLURGES

TO MY MIND, JUICY SUMMER COCKTAILS ARE THE BEST DRINKS TO SERVE WITH food. Their vibrant fruit flavors, crisp acidity, and thirst-quenching nature make many of these drinks perfect for summer entertaining. Furthermore, that predominance of fruit and acid is perfect for pairing with and complementing almost any warm-weather meal.

The lack of formality with summertime entertaining is liberating. The season's bounty offers a wealth of fruits and vegetables, making it easy for us to create fresh, inspiring food. This is no less true for cocktail making. Ripe berries and stone fruits from local farmer's markets lend their flavors to everything from fruity sangrias—there are seven in this chapter—to refreshing highballs and coolers to slushy frozen drinks. The list goes on and on. Last but not least, four recipes in this chapter, the Lemon Julep (page 176), the Mocha Rum Cooler (page 177), the Lime Tequila Frappé (page 177), and the Coconut Rum Frappé (page 178) include a summer surprise: sorbet ice cubes. These easy-to-make frozen bursts of flavor transform the drinks that feature them into extra-special summertime refreshers.

Classic Sangria
Makes ten 5-ounce servings

Sangria was originally developed as a quick way to hide the flaws in weak, acidic, or simply poor wine. Since well-made wine is so abundant today, we do not need to drink sangria out of necessity; rather, we drink it for the taste. Sangria makes a great aperitif, is always welcome at a barbecue, and jazzes up any Sunday brunch.

PLANNING AHEAD Chill all ingredients and the pitcher or punch bowl for at least 30 minutes in advance.

Place the fruit in a large pitcher or punch bowl. Sprinkle the sugar on top and muddle the fruit (see page 22) to extract some of the juice.

Add the triple sec and brandy and stir well to dissolve the sugar.

Add the orange juice and wine. Let stand for 5 minutes before serving.

1 lemon, sliced into ½-inch-thick rounds

1 lime, sliced into ½-inch-thick rounds

2 oranges, sliced into ½-inch-thick rounds

½ cup sugar

8 ounces triple sec, chilled

8 ounces brandy, chilled

8 ounces fresh orange juice (from 2 to 3 oranges), chilled

One 750-milliliter bottle dry red wine, chilled

GLASSWARE Wineglasses and large pitcher or punch bowl (see page 25)

Champagne Sangria
Makes fifteen 8-ounce servings

Very ripe red plums add both flavor and color to this sparkling beverage.

PLANNING AHEAD Chill all ingredients for at least 30 minutes before serving.

Place the plums and sugar in a punch bowl and stir well to extract juice. Add the nectar, plum wine, and brandy. Stir well and refrigerate until ready to serve.

To serve, remove the mixture from the refrigerator. Add the sparkling wine and stir briefly to combine. Float mint leaves on top and serve immediately.

4 plums, pitted and cut in thick wedges

½ cup superfine or confectioners' sugar

32 ounces apricot nectar or peach, pear, or other nectar, chilled

16 ounces plum wine, chilled

8 ounces brandy, chilled

Two 750-milliliter bottles sparkling wine, chilled

Mint leaves for garnish

GLASSWARE Punch cups and punch bowl (see page 25)

Pineapple Sangria

Makes approximately ten 8-ounce servings
(photograph opposite and on page 168, bottom)

1 small pineapple

1 cup confectioners' sugar

2 oranges, sliced into ½-inch rounds, end pieces reserved

2 lemons, sliced into ½-inch rounds, end pieces reserved

2 limes, sliced into ½-inch rounds, end pieces reserved

Two 750-milliliter bottles rosé or fruity white wine, chilled

16 ounces light rum, chilled

Mint leaves for garnish

GLASSWARE Wineglasses, large coupes, or highballs and punch bowl (see page 25)

Fresh pineapple and its juice are often included in sangria, and in this recipe they take center stage. Either a rosé or fruity white wine will work; my preference is rosé, whose extra dimensions of flavor stand up well to the pineapple. Ask your wine merchant for one that is not too dry and has some residual sugar.

PLANNING AHEAD The base requires up to 1 hour in the refrigerator. Chill the wine and rum for at least 30 minutes before preparing the sangria.

To prepare the pineapple, use a large chef's knife to cut off the green leaves and cut a thin slice off the bottom. Stand the pineapple upright on a cutting board and slice the rind off the fruit using a gentle downward sawing motion, cutting away as little of the flesh as possible. There are likely to be small "eyes" left behind; cut them out with a paring knife. Slice the pineapple lengthwise into quarters. Cut away the tough core from each quarter and chop the remaining fruit into ¼-inch chunks.

Place half of the pineapple chunks in a zippered plastic bag and place it in the freezer. Transfer the remaining pineapple to a punch bowl, stir in the sugar, and set aside.

Squeeze the juice from the end pieces of the citrus fruits over the pineapple, then discard the end pieces. Add the fruit slices to the pineapple in the bowl.

Add the wine and rum and stir well. Chill the sangria for up to 1 hour.

When ready to serve, add the frozen pineapple chunks and mint leaves to the punch bowl. Ladle into wineglasses, being sure to give a generous portion of pineapple to each guest.

Fresh Mint Sangria

Makes ten 5 ounce servings

Use a fruity white wine with this sangria. A dry white wine mixed with mint can taste astringent.

PLANNING AHEAD Chill all ingredients and the pitcher or punch bowl at least 30 minutes in advance.

Place the mint, lime slices, and sugar in a large pitcher or punch bowl. Muddle (see page 22) just until the mint is bruised.

Add the white crème de menthe and bourbon and stir well, until sugar is dissolved.

Add the white wine and white grape juice. Let stand 5 minutes before serving.

1 large bunch fresh mint, rinsed and roots trimmed

2 limes, sliced into ½-inch-thick rounds

½ cup sugar

8 ounces white crème de menthe or peppermint schnapps, chilled

8 ounces bourbon, chilled

One 750-milliliter bottle white wine, chilled

8 ounces white grape juice, chilled

GLASSWARE Wineglasses and large pitcher or punch bowl (see page 25)

Peach Sangria

Makes twenty-five 4-ounce servings

4 peaches

6 whole star anise

6 cardamom pods

1 cinnamon stick

1 vanilla bean, split in half
lengthwise

8 ounces boiling water

½ cup superfine sugar

4 ounces fresh orange juice
(from 1 to 2 oranges)

3 ounces fresh lemon juice
(from 2 lemons)

2 ounces fresh lime juice
(from 2 limes)

Two 750-milliliter bottles white wine,
chilled

16 ounces peach eau-de-vie
(see Straight Up) or
peach brandy, chilled

16 ounces peach nectar, chilled

Mint leaves for garnish

GLASSWARE Wineglasses and
punch bowl (see page 25)

Use a white wine with good fruit and acidity, such as a
Riesling or rosé, in this recipe. Sangria is such a forgiving
formula that you can substitute endlessly and practically
never go wrong.

PLANNING AHEAD The base requires up to 1 hour in the
refrigerator. Chill the wine, brandy, and peach nectar for
at least 30 minutes before preparing the sangria.

To prepare the peaches, bring a large pot of water to a boil
and have ready a large bowl of ice-cold water. Score the
bottom of each peach with a tiny X and place it in the boiling
water. Remove after 30 seconds and plunge into the cold
water. Starting at the scored bottom, use a paring knife to help
pull the skin off each peach. If it is too difficult, return the
peach to the boiling water for a few seconds. Cut the peeled
peaches into eighths, discarding the pit.

Place the star anise, cardamom, cinnamon stick, and
vanilla bean in a punch bowl and pour the boiling water over
them. Add the sugar and stir until it has fully dissolved. Add
the peaches and citrus juices and let the mixture steep in
the refrigerator for up to one hour (the longer it steeps, the
more the peach flavor will develop).

When ready to serve, add the wine, eau-de-vie, and nectar
and stir until well blended. Float several mint leaves on top of
the punch and serve.

STRAIGHT UP

Eau-de-vie is clear, unaged brandy produced by distilling wine
made from grapes or other fruit. Eaux-de-vie are often called by
the French word for whatever fruit they are made from, thus *pêche*
is peach eau-de-vie and *framboise* is raspberry eau-de-vie.
(When made from grapes, it is known as *grappa* in Italy, and
a lightly aged version made in Burgundy is called *marc*.) With a
big alcoholic bite and no sweetness, eaux-de-vie are especially
good served at the end of a rich meal. Used as mixers, eaux-de-vie
add fruit flavor without any syrupiness, so they make an interesting
substitution for brandy in mixed drinks.

Crème liqueurs are produced by macerating crushed fruit and
sugar in eaux-de-vie. The result is intensely fruit-flavored, sweet,
creamy, and alcoholic. Crème de cassis, used in the Kir Royale
(page 145), is perhaps the best-known example.

Strawberry Kiwi Sangria

Makes ten 5-ounce servings (photograph also on page 168, top)

Crème de fraise is a strawberry liqueur. It is generally easy to find, but if you have trouble, you can substitute strawberry schnapps or another berry cordial.

PLANNING AHEAD Chill all ingredients and the pitcher or punch bowl for at least 30 minutes before serving.

Place the fruit in a pitcher or punch bowl and stir in the sugar. Let stand for 5 minutes to extract the juices.

Stir in the rest of the ingredients and let stand for 5 minutes before serving.

1 pint strawberries, cleaned, hulled, and halved

3 kiwifruits, peeled and sliced into ½-inch-thick rounds

¼ cup sugar

One 750-milliliter bottle fruity rosé wine, chilled

8 ounces crème de fraise or strawberry schnapps or another berry cordial, chilled

8 ounces white rum, chilled

8 ounces white grape juice, chilled

GLASSWARE Wineglasses and large pitcher or punch bowl (see page 25)

Prickly Pear Sangria

Makes eight 5-ounce servings

6 prickly pears

¾ cup sugar

One 750-milliliter bottle
fruity rosé, chilled

8 ounces amontillado sherry,
chilled

8 ounces Spanish brandy,
chilled

GLASSWARE Wineglasses
(see page 24)

Amontillado is a medium-dry, nutty sherry. It is readily available, but you can substitute dry sac sherry. Spanish brandy is richer and somewhat sweeter on the palate than most French or American brandies. If you cannot find a Spanish brandy, substitute any brandy available.

PLANNING AHEAD Chill all ingredients and the pitcher or punch bowl at least 30 minutes in advance.

To prepare the prickly pears, cut off each end and then slice lengthwise down one side of the fruit, cutting just through the skin. Peel off and discard the skin. Cut the pears into quarters and place them in a pitcher or punch bowl. Sprinkle the sugar over the pears and stir well. Let stand for 5 to 10 minutes, stirring regularly.

Stir in the wine, sherry, and brandy and let steep for 5 minutes before serving.

Lemon Julep

Makes four 4-ounce servings

1 pint lemon sorbet

8 fresh mint sprigs

2 teaspoons sugar

8 ounces bourbon

Ice for serving

8 ounces club soda

GLASSWARE Old-fashioned glasses
(see page 23)

This recipe and the three that follow call for four different sorbet flavors. Experiment with a range of flavors to create an array of tastes.

PLANNING AHEAD The sorbet ice cubes should be made at least 1 hour before serving and can be made up to a week in advance and stored in the freezer.

To prepare the sorbet ice cubes, let the sorbet soften at room temperature for 15 minutes or microwave it for 30 seconds. Spread the sorbet in an ice cube tray and freeze until solid, at least 1 hour.

When ready to serve, place 2 mint sprigs and ½ teaspoon sugar in each old-fashioned glass. Muddle well (see page 22).

Stir in the bourbon. Divide the sorbet ice cubes among the glasses, then add enough regular ice cubes to fill each glass. Top off with club soda and serve.

Mocha Rum Cooler

Makes four 6-ounce drinks

This is an after-dinner coffee beverage, after-dinner drink, and dessert all rolled into one. You can come up with many unique variations simply by replacing the vanilla liqueur with blackberry, cherry, peach, or almost any other fruit brandy.

PLANNING AHEAD The sorbet ice cubes should be made at least 1 hour before serving and can be made up to a week in advance and stored in the freezer.

To prepare the sorbet ice cubes, let the sorbet soften at room temperature for 15 minutes or microwave it for 30 seconds. Spread the sorbet in an ice cube tray and freeze until solid, at least 1 hour.

When ready to serve, divide the sorbet ice cubes among the highball glasses, then add enough regular ice cubes to fill each glass.

Add 1½ ounces rum, ½ ounce vanilla liqueur, and 4 ounces cold coffee to each glass. Stir well. Float 1 ounce cream on each drink if desired, and serve.

1 pint chocolate sorbet

Ice for serving

6 ounces dark rum

2 ounces vanilla liqueur

16 ounces cold coffee

4 ounces heavy cream (optional)

GLASSWARE Highball glasses (see page 23)

Lime Tequila Frappé

Makes four 4-ounce drinks

For this cocktail, use a silver tequila such as Chinaco Blanco, which has a clean flavor with a great backbite and yet is still earthy, the way tequila should be. Gold and *anejo* tequilas tend to dominate too much in this drink.

PLANNING AHEAD The sorbet ice cubes should be made at least 1 hour before serving and can be made up to a week in advance and stored in the freezer.

To prepare the sorbet ice cubes, let the sorbet soften at room temperature for 15 minutes or microwave it for 30 seconds. Spread the sorbet in an ice cube tray and freeze until solid, at least 1 hour.

When ready to serve, place 2 mint sprigs and ½ teaspoon sugar in each old-fashioned glass. Gently muddle together (see page 22).

Add the tequila and stir well. Add the sorbet ice cubes and enough crushed ice to fill the glasses. Top off with club soda and serve.

1 pint lime sorbet

8 fresh mint sprigs

2 teaspoons sugar

8 ounces silver tequila

Crushed ice for serving

8 ounces club soda

GLASSWARE Old-fashioned glasses (see page 23)

Coconut Rum Frappé

Makes four 3-ounce drinks

1 pint coconut sorbet

1 lime

2 tablespoons shredded coconut for rimming the glass

2 teaspoons sugar

8 ounces dark rum

GLASSWARE Old-fashioned glasses (see page 23)

This frappé starts out tasting like a daiquiri and ends up tasting like a piña colada. Use dark, but not heavy, rum, such as Mount Gay, which is medium weight with great caramel flavor and a good kick.

PLANNING AHEAD The sorbet ice cubes should be made at least 1 hour before serving and can be made up to a week in advance and stored in the freezer.

To prepare the sorbet ice cubes, let the sorbet soften at room temperature for 15 minutes or microwave it for 30 seconds. Spread the sorbet in an ice cube tray and freeze until solid, at least 1 hour.

When ready to serve, cut the lime into 8 wedges. Pour the coconut onto a small plate. Rub the juicy side of a lime wedge along the outer edge of the lip of each old-fashioned glass—not along the inside of the rim. Holding each glass at an angle, roll the outer edge of the rim in the coconut until it is fully coated.

Place 2 lime wedges and 1/2 teaspoon sugar into each old-fashioned glass. Muddle the limes to extract the juice (see page 22). Stir in the rum.

Add the coconut sorbet ice cubes and enough crushed ice to fill each glass and serve.

Pineapple Sling

Makes four 7½-ounce drinks

This drink and the Rum Sling, which follows, demonstrate perfectly how a well-balanced classic, in this case the Singapore Sling (page 84), lends itself to improvisation. Switch one liquor for another and tweak just slightly the supporting ingredients, and you have two new distinct, delicious drinks. In this one, the combination of pineapple and gin is delicious. If you have time, try soaking the pineapple wedges in the gin—for as little as 10 minutes and up to an hour—for extra added flavor.

Fill the highball glasses with ice.

Fill a cocktail shaker with ice. Add the gin, Cherry Heering, lemon juice, and syrup. Shake vigorously until the outside of the shaker is thoroughly beaded with sweat and is extremely cold to the touch.

Strain into the glasses and top each with 4 ounces soda. Garnish each with a pineapple wedge and a cherry and serve.

Ice for serving

8 ounces gin

2 ounces Cherry Heering (see Straight Up, page 84) or cherry brandy

3 ounces fresh lemon juice (from approximately 2 lemons)

2 ounces Pineapple Syrup (page 61)

16 ounces club soda

4 pineapple wedges (see page 39) for garnish

4 Maraschino Cherries (page 53) or use store-bought for garnish

GLASSWARE Highball glasses (see page 23)

Rum Sling

Makes four 7½-ounce drinks

This variation of the Singapore Sling (page 84) uses rum instead of gin, producing a richer drink, for the rum has more weight yet less bite than gin.

Fill the highball glasses with ice.

Fill a cocktail shaker with ice. Add the rum, Cherry Heering, lemon juice, and syrup. Shake vigorously until the outside of the shaker is thoroughly beaded with sweat and is extremely cold to the touch.

Strain into the glasses. Top each with 4 ounces soda, garnish with an orange slice and a cherry, and serve.

Ice for serving

8 ounces white rum

2 ounces Cherry Heering (see Straight Up, page 84) or cherry brandy

2 ounces fresh lemon juice (from approximately 2 lemons)

2 ounces Simple Syrup (page 56)

16 ounces club soda

4 orange slices for garnish

4 Maraschino Cherries (page 53) or use store-bought for garnish

GLASSWARE Highball glasses (see page 23)

Tea & Whiskey Highball

Makes eight 11-ounce drinks (photograph opposite)

8 teaspoons or 8 bags Lapsang Souchong or other black tea

Long zest from 2 oranges (see page 39)

64 ounces boiling water

16 ounces Mint Syrup (page 57)

16 ounces scotch or bourbon

Ice for serving

8 fresh mint leaves for garnish

GLASSWARE Highball glasses (see page 23)

I prefer a rich, smoky style of whiskey for these highballs, such as an Islay malt from Laphroiag, Scotland, for example, or a robust single-cask bourbon from Kentucky, such as Blantons. For the tea I use a rich Lapsang Souchong Chinese black tea, which is smoked as part of the drying process. Feel free to substitute any other black tea.

PLANNING AHEAD The prepared tea must be refrigerated until cold.

To prepare the tea, place the loose tea or tea bags and 8 or 10 strands of the orange zest in a large pitcher. Add the boiling water. Allow to steep for 5 minutes. Remove and discard the tea leaves or bags and the orange zest and refrigerate the tea until cold.

When ready to serve, stir the mint syrup and whiskey into the tea. Fill the highball glasses with ice and add several strands of orange zest to each glass. Pour the whiskey mixture over the ice, garnish with a mint leaf, and serve.

Tenberry Highball

Makes eight 7-ounce drinks

¼ cup pitted and quartered cherries

¼ cup quartered strawberries

½ pint raspberries

½ pint blackberries

½ cup confectioners' sugar

3 ounces crème de fraise

3 ounces cherry brandy

3 ounces crème de framboise (see Straight Up, page 125)

3 ounces blackberry liqueur

8 ounces gin, vodka, or rum

16 ounces fresh lime juice (from approximately 16 limes)

16 ounces fresh orange juice (from approximately 5 oranges)

GLASSWARE Highball glasses (see page 23)

Okay, so there are not *really* ten different berries in this highball, but it sure tastes as if there are! It's summer in a glass.

PLANNING AHEAD Infuse the fruits for at least 1 hour before serving; they are better if left overnight. They can be made up to 1 week in advance and stored in the refrigerator.

Mix the cherries, berries, and sugar in a bowl and stir well. Let stand for 10 minutes. Stir in all the liquors and store in the refrigerator until ready to serve.

Fill each highball glass halfway with ice and divide the fruit among the glasses. Fill each the rest of the way with ice and divide the fruit liquor among the glasses.

Add 2 ounces each of the lime juice and orange juice. Stir well and serve.

Cider Highball

Makes four 7-ounce drinks

Ice for serving

1 orange for zesting, plus another for garnish

4 ounces vanilla vodka

4 ounces calvados or applejack (see Straight Up, page 112)

One 750-milliliter bottle nonalcoholic sparkling apple cider, chilled

4 long orange twists (see page 39) for garnish

GLASSWARE Highball glasses (see page 23)

Cold and refreshing, this is a lovely summer drink, though the apples make it a natural for fall and winter, as well. Using sparkling cider instead of soda makes a traditional highball more unique. Hard cider can make the drink too strong and out of balance.

PLANNING AHEAD Chill the sparkling cider for at least 30 minutes before serving.

Fill the highball glasses with ice. Grate some orange zest over the ice in each glass.

Pour 1 ounce vodka and 1 ounce calvados into each glass.

Fill each glass with cider, garnish with an orange twist, and serve.

Maraschino Highball

Makes four 6-ounce drinks

Ice for serving

12 Maraschino Cherries (page 53) or use store-bought

4 teaspoons syrup from maraschino cherries

8 ounces fresh lemon juice (from approximately 6 lemons)

8 ounces fresh orange juice (from approximately 3 oranges)

4 ounces Limoncello (page 69) or use store-bought

4 ounces maraschino liqueur (see Straight Up, page 74) or cherry brandy

4 orange twists (see page 39) for garnish

GLASSWARE Highball glasses (see page 23)

Since both limoncello and maraschino liqueur are lower-alcohol spirits, this cocktail makes a nice afternoon drink. For a simpler cocktail, stir equal parts limoncello and maraschino liqueur in a pitcher with ice, then strain into highball glasses and serve.

Fill the highball glasses with ice.

Add three maraschino cherries and 1 teaspoon syrup to each glass.

Pour into each glass 2 ounces lemon juice, 2 ounces orange juice, 1 ounce limoncello, and 1 ounce maraschino liqueur. Stir briskly.

Garnish each with an orange twist and serve.

Summer Buck

Makes four 6-ounce drinks

Bucks are basically gin and ginger ale with lots of fruit added. This version uses ripe mangoes, but you can use papaya, any melon, or citrus fruit instead.

Peel the mango and cut the flesh into $\frac{1}{2}$-inch cubes, discarding the hard pit.

Fill each highball glass by $\frac{1}{2}$ with ice. Spoon a generous amount of mango into each glass, then fill the rest of the way with ice.

Add a dash of bitters to each glass. Squeeze 1 lemon wedge into each, then drop the wedge into the glass.

Pour 2 ounces gin and 4 ounces ginger ale into each glass and serve.

1 small ripe mango

Ice for serving

4 dashes Angostura bitters

1 lemon, quartered

8 ounces gin

16 ounces ginger ale

GLASSWARE Highball glasses (see page 23)

Bitter Pill

Makes four 6½-ounce drinks

This blend of bitter and sweet is very refreshing and thirst quenching. Serve it as an aperitif before dinner.

Pour the sugar onto a small plate. Rub the juicy side of the lemon wedge along the outer edge of the lip of each highball glass—not along the inside of the rim. Holding each glass at an angle, roll the outer edge of the rim in the sugar until it is fully coated.

Fill the glasses with ice. Add 4 ounces grapefruit juice, 1 ounce Campari, and 1 ounce sweet vermouth to each glass and stir.

Float $\frac{1}{2}$ ounce berry syrup on each drink and serve.

Sugar for rimming the glass

Lemon wedge for rimming the glass

Ice for serving

16 ounces fresh grapefruit juice (from approximately 3 grapefruits)

4 ounces Campari

4 ounces sweet vermouth

2 ounces Berry Syrup (page 62)

GLASSWARE Highball glasses (see page 23)

Watermelon Cooler

Makes four 12-ounce drinks

½ small watermelon

8 ounces Simple Syrup (page 56)

4 ounces fresh lemon juice
(from approximately 3 lemons)

4 ounces fresh lime juice
(from approximately 4 limes)

Ice for serving

12 ounces dark rum

8 ounces vanilla liqueur

12 fresh mint leaves for garnish

GLASSWARE Cooler glasses
(see page 25) or any other
large glasses

This has become the barbecue beverage of choice at our house. After a day at the beach, there's nothing better to sip while you are waiting for the dogs to grill. For a punch version of this recipe, see Watermelon Punch (page 193). Use seedless watermelon if available; if not, remove the seeds or just ignore them.

PLANNING AHEAD The watermelon must be frozen for at least 30 minutes.

To prepare the watermelon, cut off the rind and discard. Cut the flesh into 1-inch cubes (you should have about 4 cups) and place them in a colander set inside a bowl. Stir the cubes gently to extract as much juice as possible. The more you stir, the more juice will be extruded; just be careful not to overdo it and break down the melon. You should have at least 8 ounces of juice. Set the watermelon juice aside.

Place the watermelon cubes in a freezer bag and freeze for at least 30 minutes.

Mix the syrup, lemon juice, and lime juice with the extracted watermelon juice.

When ready to serve, divide the frozen watermelon among the 4 cooler glasses. Add ice cubes to top off the glass. Evenly divide the rum, vanilla liqueur, and watermelon juice mixture among the glasses and stir thoroughly. Don't worry if the watermelon breaks down a bit—this adds flavor to the drink. Garnish with the mint leaves and serve.

Pear Cider Cooler

Makes four 8-ounce drinks

Ice for serving

4 ounces Limoncello (page 69)
or use store-bought

4 ounces Belle de Brillet
pear liqueur

One 750-milliliter bottle sparkling
pear cider

4 long lemon twists
(see page 39) for garnish

GLASSWARE Highball glasses
(see page 23)

This makes both a great precursor to a meal and a refreshing restorative afterward.

PLANNING AHEAD Chill the pear cider for at least 30 minutes before preparing the coolers.

Fill the highball glasses with ice.

Pour 1 ounce limoncello and 1 ounce pear liqueur into each glass. Stir well.

Fill the glasses with cider, garnish each with a lemon twist, and serve.

Moscato Cooler

Makes five 7-ounce drinks

Slightly sweet, low-alcohol Moscato is a sparkling counterpoint to the orange juice and Cointreau in this version of the Magnificent Mimosa (page 142), adapted for slow drinking on summer afternoons.

PLANNING AHEAD Chill the Moscato for at least 30 minutes before preparing the coolers.

Mix the sugar and orange zest on a small plate. Cut a wedge from the reserved orange. Rub the juicy side of the orange wedge along the outer edge of the lip of each wineglass—not along the inside of the rim. Holding each glass at an angle, roll the outer edge of the rim in the sugar until it is fully coated.

Fill the wineglasses with ice.

Add 1 ounce Cointreau and 1 ounce orange juice to each glass.

Fill with Moscato, stir gently, and serve.

1 tablespoon sugar for rimming the glass

1 tablespoon grated orange zest (see page 39), flesh reserved for rimming the glass

Ice for serving

5 ounces Cointreau

5 ounces fresh orange juice (from approximately 2 oranges)

One 750-milliliter bottle sparkling Moscato

GLASSWARE Wineglasses (see page 24)

Blackberry Cooler

Makes four 7-ounce drinks

If you cannot find fresh blackberries for this fresh berry cooler, substitute raspberries and use raspberry liqueur in place of the blackberry liqueur.

Place 3 blackberries, ½ teaspoon sugar, and 1 ounce lemon juice in each cooler glass. Muddle the blackberries (see page 22).

Fill each glass with ice, then add 1 ounce blackberry liqueur and 1 ounce Grand Marnier, and top off with club soda. Stir well.

Sprinkle orange zest on top and serve.

12 blackberries, rinsed if necessary

2 teaspoons sugar

4 ounces fresh lemon juice (from approximately 3 lemons)

Ice for serving

4 ounces blackberry liqueur

4 ounces Grand Marnier

16 ounces club soda

Grated orange zest (see page 39) for garnish

GLASSWARE Cooler glasses (see page 25) or any other large glasses

Plum Sake

Makes two 3-ounce drinks

4 ounces sake (see Straight Up)

4 ounces plum wine

4 ounces fresh lime juice
(from approximately 4 limes)

1 teaspoon confectioners' or
superfine sugar

2 slices dark red plums
or 2 dried plum halves or
2 slices lime for garnish

GLASSWARE Cocktail glasses
(see page 24)

This is a wonderful summer cocktail that takes advantage of fresh seasonal plums. It's just as nice in the winter made with dried plums.

Fill a cocktail shaker with ice. Add the sake, plum wine, lime juice, and sugar. Shake vigorously until the outside of the shaker is thoroughly beaded with sweat and is extremely cold to the touch.

Place a plum slice in each cocktail glass. Add the sake mix and serve.

STRAIGHT UP

Sake, made from rice, has as wide a range of textures and flavors as wine or beer. Some sakes are robust and dry and some are soft and fruity. For this plum sake cocktail, choose an off-dry or medium-dry style. Not all sake is meant to be drunk hot, though that is the only way many Americans have ever had it. Some sake is best served ice-cold.

Nevisian Smile

Makes four 14-ounce drinks

A bartender on the Caribbean island of Nevis gave me this recipe, which is guaranteed to make you smile. The Baileys Irish Cream and Tia Maria make a very rich and thick drink with many layers of flavors. While at first sip it tastes like a piña colada, the coffee and chocolate flavors of the Tia Maria and Baileys subtly come through.

PLANNING AHEAD The base can be made up to 8 hours in advance and stored in the refrigerator.

In a large pitcher, combine all the ingredients except the ice and the pineapple wedges.

Process in a blender in two batches, using 22 ounces of mix and 2 cups of crushed ice per batch. Blend until smooth.

Pour into hurricane glasses, garnish with pineapple wedges, and serve.

12 ounces pineapple juice

8 ounces coconut rum

8 ounces Baileys Irish Cream

6 ounces coconut milk

6 ounces Coco Lopez cream of coconut

4 ounces Tia Maria

4 cups crushed ice

4 pineapple wedges (see page 39) for garnish

GLASSWARE Hurricane glasses (see page 25) or any other large glasses

Frozen Raspberry Daiquiri

Makes four 12-ounce drinks

The texture of raspberries and their intense flavor help make a truly great blended daiquiri.

PLANNING AHEAD The base can be made up to 8 hours in advance and stored in the refrigerator.

In a large pitcher, mix the tequila, triple sec, crème de framboise, and lime juice.

When ready to serve, pour the salt onto a small plate. Rub the juicy side of the reserved lime rind along the outer edge of the lip of each glass—not along the inside of the rim. Holding each glass at an angle, roll the outer edge of the rim in the salt until it is fully coated.

Blend the daiquiri in 2 batches, using 16 ounces of mix, 2 cups of crushed ice, and half of the raspberries for each batch. Blend until smooth.

Pour into the hurricane glasses and serve.

8 ounces tequila

3 ounces triple sec

3 ounces crème de framboise

6 ounces fresh lime juice (from approximately 6 limes), some rinds reserved for rimming the glasses

Kosher salt for rimming the glasses

Crushed ice for serving

1/2 pint fresh raspberries

GLASSWARE Hurricane glasses (see page 25) or any other large glasses

Lava Flow

Makes four 14-ounce drinks

12 ounces pineapple juice

12 ounces coconut rum

12 ounces white rum

6 ounces coconut milk

6 ounces Coco Lopez cream
of coconut

4 cups crushed ice

4 ounces Grenadine
(page 64) or use store-bought

GLASSWARE Hurricane glasses
(see page 25) or any other
large glasses

Frozen drinks are better served in the late afternoon rather than right before dinner, when they tend to fill you up. This drink is a flowing version of the Piña Colada (page 90).

PLANNING AHEAD The base can be made up to 8 hours in advance and stored in the refrigerator.

In a large pitcher, combine all the ingredients except the ice and the grenadine.

Process in a blender in two batches, using 24 ounces of mix and 2 cups of crushed ice per batch. Blend until smooth.

Pour into the hurricane glasses. Float 1 ounce grenadine on each and watch the lava flow.

The Nick-o-cino

Makes four 14-ounce drinks

I first started making this version of a frozen cappuccino at C. D. Tweeds in Greenwich, Connecticut. I began with a hot version, which was christened the Nick-o-cino. Once summer hit, we simply tossed the ingredients in the blender with some ice and kept selling them.

PLANNING AHEAD The base can be made up to 8 hours in advance and stored in the refrigerator.

In a large pitcher, combine all the ingredients except the ice and the coffee beans.

Process in a blender in two batches, using 14 ounces of mix and 2 cups of crushed ice per batch. Blend until smooth.

Pour into hurricane glasses, garnish each drink with 3 coffee beans, and serve.

8 ounces cold black coffee

8 ounces heavy cream

8 ounces Sylk Cream Liqueur (see Straight Up)

4 ounces Kahlúa

4 cups crushed ice for serving

12 chocolate-covered coffee beans for garnish

GLASSWARE Hurricane glasses (see page 25) or any other large glasses

STRAIGHT UP

Sylk Cream Liqueur is a blend of malt whiskey, honey, and cream. It is similar to Baileys Irish Cream but has a little more bite.

Frozen Mango Smash

Makes four 12-ounce drinks

The creamy texture of mangoes makes them perfect for frozen drinks. Overripe fruit works especially well in this recipe.

Carefully peel the mango and cut the flesh into 1-inch cubes, discarding the pit. Scrape the remaining fruit off the skin of the mango and add it to the cubes. Cut the longest strips of skin into 4 long strips for garnishing and set aside.

In a large pitcher, combine the rum, triple sec, apricot brandy, and lime juice.

Process in a blender in two batches, using half the mango, half the rum mixture, and 1 cup crushed ice per batch. Blend until smooth.

Pour into hurricane glasses, garnish with the strips of mango peel, and serve.

1 ripe mango

8 ounces white rum

3 ounces triple sec

3 ounces apricot brandy

6 ounces fresh lime juice (from approximately 6 limes)

Crushed ice for serving

GLASSWARE Hurricane glasses (see page 25) or any other large glasses

193 WATERMELON PUNCH

194 POMEGRANATE PUNCH

195 DARK AND STORMY II

195 GINGER CHAMPAGNE PUNCH

196 RUM AND CHERRY PUNCH

196 PORT PUNCH

197 PINEAPPLE PUNCH

198 WHISKEY AND GINGER PUNCH

199 PHILADELPHIA FISH HOUSE PUNCH

199 SLOE COMFORTABLE PUNCH

KNOCKOUT PUNCHES

PUNCHES ARE AN EXCELLENT WAY TO ENTERTAIN LARGE NUMBERS OF GUESTS.
Often colorful centerpieces at a party, punches make any occasion more festive, and the fact that they make your entertaining easier is purely a bonus. Almost anything can be converted to a punch—within reason, that is: A large bowl of strongly alcoholic Dirty Martinis (page 74) may well kill the party before it begins. But certainly feel free to experiment. All you have to do is mix a spirit or sparkling wine with juice in a large bowl and you have a punch. Just remember that the ingredients should compose a mix that works well with both your meal and your tastes. When making these recipes or creating your own, avoid the urge to make them stronger by adding more liquor—punches, like any cocktail, should be balanced. The sweetness of most punches sometimes masks the alcohol, making it seem, by taste anyway, that they contain less alcohol than they actually do. While the term "packs a punch" might seem as though it fits in this chapter, punches should above all be refreshing, with a good kick but not over the top.

The punches in this chapter are fairly easy to prepare and are unique marriages of ingredients. Most, like the Rum and Cherry Punch (page 196) and the Watermelon Punch (page 193) have a vibrant fruitiness. For those who love ginger, the Dark and Stormy II (page 195), which contains ginger beer, fresh ginger, and pickled ginger, is a must. And don't miss the Philadelphia Fish House Punch (page 199), so delicious it's easy to see why it's been around since before the American Revolution.

Watermelon Punch

Makes twenty 4-ounce or fifteen 5-ounce servings

This refreshing and fun summer cocktail is the perfect accompaniment to a homemade Mexican meal of chicken quesadillas or steak fajitas. Use seedless watermelon if available; if not, you can remove the seeds or just ignore them.

PLANNING AHEAD Watermelon cubes will need to be frozen at least 45 minutes before serving. The watermelon base requires at least 1 hour chilling time, but it is really best if left to chill overnight. It can be made up to 1 day in advance and stored in the refrigerator.

Cut the watermelon flesh into 1/2-inch cubes, discarding the rind. Place 1/4 of the watermelon cubes in a freezer bag and freeze until ready to use. Place the remaining melon in a punch bowl.

Tear the mint leaves off of the stems. Place the leaves in a bowl and cover with cold water. Swish the leaves around once or twice, and when the water settles, transfer the leaves to a paper towel. Pat dry. Set aside 1/2 of the leaves and add the remaining leaves to the watermelon in the punch bowl.

Add the confectioners' sugar to the punch bowl. Stir the melon cubes to extract as much of the juice as possible.

Stir in the rum, white grape juice, vanilla liqueur, and lemon juice. Let chill in the refrigerator for at least 1 hour and up to 1 day (longer is better).

When ready to serve, you may rim the punch cups, if desired: On a small plate, combine the chipotle powder with the sugar and salt. Rub the juicy side of the reserved lemon rind along the outer edge of the lip of each cup—not along the inside of the rim. Holding each cup at an angle, roll the outer edge of the rim in the spice mix until it is fully coated.

To serve, place a few cubes of frozen watermelon in each punch cup. Ladle in the punch and garnish with mint.

1/2 small watermelon

2 large bunches fresh mint

1 1/2 cups confectioners' or superfine sugar

1 liter white rum

16 ounces white grape juice

8 ounces vanilla liqueur

18 ounces fresh lemon juice (from approximately 12 lemons), some rinds reserved for rimming the glasses

2 tablespoons chipotle powder or smoked paprika (see Straight Up, page 215) for rimming the glasses (optional)

1 tablespoon sugar for rimming the glasses (optional)

1 tablespoon kosher salt for rimming the glasses (optional)

GLASSWARE Punch cups and punch bowl (see page 25)

Pomegranate Punch

Makes sixteen 4-ounce servings (photograph also on page 190)

1 large pomegranate

32 ounces fresh blood orange juice (from approximately 10 blood oranges), chilled

8 ounces vodka, chilled

8 ounces Mandarine Napoleon liqueur, chilled

1 blood orange, cut into ¼-inch slices, for garnish

GLASSWARE Punch cups and punch bowl (see page 25)

This is a great winter punch to serve when blood oranges are in season. The bright colors and complementary tanginess of pomegranates and blood oranges make them an ideal combination. Full-flavored yet light in body and texture, this punch is not overly filling and is thus a very refreshing aperitif to a rich winter meal.

PLANNING AHEAD The punch should be served very cold, so either refrigerate all of the ingredients the night before you assemble the punch, or chill the prepared punch overnight.

Cut the pomegranate in half. Holding each half over a large bowl, squeeze firmly to extract the juice. Use a large spoon to scoop out as many seeds as possible and add them to the juice. Be careful not to spray the seeds everywhere, as they can stain.

Transfer the pomegranate seeds and juice to a punch bowl. Add the blood orange juice, vodka, and Mandarine Napoleon, and stir well to combine. Float the blood orange slices on top and serve.

Dark and Stormy II

Makes sixteen 4-ounce servings

The Dark and Stormy is a specialty of Bermuda, where dark, heavy rums and ginger beer are produced. The highball version (page 94) is made from 2 ounces of rum topped off with 4 ounces of ginger beer and a squeeze of lime. This punch takes that drink to a higher level, with the addition of fresh and pickled ginger.

PLANNING AHEAD The punch should be served very cold, so either refrigerate all of the ingredients the night before you assemble the punch, or chill the prepared punch overnight. Alternatively, the base can be made up to 8 hours in advance and stored in a tightly covered container in the refrigerator.

Place the sugar, pickled ginger, fresh ginger, and lime slices in a punch bowl. Muddle the ingredients together to extract the juice from the limes and essential oils from the ginger (see page 22).

Add the rum and stir to combine. At this point, you may store the mixture in the refrigerator for up to 8 hours.

When ready to serve, add the ginger beer, stir well to combine, and serve.

½ cup turbinado sugar (see page 41)

8 strips pickled ginger

One 2-inch piece fresh ginger, peeled and cut into eight ¼-inch slices

2 limes, cut into ¼-inch-thick slices

16 ounces Goslings Black Seal Rum, chilled

Four 12-ounce bottles ginger beer, chilled

GLASSWARE Punch cups and punch bowl (see page 25)

Ginger Champagne Punch

Makes eighteen 4-ounce or twelve 6-ounce servings

The tangy sweetness of ginger, lime, and sparkling wine makes this cocktail a wonderful palate opener before dinner or a soothing restorative after dinner. Or serve it with food—it's especially good with Asian dishes.

PLANNING AHEAD The punch should be served very cold, so either refrigerate all of the ingredients the night before you assemble the punch, or chill the prepared punch overnight.

Place the ginger syrup and lime juice in a punch bowl. Stir well to blend.

Add the sparkling wine and mix gently but thoroughly.

Float the lime slices on top and serve.

16 ounces Ginger Syrup (page 59), chilled

8 ounces fresh lime juice (from approximately 8 limes), chilled

Two 750-milliliter bottles sparkling wine, chilled

1 lime, cut into 8 thin slices

GLASSWARE Punch cups or champagne glasses and punch bowl (see page 25)

TRICK OF THE TRADE

If you are serving this punch in champagne glasses, you can rim the glasses (see page 22) with a mixture of equal parts powdered ginger and granulated sugar.

Rum and Cherry Punch

Makes about fifteen 8-ounce servings

½ pound cherries, pitted and halved

¼ cup superfine sugar

1 liter dark rum, chilled

8 ounces amaretto, chilled

8 ounces Cointreau, chilled

32 ounces fresh orange juice (from approximately 10 oranges), chilled

32 ounces pineapple juice, chilled

4 ounces fresh lemon juice (from approximately 3 lemons), chilled

4 ounces fresh lime juice (from approximately 4 limes), chilled

1 pint very well frozen coconut sorbet

2 lemons, sliced crosswise into thin rounds

2 limes, sliced crosswise into thin rounds

Mint leaves for garnish

Ice for serving

GLASSWARE Highball or cooler glasses and punch bowl
(see page 25)

This great mix of fruits, juices, and liquors makes it an exotic and refreshing punch, meant to be savored and sipped. As the sorbet melts, it extends the life of the punch and lowers the alcohol level. It also changes the flavor, so that over the course of a party, it seems as though more than one punch has been served.

PLANNING AHEAD This punch should be served very cold, so either refrigerate all of the ingredients the night before you assemble the punch, or chill the prepared punch overnight.

Place the cherries and sugar in a punch bowl and stir well to extract juice. Add the rum, amaretto, Cointreau, orange juice, pineapple juice, lemon juice, and lime juice and stir well. Chill overnight in the refrigerator.

When ready to serve, unmold the sorbet into the middle of the punch bowl. Float the lemon slices, lime slices, and mint leaves on top.

To serve, fill the highball glasses with ice and ladle the punch over it.

RUM AND CHERRY FIZZ Prepare the Rum and Cherry Punch, above, omitting the sorbet and adding 32 ounces club soda just before serving.

Port Punch

Makes fourteen 4-ounce servings

2 oranges, cut into ¼-inch rounds

16 ounces brandy, chilled

One 750-milliliter bottle ruby port, chilled

16 ounces dry sherry, chilled

Finely grated zest of 1 lemon (see page 39) for garnish

GLASSWARE Punch cups and punch bowl (see page 25)

This is a good punch to serve in the late fall or winter. Although it includes port, sherry, and brandy, the port adds the biggest flavor, hence its star billing. Choose a ruby port, which is the most economical, and whose fruitier style works well in this punch. The port itself is sweet, so no sugar is needed.

PLANNING AHEAD The punch should be served very cold, so either refrigerate all of the ingredients the night before you assemble the punch, or chill the prepared punch overnight.

Place the orange slices and brandy in a punch bowl and muddle them together to extract the orange juice (see page 22). Add the port and sherry and stir well. Sprinkle the lemon zest over the top and serve.

Pineapple Punch

Makes fourteen to sixteen 5-ounce servings

This versatile punch base is perfect to keep on hand for the holidays and pairs very well with most hors d'oeuvres and cheeses. You can make individual servings: Fill champagne glasses one-third full with the base and top them off with chilled sparkling wine. Depending on the size of your pineapple and your glasses, the recipe may yield from twelve to eighteen drinks.

PLANNING AHEAD Requires at least 2 hours chilling. Punch base can be made up to 2 weeks in advance and stored in the refrigerator. Chill the sparkling wine for at least 30 minutes before preparing the punch.

To make the punch base, prepare the pineapple as on page 172, then chop the remaining fruit into 1/4-inch chunks.

Tear the mint leaves off the stems. Place the leaves in a bowl and cover with cold water. Swish the leaves around once or twice, and when the water settles, transfer the leaves to a paper towel. Pat dry. Give the leaves two or three whacks with a sharp knife, being careful not to chop them up (you only want to release some of the essential oils from the leaves).

Place the pineapple in a bowl and add the mint and confectioners' sugar. Stir gently, cover tightly with plastic wrap, and chill for up to 24 hours, stirring occasionally.

Pour the apricot brandy over the pineapple mixture and refrigerate for at least 1 hour, or until needed. The mixture can be refrigerated for up to 2 weeks.

To serve, place the pineapple mixture in a punch bowl and top with the sparkling wine. Stir thoroughly and serve well chilled in champagne glasses or punch cups.

NONALCOHOLIC PINEAPPLE PUNCH Prepare the pineapple punch, above, replacing the apricot brandy with peach or apricot nectar and using ginger ale or nonalcoholic sparkling cider in place of the sparkling wine.

TRICK OF THE TRADE

To keep the punch chilled without diluting the flavor, pour 1 quart of pineapple juice into a small bowl and freeze it. When ready to assemble the punch, dip the bowl into warm water briefly to loosen the pineapple ice. Invert the bowl over the empty punch bowl, drop the pineapple ice in, then add the pineapple mixture and sparkling wine.

FOR THE PUNCH BASE

1 ripe pineapple

1 small bunch mint

3/4 to 1 cup confectioners' sugar, depending on the sweetness of the pineapple

16 ounces apricot brandy

FOR THE PUNCH

Two 750-milliliter bottles sparkling wine, thoroughly chilled

GLASSWARE Champagne glasses or punch cups and punch bowl (see page 25)

Whiskey and Ginger Punch
Makes sixteen 4-ounce servings

One 3-inch piece fresh ginger, peeled and cut into ¼-inch slices

½ cup sugar

16 ounces Maker's Mark bourbon, chilled

4 ounces fresh lime juice (from approximately 4 limes), chilled

Four 12-ounce bottles ginger beer, chilled

2 limes, cut into ¼-inch rounds

Freshly grated nutmeg for garnish

GLASSWARE Punch cups and punch bowl (see page 25)

Spicy ginger beer and bone-warming bourbon make this a great punch to serve in the late fall and winter when you need something to ward off the chill. This variation of the Whiskey and Ginger Muddle (page 135) calls for Maker's Mark bourbon, for its sweetness, but feel free to substitute your favorite scotch, rye, or other bourbon.

PLANNING AHEAD The punch should be served very cold, so either refrigerate all of the ingredients the night before you assemble the punch, or chill the prepared punch overnight.

Place the ginger and sugar in a punch bowl and muddle to extract the ginger's essential oils (see page 22).

Add the bourbon and lime juice and stir well to combine. Let stand for 5 minutes.

Add the ginger beer and limes and stir well. Sprinkle fresh nutmeg over the top and serve.

Philadelphia Fish House Punch

Makes twelve 4-ounce servings

There are many theories about the origins of this punch, and the one I like best begins in pre–Revolutionary War Philadelphia. Colonists in the fishing ports who were trading with Caribbean countries stocked great quantities of rum and citrus fruits. These trading posts were called fish houses, and bowls of fish house punch were always kept in the foyers, ready to entertain guests. This recipe is adapted from Jerry Thomas's 1865 book *The Bon Vivant's Companion or How to Mix Drinks*.

PLANNING AHEAD The punch should be served very cold, so either refrigerate all of the ingredients the night before you assemble the punch, or chill the prepared punch overnight.

Place the lemon juice and sugar in a punch bowl and stir until the sugar has almost fully dissolved. Add the remaining ingredients, except the garnishes, and stir well.

Garnish with the peach wedges and mint leaves and serve.

8 ounces fresh lemon juice (from approximately 6 lemons), chilled

1 cup sugar

8 ounces peach brandy, chilled

8 ounces brandy, chilled

8 ounces dark rum, chilled

16 ounces cold water

1 to 2 fresh peaches, cut into 12 wedges for garnish

12 fresh mint leaves for garnish

GLASSWARE Punch cups and punch bowl (see page 25)

Sloe Comfortable Punch

Makes sixteen 4-ounce servings

In the 1980s a very popular highball was the sloe comfortable screw (short for screwdriver), a blend of sloe gin, Southern Comfort, and orange juice. The sweet and tasty combination of flavors in this drink makes a refreshing summer punch for a group. Sloe gin is not actually gin at all, but a wonderful cordial made from the sloe berry, a type of wild plum. It is very red, tastes like an alcoholic grenadine, and is a great way to add a little sweetness and color to any cocktail.

PLANNING AHEAD The punch should be served very cold, so either refrigerate all of the ingredients the night before you assemble the punch, or chill the prepared punch overnight.

Place all the ingredients except the mint in a punch bowl and stir well to combine.

Float the mint on top and serve.

32 ounces fresh orange juice (from approximately 10 oranges), chilled

16 ounces Southern Comfort, chilled

8 ounces vodka, chilled

8 ounces sloe gin, chilled

2 peaches, each cut into 8 wedges

8 fresh mint leaves for garnish

GLASSWARE Punch cups and punch bowl (see page 25)

203 VANILLA ALEXANDER

203 CHOCOLATE ALEXANDER

204 WHITE CHOCOLATE MARTINI

204 VANILLA FRAPPÉ

205 CREAM-SICLE

205 POIRE FRAPPÉ

207 GRAND GALLIANO

207 ISLAND ROSE

208 CHOCOLATE-COVERED CHERRY

208 BLACKBERRY CARAMELS

210 GOOSE BERRY

210 43 LICKS

211 FLUTTER

211 GRASSHOPPER

211 GLOOM CHASER

THE AFTER-PARTY

IF SOME HOSTS MISS THE "WHAT TO DO BEFORE DINNER" PART OF ENTERTAINING, many more get lost after dinner. Pat Cetta, the late great restaurateur and owner of Sparks steakhouse in New York City, had a unique approach. After the entrée plates were cleared, the waiter would remove all evidence of dinner, including the dirty tablecloth. Then, with the guests still seated at the table, the waiter would reset the entire table. This gave guests a few extra moments to digest, and a clean and empty table subliminally suggested to them that they had not eaten or drunk too much and had plenty of room for dessert and after-dinner drinks.

Rushing right into dessert after a large meal leaves many people uncomfortably full. I much prefer to clear everything away and tidy up the kitchen. Then I can relax with my guests over an after-dinner drink. In many cases the drink itself is dessert or at least as much a part of dessert as the accompanying cookies, dried fruits, chocolates, or nuts.

Choose the after-dinner beverage based on what was served during the meal. If dinner is rich and heavy, serve a light after-dinner cocktail, such as the Poire Frappé (page 205). If the meal is lighter, serve a richer after-dinner beverage such as 43 Licks (page 210). This way you'll neither overstuff your guests nor leave them wanting more.

Some people choose not to have after-dinner drinks either because they are driving or because they prefer to continue drinking the wine they were served at dinner. Since you shouldn't push drinks on anyone or waste a pitcherful of good cocktails, the yields for the drinks in this chapter are a bit more conservative. If you are serving a larger group, all the recipes can easily be doubled.

Vanilla Alexander

Makes four 3-ounce drinks (photograph on page 200, left)

The classic Brandy Alexander (page 83) is a heavenly combination of brandy, white crème de cacao, and cream. This recipe produces a more subtle, vanilla-flavored variation. Vanilla vodka syrup adds a little more zip and complexity to the final product, but you can substitute a plain simple syrup as well.

Fill a cocktail shaker with ice and add all the ingredients except the nutmeg. Shake vigorously until the outside of the shaker is beaded with sweat and frosty.

Strain into the wineglasses, grate nutmeg on top, and serve.

4 ounces heavy cream

4 ounces brandy

4 ounces Galliano (see Straight Up)

2 ounces Vanilla Vodka Syrup (page 60) or Simple Syrup (page 56)

Freshly grated nutmeg for garnish

GLASSWARE Small wineglasses (see page 24)

STRAIGHT UP

Galliano is an Italian liqueur made from unaged grape brandy and many different herbs. It tastes of pungent vanilla. You can substitute Licor 43 (see Straight Up, page 114) if you can't find Galliano.

Chocolate Alexander

Makes four 3-ounce drinks (photograph on page 200, right)

This variation of the Brandy Alexander (page 83) is aimed to please chocolate lovers. Godiva Liqueur is very rich and is wonderful on its own as well as in this drink. Make sure you serve this one to your guests—after the table has been cleared and the dishes put away—alongside a couple of chocolate truffles.

Fill a cocktail shaker with ice and add the cream, brandy, and chocolate liqueur. Shake vigorously until the outside of the shaker is beaded with sweat and frosty.

Strain into the sherry glasses, sprinkle cocoa on top, and serve.

4 ounces heavy cream

4 ounces brandy

4 ounces Godiva Liqueur or other chocolate liqueur

Cocoa powder for garnish

GLASSWARE Sherry copitas (see page 25) or small wineglasses (see page 24)

White Chocolate Martini

Makes four 3-ounce drinks

1 ounce shaved white chocolate or 12 coffee beans for garnish

6 ounces vanilla vodka

6 ounces white crème de cacao

GLASSWARE Cocktail glasses (see page 24)

Sweet but not too sweet, flavorful but not over the top, this drink makes a sublime nightcap, especially for those who do not care for cream-based drinks but still have a sweet tooth.

To prepare chocolate shavings, hold the chocolate bar in one hand and, using a vegetable peeler, cut shavings from a long edge of the bar—you'll want several shavings for each drink. Set aside. If not using immediately, cover and store in the refrigerator.

Fill a pitcher with ice and add the vodka and crème de cacao. Stir briskly until the outside of the pitcher is beaded with sweat and frosty.

Strain into cocktail glasses, garnish with the chocolate shavings or 3 coffee beans per glass, and serve.

Vanilla Frappé

Makes four 3-ounce drinks

Crushed ice for serving

1 vanilla bean

4 ounces heavy cream

4 ounces Licor 43 (see Straight Up, page 114)

4 ounces vodka

GLASSWARE Rocks glasses (see page 23)

This frappé is intensely flavorful and makes a great centerpiece to a light dessert of dried fruits and nuts.

Fill the rocks glasses with crushed ice.

Fill a cocktail shaker with ice. Split the vanilla bean in half lengthwise. Scrape out the seeds and add them to the cocktail shaker. Cut the bean halves in half crosswise and set aside.

Add the cream, Licor 43, and vodka to the shaker. Shake vigorously until the outside of the shaker is beaded with sweat and frosty.

Strain into the rocks glasses, garnish with the reserved vanilla bean sections, and serve.

Cream-Sicle

Makes four 4-ounce drinks

My brother and I used to chase the Good Humor man down the street in hot pursuit of those creamy sticks of vanilla ice cream and orange sherbet. Here's a grown-up version served in a glass.

Fill the rocks glasses with ice.

Fill a cocktail shaker with ice and add all ingredients except the orange zest. Shake vigorously until the outside of the shaker is beaded with sweat and frosty.

Strain into the glasses, add the orange zest, and serve.

BLENDED CREAM-SICLE For a wonderful blender drink, place all of the ingredients for the Cream-Sicle above in a blender with 2 cups of crushed ice and blend until smooth.

Ice for serving

4 ounces fresh orange juice (from approximately 1 orange), rind reserved for zesting

4 ounces heavy cream

4 ounces Galliano (see Straight Up, page 203)

4 ounces vodka

Grated orange zest (see page 39) for garnish

GLASSWARE Rocks glasses (see page 23)

Poire Frappé

Makes four 2½-ounce drinks

I first made this after Grey Goose came out with its naturally flavored vanilla vodka, which has a cleaner, less medicinal taste than most others. Poires are pear eaux-de-vie (see Straight Up, page 174) that are infused with fresh pear. The resulting drink is intensely pear flavored with a good backbite. I use Massanez Poire because it is less harsh than some of the others. This drink can be served several ways: as it is written, for a frappé nightcap, or without the ice and served up as an aperitif or with strong coffee or espresso as a digestif.

Fill a pitcher with ice. Add the poire, vodka, and syrup and stir briskly until the outside of the pitcher is beaded with sweat and frosty.

Fill the cocktail glasses with crushed ice. Strain the frappé into the glasses, garnish each with a pear slice, and serve.

5 ounces Massanez Poire

5 ounces vanilla vodka

2 teaspoons Simple Syrup (page 56)

Crushed ice for serving

1 dried pear half, cut lengthwise into 4 slices for garnish

GLASSWARE Cocktail glasses (see page 24)

Grand Galliano

Makes two 3-ounce drinks (photograph opposite)

This is a more adult, slightly more potent version of the Cream-Sicle (page 205). If you have the stamina, shake it until you can't shake anymore. The result will be an ethereally light cocktail perfect for a slow-sipping nightcap. Served over crushed ice, it makes a wonderful frappé.

Fill a cocktail shaker with ice and add the Galliano, Grand Marnier, and cream. Shake vigorously until the outside of the shaker is beaded with sweat and frosty.

Strain into cocktail glasses, garnish with the orange twists, and serve.

2 ounces Galliano
(see Straight Up, page 203)

2 ounces Grand Marnier

2 ounces heavy cream

2 orange twists (see page 39)
for garnish

GLASSWARE Cocktail glasses
(see page 24)

Island Rose

Makes two 4½-ounce drinks

When we first moved into our Long Island, New York, house in the early fall, after most of the plants had given up their flowers, I found one large row of plants so ugly that I resolved to pull them out next season. The following spring I created this drink the very same evening a friend pointed out the now-flowering bushes and explained that they were actually fruit-bearing plants variously called island roses, beach roses, or beach plums. This plum-based drink was spontaneously christened the Island Rose.

Fill a cocktail shaker with ice and add all of the ingredients. Shake vigorously until the outside of the shaker is beaded with sweat and frosty.

Strain into cocktail glasses and serve.

4 ounces Plum Brandy (page 68) or
plum wine

2 ounces orange vodka

2 ounces cream

1 ounce Grenadine (page 64) or
use store-bought

GLASSWARE Cocktail glasses
(see page 24)

Chocolate-Covered Cherry

Makes two 3-ounce drinks (photograph opposite, left)

3 ounces Cherry Heering
(see Straight Up, page 84)
or cherry brandy

3 ounces dark crème de cacao

2 Maraschino Cherries (page 53)
or use store-bought

GLASSWARE Cocktail glasses
(see page 24)

I first experienced this combination of flavors served as a shooter, which is a shot, or small drink, that you gulp down in one sip. I quickly realized what a delight a slow-sipping version would be for lovers of chocolate-covered cherries.

Fill a pitcher with ice and add the Cherry Heering and crème de cacao. Stir briskly until the outside of the pitcher is beaded with sweat and frosty.

Strain into cocktail glasses, garnish with cherries, and serve.

Blackberry Caramels

Makes four 3-ounce drinks (photograph opposite, right)

4 ounces Echte Kroatsbeere
Blackberry liqueur

4 ounces Frangelico

2 ounces brandy

2 ounces cream

2 teaspoons Brown Sugar Syrup
(page 56)

4 blackberries for garnish

GLASSWARE Cocktail glasses
(see page 24)

This is a great cocktail to serve alongside strong coffee. Frangelico is an Italian liqueur made from hazelnuts. It is light and delicate compared to other cordials and has a dry—as opposed to cloying—finish. It is wonderful to drink on its own and is fabulous as a mixer.

Fill a pitcher with ice and add all the ingredients. Stir vigorously until the outside of the pitcher is beaded with sweat and frosty.

Strain into cocktail glasses, garnish each with a blackberry, and serve.

Goose Berry

Makes four 3-ounce drinks

Crushed ice for serving

4 ounces Grey Goose Le Citron vodka

4 ounces blackberry liqueur

2 ounces Vanilla Vodka Syrup (page 60)

4 tablespoons heavy cream for floating

GLASSWARE Rocks glasses (see page 23)

A neat bartending trick is the "float," which involves setting a small amount of brightly flavored liqueur or, as in this case, cream atop the cocktail. This technique has both aesthetic and practical benefits (see page 22). First, it makes the drink look quite festive. Second, rather than blending the cream directly into the drink, floating it on top effectively divides the drink into two distinct levels in the drinker's mouth so that the rich cream is followed by the fruity liquor.

Fill the rocks glasses with crushed ice.

Fill a pitcher with ice and add the vodka, blackberry liqueur, and syrup. Stir briskly until the pitcher is beaded with sweat and frosty.

Strain into the rocks glasses. Float 1 tablespoon cream on each drink and serve.

43 Licks

Makes four 5-ounce drinks

4 ounces Licor 43 (see Straight Up, page 114)

4 ounces Godiva White Chocolate Liqueur

1 scoop vanilla ice cream

1 cup ice

GLASSWARE Wineglasses (see page 24)

Vanilla ice cream makes this truly a dessert beverage. Serve it with tuiles or sugar cookies on the side for a whimsical deconstructed ice cream cone.

Mix all ingredients in a blender and blend until smooth.

Pour into wineglasses and serve.

Flutter

Makes two 4½-ounce drinks

I had something like this in a bar in London several years ago and came up with this version upon my return. The surprising blend of ingredients makes a delicious cocktail.

Fill a cocktail shaker with ice and add all of the ingredients. Shake vigorously until the outside of the shaker is beaded with sweat and frosty.

Strain into cocktail glasses and serve.

4 ounces silver tequila

3 ounces pineapple juice

2 ounces Kahlúa

GLASSWARE Cocktail glasses (see page 24)

Grasshopper

Makes two 3-ounce drinks

The grasshopper is a classic after-dinner drink made with green crème de menthe, white crème de cacao, and cream. This updated version uses fresh mint and vodka.

Place into each rocks glass 4 sprigs of mint and 1 teaspoon sugar. Muddle gently just until the mint has been bruised and releases its aroma (see page 22).

Add 1 ounce vodka to each glass and gently muddle once more. Add ice and 1 ounce each crème de cacao and cream to each glass. Stir well until blended.

Garnish each glass with fresh mint leaves and serve.

8 fresh mint sprigs, plus fresh mint leaves for garnish

2 teaspoons sugar

2 ounces vodka

Ice for serving

2 ounces white crème de cacao

2 ounces heavy cream

GLASSWARE Rocks glasses (see page 23)

Gloom Chaser

Makes two 3½-ounce drinks

With this drink the color alone—bright orange with a hint of pink, reminiscent of a sunset—will help chase away the blues. It is a great nightcap that blends sweet and acid in perfect harmony. Mandarine Napoleon is a tangerine liqueur similar to Grand Marnier.

Fill a pitcher with ice and add all of the ingredients except the blackberries. Stir vigorously until the outside of the pitcher is beaded with sweat and frosty.

Strain into cocktail glasses, add a blackberry to each, and serve.

2 ounces triple sec

2 ounces Mandarine Napoleon Liqueur

2 ounces fresh orange juice (from approximately 1 orange)

1 ounce Berry Syrup (page 62) or Grenadine (page 64) or use store-bought

2 fresh blackberries for garnish

GLASSWARE Cocktail glasses (see page 24)

215 **BLOODY MARY**

216 **MEDITERRANEAN MARY**

217 **PICKLE MARY**

217 **ASIAN MARY**

218 **BARBECUE COCKTAIL**

219 **JALAPEÑO VODKA**

220 **BLOOD ORANGE SUNRISE**

220 **TANGERINE DREAM**

221 **MORNING GLORY DAISY**

221 **CHERRY HEAVEN**

223 **RUM AND PLUM**

223 **GINGER ZIP**

MORNING GLORIES AND TONICS TO CURE WHAT AILS YOU

THIS CHAPTER IS A COMBINATION OF CELEBRATORY DRINKS CUSTOM-MADE FOR drinking early in the day and reliable remedies for celebrations whose effects are lingering a little too long. While I certainly do not endorse heavy drinking of alcohol first thing in the morning, there is a reason weekend brunch and a spicy Bloody Mary (opposite) have become a cliché. It must be said that there are also times when the night before got a little late and you're moving a little sluggishly the next morning. In those cases, a bit of the hair of the dog that bit you is the best medicine.

Besides the tried-and-true Bloody Mary, perhaps the most famous hangover remedy of all, you'll find some alternative concoctions here as well. For those who prefer something a little sweeter in the morning, try the Morning Glory Daisy (page 221) or Cherry Heaven (page 221), which are equally welcome accompaniments to weekend brunch. The spicy Jalapeño Vodka (page 219), whether drunk alone or in the Barbecue Cocktail (page 218), and the zesty Ginger Zip (page 223) will clear your head at any time of day.

Bloody Mary

Makes eight 7-ounce drinks (photograph on page 212, right)

A pickle—whether it's an ordinary dill spear or one of my own Quick Carrot Pickles—is my garnish of choice for the Bloody Mary. Its tanginess and acidity offset the richness of the tomato and accentuate the spices. Don't think of the Bloody Mary as only a brunch beverage. It is fantastic for a cocktail party or before dinner, especially when served with Spicy Roasted Chickpeas (page 252) or a cold platter of vegetables, meats, and cheeses.

PLANNING AHEAD The mix can be made 3 to 4 days ahead and refrigerated. If you make it much further in advance, the horseradish will begin to lose its kick and the tomato juice will begin to turn.

To prepare the Bloody Mary mix, combine all the ingredients for the mix in a pitcher with a tight-fitting lid. Close the pitcher tightly and shake vigorously.

When ready to serve, pour the celery salt onto a small plate. Rub the juicy side of the lemon or lime wedge along the outer edge of the lip of each rocks glass—not along the inside of the rim. Holding each glass at an angle, roll the outer edge of the rim in the salt until it is fully coated.

Fill each glass with ice cubes, fill ⅓ of the way with vodka, and top off with the Bloody Mary mix.

Add one pickle spear to each glass, stir once with the spear, and serve.

BASIL MARY The warm basil undertones of the infused vodka marry beautifully with the tomato-based Bloody Mary.

Prepare the Bloody Mary, above, replacing the vodka with an equal amount of Basil-Infused Vodka (page 126). Float a few strips of fresh basil on each drink if desired.

STRAIGHT UP

Paprika is made from pimiento peppers that are dried and ground into a fine powder. Paprika is generally sweet and mild or hot. My favorite paprika is *smoked*. It is produced in Jarandilla de la Vera (more commonly known simply as La Vera) in Spain's western province of Extremadura. The peppers are slowly smoked over an oak fire, then stone-ground to a fine powder with a robust, smoky, and toasty flavor. There are three flavors of smoked paprika: sweet, bittersweet, and hot. The sweet variety is best for a Bloody Mary. Smoked paprika is available at specialty food stores or by mail order (see Mail-order Sources).

FOR THE BLOODY MARY MIX

32 ounces tomato juice

2 ounces fresh lemon juice
(from approximately 2 lemons)

2 ounces fresh lime juice
(from approximately 2 limes)

4 teaspoons Tabasco sauce

2 heaping tablespoons prepared horseradish

1 tablespoon Worcestershire sauce

1 heaping teaspoon celery salt

1 teaspoon freshly ground
black pepper

½ teaspoon kosher salt

½ teaspoon sweet paprika

½ teaspoon smoked paprika
(see Straight Up)

FOR THE COCKTAIL

2 tablespoons celery salt for rimming the glasses

1 lemon or lime wedge for rimming the glasses

Ice for serving

24 ounces vodka

8 long pickle spears or Quick Carrot Pickles (page 50) or fresh cucumber spears for garnish

GLASSWARE Rocks glasses
(see page 23)

Mediterranean Mary

Makes eight 7-ounce drinks (photograph on page 212, top left)

(photograph on page 212, top left)

FOR THE MEDITERRANEAN MARY MIX

2 dozen pitted oil-cured black olives, or your favorite olives

2 tablespoons olive oil

1 tablespoon capers

1 tablespoon coarsely chopped roasted red peppers (see Trick of the Trade)

1 teaspoon fresh oregano leaves

32 ounces tomato juice

5 teaspoons Tabasco sauce

1 heaping teaspoon celery salt

1 heaping teaspoon freshly ground black pepper

½ teaspoon kosher salt

4 ounces fresh lemon juice (from approximately 3 lemons)

4 ounces fresh lime juice (from approximately 4 limes)

FOR THE COCKTAIL

16 ounces vodka

8 ounces dry sherry

2 tablespoons coarse salt for rimming the glasses

1 lemon or lime wedge for rimming the glasses

Ice for serving

8 Quick Carrot Pickles (page 50) or 8 oil-cured black olives (more if desired)

GLASSWARE Rocks glasses (see page 23)

This drink was inspired by my buddy Mark Lassi, who used to sit at the bar at Gramercy Tavern on Friday afternoons drinking Bloody Marys and eating oysters on the half shell with cocktail sauce. One day I remarked that I prefer my oysters with sherry and a bowl of good olives to nibble. Mark challenged me to put my words into action and the result was the Mediterranean Mary—essentially a combination of the cocktail sauce, sherry, and olives. Oysters are the best accompaniment to this drink.

PLANNING AHEAD The Mediterranean Mary mix can be prepared up to 1 week in advance and stored in the refrigerator.

To prepare the Mediterranean Mary mix, combine the olives, olive oil, capers, roasted peppers, and oregano in a food processor or in a large mortar with a pestle. Process or crush until a coarse paste is formed. Alternatively, you can finely chop the ingredients, place them in a bowl, add the oil, and stir to combine.

Place the olive paste and all other mix ingredients in a large pitcher with a tight-fitting lid. Close the pitcher tightly and shake vigorously to combine.

When ready to serve, add the vodka and sherry to the Mediterranean Mary mix, close the pitcher tightly, and shake vigorously to combine.

Pour the coarse salt onto a small plate. Rub the juicy side of the lemon or lime wedge along the outer edge of the lip of each glass—not along the inside of the rim. Holding each glass at an angle, roll the outer edge of the rim in the salt until it is fully coated.

Fill each rocks glass with ice cubes and add the Mary mix. Add 1 pickled carrot spear or black olive to each glass and serve immediately.

TRICK OF THE TRADE

ROASTING PEPPERS Preheat the broiler to high. Place one or more whole red peppers in a small shallow roasting pan or on a rimmed baking sheet and brush lightly with olive oil. Broil until the skin is blackened and bubbling, turning the peppers to brown them on all sides. Transfer the peppers to a bowl and cover with plastic wrap or a towel. When the peppers are cool enough to handle, use a paring knife to scrape off the skin.

Pickle Mary

Makes two 6½-ounce drinks (photograph on page 212, bottom left)

If you are in search of the perfect burger in New York, you will no doubt end up at the Corner Bistro in Greenwich Village. After dreaming of a cheeseburger topped with relish and ketchup, I woke up and headed directly to the bistro. Waiting to sate my craving, I slaked my thirst with a spicy Bloody Mary. When at last I bit into my cheeseburger with relish and ketchup, I washed it down with a big sip of Bloody Mary, and inspiration struck.

Pour the celery salt onto a small plate. Rub the juicy side of the lemon or lime wedge along the outer edge of the lip of each rocks glass—not along the inside of the rim. Holding each glass at an angle, roll the outer edge of the rim in the salt until it is fully coated.

Fill a cocktail shaker with ice and add the Bloody Mary mix, vodka, and pickle relish. Shake vigorously until the outside of the shaker is thoroughly beaded with sweat and is extremely cold to the touch.

Remove the entire top of the shaker and pour the drink along with the ice into the rocks glasses. Garnish each with a pickled carrot or 2 bread and butter pickles and serve.

Celery salt for rimming the glass

1 lemon or lime wedge for rimming the glass

8 ounces Bloody Mary mix (page 215)

4 ounces vodka

2 tablespoons pickle relish, or to taste

2 Quick Carrot Pickles (page 50) or 4 bread and butter pickles

GLASSWARE Rocks glasses (see page 23)

Asian Mary

Makes four 5½-ounce drinks

This unique flavor blend is the perfect accompaniment to a shellfish appetizer or a bagel and lox Sunday brunch. If you cannot find shiso, cilantro leaves make a flavorful substitute.

Fill the rocks glasses with ice.

Fill a cocktail shaker with ice and add all of the ingredients except the garnish. Shake vigorously until the outside of the shaker is thoroughly beaded with sweat and is extremely cold to the touch.

Pour into glasses, garnish each with a shiso leaf, and serve.

Ice for serving

12 ounces tomato juice

6 ounces vodka

2 ounces sake

4 teaspoons wasabi paste

2 teaspoons soy sauce

4 shiso leaves (see Straight Up) or several cilantro leaves for garnish

GLASSWARE Rocks glasses (see page 23)

STRAIGHT UP

Shiso leaves come from a member of the plant family that includes basil and mint. The green leaves have jagged edges and are flavorful in salads. Green shiso is in season during the summer and fall and can be found in Asian markets.

Barbecue Cocktail

Makes two 3-ounce drinks

1 teaspoon smoked paprika
for rimming the glass
(see Straight Up, page 215)

½ teaspoon kosher salt for
rimming the glass

½ teaspoon sugar for rimming
the glass

1 lime

4 ounces Jalapeño Vodka
(page 219)

1 ounce dry vermouth

1 ounce tomato juice

GLASSWARE Cocktail glasses
(see page 24)

The Barbecue Cocktail balances the heat of jalapeños
with vermouth and tomato juice to produce intriguing
and complex flavors. Serve this any time a little heat
is desired. It is a perfect aperitif before any grilled entrée
and is a nice accompaniment to Guacamole (page 256).

Mix the paprika, salt, and sugar on a small plate. Cut twists
(see page 39) from the lime for garnish, then halve the lime
crosswise. Rub the juicy side of the lime along the outer edge
of the lip of each cocktail glass—not along the inside of the
rim. Holding each glass at an angle, roll the outer edge of the
rim in the paprika until it is fully coated.

Fill a pitcher with ice. Squeeze the juice from the lime into
the pitcher. Add the jalapeño vodka, vermouth, tomato juice,
and any remaining paprika mixture. Stir vigorously until the
outside of the pitcher is beaded with sweat and frosty.

Strain into the prepared glasses, garnish with lime twists,
and serve.

Jalapeño Vodka

Makes enough vodka for about sixteen 2-ounce drinks

Not only does this vodka taste great, it also wakes you up, clears your sinuses, and stimulates your thoughts! You can use it as a replacement for straight vodka in the Classic Martini (page 73) or to make the spiciest Bloody Mary (page 215) around.

PLANNING AHEAD The infusion requires at least a few hours, but is really best after 2 days. It can be made several weeks in advance and stored in the refrigerator.

Beginning at the pointy end, cut a slit halfway up each jalapeño pepper. Set aside.

Preheat a small nonstick pan on high heat. Add the peppercorns, and the allspice berries and juniper berries if desired, and cook for 30 seconds. Immediately toss into a pitcher with a tight-fitting lid.

Return the pan to the heat and add the jalapeños. Cook them until all sides are slightly toasted and blistered, about 30 seconds per side. Immediately add them to the pitcher.

Pour the vodka over the peppers and spices and tightly close the pitcher. The vodka will be ready after a few hours but is best after 2 days.

Before serving the vodka, remove the jalapeños. You can either discard the peppers or use them immediately for cooking.

BONUS FROM THE BAR

JALAPEÑO MARINADE The jalapeño infusion has lots of heat and acid, which makes it a very useful ingredient in the kitchen. Use it for deglazing the pan after a quick sauté or as a great substitute for straight vodka in penne à la vodka. Or use it as the base of a marinade for two steaks: Mix together ¾ cup jalapeño vodka, ¼ cup lime juice (from approximately 2 limes), a good handful of chopped cilantro, and 1 tablespoon crushed garlic. Pour the mixture over the steaks and let sit for 30 minutes before grilling or broiling.

6 fresh jalapeño peppers

1 teaspoon black peppercorns

½ teaspoon whole allspice berries (optional)

½ teaspoon whole juniper berries (optional)

1 liter vodka

GLASSWARE Cocktail glasses (see page 24)

Blood Orange Sunrise

Makes four 6-ounce drinks

Sugar, for rimming the glasses

16 ounces fresh blood orange juice (from approximately 5 blood oranges), some rinds reserved for rimming the glasses

1 pomegranate

Ice for serving

8 ounces tequila

GLASSWARE Highball glasses (see page 23)

The classic tequila sunrise is made with tequila, orange juice, and grenadine. This version uses blood oranges and pomegranate for its intense color and flavor. Use a vibrant tequila such as Porfidio *Anejo,* which will stand up to the full-flavored blood oranges. If you cannot find fresh pomegranates or would like to save time, you can substitute Grenadine (page 64) or Pom, a pure pomegranate juice available in many markets. Just spoon two teaspoons of either into each glass immediately before serving.

Pour the sugar onto a small plate. Rub the juicy side of the orange rind along the outer edge of the lip of each highball glass—not along the inside of the rim. Holding each glass at an angle, roll the outer edge of the rim in the sugar until it is fully coated.

If using the pomegranate, cut it in half crosswise. Over a bowl, squeeze the pomegranate as you would a lemon, letting the juice and many seeds run out. If you have trouble, use a spoon to dislodge more of the seeds.

Fill the glasses with ice. Into each highball glass, pour 2 ounces tequila and 4 ounces blood orange juice.

Into each glass, spoon a generous amount of the pomegranate juice and seeds (or 2 teaspoons grenadine or Pom) and serve.

Tangerine Dream

Makes four 3-ounce drinks

1 tangerine

1 teaspoon sugar

8 ounces tequila

Ice, for serving

Grated lime zest (see page 39) for garnish

GLASSWARE Rocks glasses (see page 23)

Using different citrus fruits and different textures together—in this case the fruit of a tangerine and the zest of a lime—adds dimension to a drink. Choose a full-flavored tequila such as Sauza Tres Generaciónes for this drink.

Peel the tangerine and cut it into 4 wedges. Into each rocks glass place a tangerine wedge and 1/4 teaspoon sugar. Muddle the tangerine (see page 22) to extract as much of the juice as possible. Pour 2 ounces tequila into each glass and stir well.

Fill the glasses with ice and stir once again.

Sprinkle lime zest over each drink and serve.

Morning Glory Daisy

Makes two 3-ounce drinks

Trader Vic considered the Daisy (page 104) the perfect hangover remedy because it is juicy and sweet. Here is a variation of his morning libation.

Fill a cocktail shaker with ice and add all of the ingredients. Shake vigorously until the outside of the shaker is beaded with sweat and frosty.

Strain into dessert wineglasses and serve.

STRAIGHT UP

Pernod is an anise-flavored liqueur originally created as a sort of absinthe without the outlawed wormwood. Although Pernod smells as if it should be sweet like anisette or sambuca, it is, in fact, fairly dry, quite aromatic, and extremely potent. Like other anise-based liquors, Pernod becomes cloudy as soon as it comes in contact with water.

2 ounces vodka

2 ounces Berry Syrup (page 62) or Grenadine (page 64) or use store-bought

2 ounces fresh lemon juice (from approximately 2 lemons)

1 ounce Pernod (see Straight Up)

1 tablespoon pasteurized egg whites

GLASSWARE Dessert wineglasses (see page 24)

Cherry Heaven

Makes four 7-ounce drinks

Tangerines are a little less acidic and somewhat sweeter than oranges. They work well here as a backdrop to the cherries, which have such vibrant flavor. This is a great brunch cocktail as well as a refreshing highball before a summer dinner.

Place the cherries and syrup in a small bowl. Peel the tangerine, then break it apart into individual sections, remove any seeds, and add the sections to the cherries.

Muddle the cherries and tangerines (see page 22) into a juicy and chunky fruit mash.

Fill highball glasses halfway with ice, then divide the mash evenly among the glasses. Fill the glasses the rest of the way with ice.

Add 1 ounce Cherry Heering and 1 ounce brandy to each glass. Stir gently. Top off each glass with tangerine juice and serve.

20 Maraschino Cherries (page 53) or use store-bought

4 teaspoons syrup from maraschino cherries

1 tangerine

Ice for serving

4 ounces Cherry Heering (see Straight Up, page 84) or cherry brandy

4 ounces brandy

12 ounces fresh tangerine juice (from 6 to 8 tangerines)

GLASSWARE Highball glasses (see page 23)

Rum and Plum

Makes four 3-ounce drinks (photograph opposite)

There are dozens of varieties of plums on the market to choose from. One of my favorites is the dinosaur plum, whose speckled appearance, firm texture, and bright acidity are in this drink.

Cut the plum into bite-size chunks and place in a bowl. Sprinkle the sugar over the fruit and squeeze the lime over the top. Stir and gently muddle the fruit (see page 22).

Fill each glass by 1/4 with ice. Divide the plum mixture among the glasses, then fill the glasses with the ice.

Add 1 ounce plum brandy and 1 ounce rum to each glass. Stir well and serve.

1 large or 2 small ripe dinosaur or other red plums

1 teaspoon sugar

Juice of 1 lime

Ice for serving

4 ounces Plum Brandy (page 68) or plum wine

4 ounces white rum

GLASSWARE Rocks glasses (see page 23)

Ginger Zip

Makes four 4-ounce drinks

Paper-thin pickled ginger is available in the Asian foods section of most grocery stores. If you cannot find it, cut the longest piece of fresh, unpeeled ginger you can find into four long spears, about 3 inches long by 1/4 inch thick, and use them as swizzle sticks in the drink.

Fill the rocks glasses with ice.

Fill a cocktail shaker or pitcher with ice and add all the ingredients except the pickled ginger. Shake or stir vigorously until the outside of the shaker or pitcher is beaded with sweat and frosty.

Strain into the rocks glasses, twirl a strip of pickled ginger on top of each, and serve.

Ice for serving

8 ounces fresh lime juice (from approximately 8 limes)

3 ounces Ginger Syrup (page 59)

3 ounces bourbon

3 ounces Southern Comfort

4 strips pickled ginger for garnish

GLASSWARE Rocks glasses (see page 23)

227   MILLENNIUM BLEND

227   COCO YAUCO BLEND

228   CAFÉ CACAO BLEND

228   VANILLA SPICE BLEND

229   CINNAMON CARDAMOM BLEND

229   PUMPKIN SPICE BLEND

230   KENTUCKY CAPPUCCINO

230   MOCHA RUM TODDY

230   CAFÉ FRAPPÉ

232   CAFÉ BRULOT

232   VANILLA COFFEE

233   CAFFÈ SHAKERATA

233   WARM AND RUSTY

233   LAPSANG AND ARMAGNAC

234   ICED TEA

234   GRAND MARNIER TEA COOLER

235   GREEN TEA TODDY

JAVA HEAVEN AND SPIKED TEA TIME

FLAVORED COFFEES HAVE BEEN GIVEN A BAD REPUTATION BY COMPANIES THAT heap artificial ingredients into their blends. When natural ingredients are used, flavored coffees are delicious and versatile.

I like to blend a full pound of flavored coffee at a time and store it in the refrigerator for up to two weeks or in the freezer for up to one month. As the mixture sits, the flavors infuse and improve. When you're ready to brew a potful, measure the blend, spices and all, as you would regular unflavored coffee. My general rule for brewing coffee is two tablespoons of coffee to six ounces of water. Brewing these blends in a French press yields rich, full flavor. They work equally well in an automatic drip, though the flavor is slightly less rich.

You'll notice that the following coffee blends are made with ground coffee. One advantage to coffee blends is that they are made so flavorful by the additional ingredients that the slight degradation caused by grinding the coffee in advance is unnoticeable.

All tea starts out green. Black tea becomes so via various stages of processing and fermentation. Green tea has a more delicate flavor than black tea. In general, use one tablespoon of fresh tea leaves to eight ounces of water and let it steep for three minutes for a good strong cup. Don't leave the tea steeping too long, however, for it will become astringent and bitter, as tea has a great deal of tannin.

Like many people, I love the stimulating effect of coffee and tea, but I hope the recipes in this chapter will demonstrate how much more there is to these beverages and what versatile mixers they make. I use them in many different cocktails, toddies, and coolers, the best of which follow here.

Millennium Blend

Makes 1½ pounds

Nicknamed "the Monster," this flavorful brew is so potent that a cup or two will keep you going through the next millennium. This is a great brunch coffee and is wonderful spiked with rum and curaçao or brandy and Kahlúa. The roasted chicory root can be found at specialty coffee shops (see Mail-order Sources).

Place the coffee, chicory root, and orange zest in a zippered plastic bag or other airtight container.

Place the cinnamon sticks on a cutting board. Using a kitchen knife, crack the cinnamon into ½-inch-long pieces. Add them to the coffee mixture.

Seal the bag and shake to mix all ingredients. Store in an airtight container in the refrigerator or freezer.

1 pound ground French roast coffee

2 ounces ground roasted chicory root

Long zest from 1 orange (see page 39)

4 cinnamon sticks

Coco Yauco Blend

Makes about 1½ pounds

For this blend, use Yauco Selecto coffee beans if you can find them or choose your favorite single-estate coffee, such as Ethiopian Moka Harrar or Kenya AA. These coffees are robustly flavored, with spicy notes, yet are smooth and medium bodied, so they blend well with macadamia nuts and coconut.

Place the macadamia nuts in an unheated heavy-bottomed pan. Place the pan over high heat and heat until the nuts are darkened but not black and begin to look slightly oily. Add the coconut and toast gently with the nuts just until the coconut is lightly browned. Immediately transfer the mixture to a bowl and let it cool.

Coarsely chop the cooled nuts and coconut and add them to the ground coffee. Mix thoroughly. The blend tastes great immediately but gets better and better if you let it sit for several hours before using.

Store in an airtight container in the refrigerator or freezer.

1 cup macadamia nuts

1 cup unsweetened shredded coconut

1 pound ground Yauco Selecto coffee beans

Café Cacao Blend

Makes 1½ pounds

1 pound ground French roast coffee

4 ounces cocoa nibs

4 ounces ground roasted chicory root

2 vanilla beans

This subtle chocolate-laced coffee showcases the natural affinity chocolate and coffee flavors have for each other. For this blend, try to use a full-flavored and robust Costa Rican or Sumatran bean that has been French roasted. Roasted chicory root binds all the flavors together, and the vanilla bean adds a natural sweetness and mellows any astringency. Cocoa nibs are the ground pods of cocoa beans (see Mail-order Sources).

Place the coffee, cocoa nibs, and chicory root in a zippered plastic bag or other airtight container.

Split the vanilla beans lengthwise down the middle and roughly chop each half into 4 pieces. Add the vanilla to the coffee mixture.

Seal the bag and shake to mix all ingredients. Store in an airtight container in the refrigerator or freezer.

Vanilla Spice Blend

Makes 1 pound

1 pound ground coffee, preferably Indian Malabar

4 vanilla beans

4 whole star anise

The scent of vanilla in this blend is intoxicating, and the hint of star anise gives it more complexity. If you can find Indian Malabar coffee, give it a whirl. It is a spicy, somewhat racy, medium-bodied coffee. Spiked with a little Strega—an aromatic vanilla-scented liqueur from Italy—this blend makes an unbelievable after-dinner coffee.

Place the coffee in a zippered plastic bag or other airtight container.

Cut the vanilla beans in half lengthwise. Scrape out the seeds with a paring knife and add them to the coffee. Cut the beans into ½-inch pieces and add them to coffee.

Crack the star anise in half and add it to the coffee. Seal the bag and shake vigorously to mix.

Store in the refrigerator or freezer.

Cinnamon Cardamom Blend

Makes 1 pound

In his great book *Uncommon Grounds,* Mark Pendergrast vividly describes how Ethiopian women ritualistically roast coffee beans over an open fire, add cinnamon and cardamom, grind the beans together, and brew an incredible aromatic coffee. That passage was the inspiration for this blend. If you can find Ethiopian Yrgacheffe coffee, do try it (see Mail-order Sources).

Because of its robust flavor and intense spiciness, I like to brew this blend in a French press and serve it as you would espresso, in small cups. It is delicious, well sweetened or straight, with a healthy shot of grappa.

1 pound ground dark roast coffee

4 cinnamon sticks

24 whole cardamom pods

Place the coffee in a zippered plastic bag or other airtight container.

Heat a nonstick skillet over medium heat. Place the cinnamon and cardamom in the pan and heat until the cardamom just begins to brown. Immediately remove the spices from the pan.

Using a kitchen knife, coarsely crack the spices. They do not need to be pulverized. Add the spices to the coffee. Seal the container and shake vigorously to mix.

Store in the refrigerator or freezer.

BONUS FROM THE BAR

This brewed coffee is an excellent base for a frozen blender drink with Kahlúa and cream. Use 2 parts brewed cold coffee to 1 part Kahlúa and 1 part cream. Blend with 1 cup ice until smooth.

Pumpkin Spice Blend

Makes 1 pound

I never get enough pumpkin pie or sweet potato pie during the holiday season, so I created this coffee to remind me of Thanksgiving all year round. It makes a great dessert coffee or an afternoon pick-me-up.

1 pound ground coffee

1 tablespoon ground cinnamon

1 teaspoon ground ginger

¼ teaspoon ground cloves

¼ teaspoon ground mace

¼ teaspoon freshly grated nutmeg

Mix all ingredients in a zippered plastic bag or other airtight container. Shake to mix.

Store in the refrigerator or freezer.

Kentucky Cappuccino

Makes four 9½-ounce drinks (photograph opposite)

24 ounces freshly brewed coffee

8 ounces bourbon

4 ounces white crème de menthe

4 teaspoons Brown Sugar Syrup
(page 56) or 4 teaspoons
brown sugar

1 cup Whipped Cream (page 54)

2 ounces green crème de menthe

Mint leaves for garnish

GLASSWARE Mugs (see page 25)

This is essentially a variation of classic Irish coffee, using bourbon instead of Irish whiskey. It hits the spot after a hardy brunch, or serve it after dinner to those folks who are not going to sleep anytime soon.

Stir together the coffee, bourbon, white crème de menthe, and syrup.

Divide the coffee mixture among the mugs.

Top with the whipped cream. Float ½ ounce green crème de menthe over the whipped cream in each mug, garnish with mint leaves, and serve.

Mocha Rum Toddy

Makes four 6-ounce drinks

4 teaspoons sugar (optional)

16 ounces freshly brewed coffee

4 ounces dark crème de cacao

4 ounces dark rum

1 cup Whipped Cream (page 54)

1 teaspoon cocoa powder for
garnish

GLASSWARE Mugs (see page 25)

This flavorful toddy is based on a natural combination of rich coffee and creamy, molasses-based dark rum. For warm and spicy undertones, add 1 teaspoon cocoa powder to the coffee grounds before brewing the coffee.

Add the optional sugar to the hot coffee and stir until dissolved. Stir in the crème de cacao and rum.

Pour the coffee into the mugs. Top with whipped cream, dust each serving with ¼ teaspoon cocoa, and serve.

Café Frappé

Makes four 4-ounce drinks

4 teaspoons sugar

12 ounces freshly brewed French
roast coffee

4 ounces brandy

Crushed ice for serving

GLASSWARE Rocks glasses
(see page 23)

Coffee works particularly well as a frappé, where the bitterness inherent in coffee is made milder by crushed ice. In this version, well-sweetened coffee is spiked with brandy for a smooth drink with a bit of buzz.

PLANNING AHEAD Brew the coffee at least 30 minutes before serving and allow it to come to room temperature, or make it up to 8 hours ahead and store in the refrigerator.

Add the sugar to the hot coffee. Stir well and let cool to room temperature, about 30 minutes, or refrigerate for 15 minutes.

Add the brandy to the cooled coffee.

Fill four rocks glasses with crushed ice, fill with the coffee mixture, and serve.

Café Brulot

Makes six 7-ounce drinks

8 ounces brandy

4 ounces Grand Marnier

¼ cup sugar

4 cinnamon sticks, cracked into several large pieces

Long zest from 1 orange (see page 39)

32 ounces freshly brewed dark roast coffee

GLASSWARE Mugs (see page 25)

This New Orleans classic typically calls for igniting the liquor and allowing it to burn off. I don't recommend doing this unless you are well practiced in flambéing food.

Place all the ingredients except the coffee in a heavy-bottomed saucepan over medium-high heat. Warm the mixture until hot.
   Add the coffee and stir well.
   Ladle into mugs and serve.

SPICY CAFÉ BRULOT To make the coffee even richer and spicier, brew it with 2 ounces of chicory added to the coffee grounds. Also try replacing 1 cinnamon stick with 1 whole star anise for a slightly more exotic flavor.

Vanilla Coffee

Makes four 8-ounce drinks

24 ounces freshly brewed Vanilla Spice Blend (page 228)

4 ounces bourbon

4 ounces Galliano (see Straight Up, page 203) or Licor 43 (see Straight Up, page 114)

4 teaspoons brown sugar

1 cup Whipped Cream (page 54)

2 teaspoons cocoa powder

GLASSWARE Mugs (see page 25)

This is a potent and flavorful coffee. Vanilla and bourbon enhance each other, so the flavors of both are heightened in this blend. It's perfect for dunking shortbread cookies.

Stir together the coffee, bourbon, Galliano, and sugar.
   Divide the coffee mixture among the mugs.
   Top with whipped cream, sprinkle ½ teaspoon cocoa powder over the cream in each mug, and serve.

Caffè Shakerata

Makes four 4-ounce drinks

This is a simple version of Caffè Shakerata, an Italian specialty, to make at home. The formula lends itself to endless variations: Try replacing the simple syrup with Vanilla Syrup (page 58) or Mint Syrup (page 57) or your favorite cordial, such as sambuca, Frangelico, or Godiva.

Fill the rocks glasses with crushed ice.

Fill a cocktail shaker with ice. Add the espresso and syrup and shake vigorously until the outside of the shaker is thoroughly beaded with sweat and is extremely cold to the touch.

Strain into the glasses and serve.

Crushed ice for serving

8 ounces freshly brewed espresso

8 ounces Simple Syrup (page 56)

GLASSWARE Rocks glasses (see page 23)

Warm and Rusty

Makes four 8-ounce drinks

This is a hot toddy version of the Rusty Nail (page 106), a classic cocktail that is two parts scotch and one part Drambuie.

Place the tea bags in a pitcher and add the boiling water. Let steep for 3 minutes.

Into each mug place 1 lemon twist and 1 ounce each of scotch and Drambuie.

Add the tea and stir well. Grate the nutmeg over the top and serve.

4 tea bags

24 ounces boiling water

4 large lemon twists (see page 39) for garnish

4 ounces scotch

4 ounces Drambuie (see Straight Up, page 106)

Freshly grated nutmeg for garnish

GLASSWARE Mugs (see page 25)

Lapsang and Armagnac

Makes four 8-ounce drinks

Lapsang Souchong is a smoked black tea from China that I am particularly fond of. Armagnac is used in this drink because it has more bite than other brandies and stands up well to the smoky tea.

Place 1 teaspoon sugar and 2 sprigs of mint in each of the mugs. Muddle together (see page 22). Add the Armagnac and stir.

Place the tea bags in a pitcher. Add the boiling water. Let steep for 3 minutes.

Pour the tea over the Armagnac mixture and serve.

4 teaspoons sugar

8 fresh mint sprigs

8 ounces Armagnac

4 Lapsang Souchong tea bags

24 ounces boiling water

GLASSWARE Mugs (see page 25)

Iced Tea

Makes eight 8-ounce drinks

12 tea bags

1 lemon or orange

64 ounces boiling water

Ice for serving

Simple Syrup (page 56) for serving
(optional)

GLASSWARE Iced-tea glasses
(see page 25)

In the summer, I make batches and batches of iced tea, sometimes mixing it with lemonade or limeade, other times with Southern Comfort or Limoncello (page 69). The tea can be steeped with cinnamon, clove, or star anise for warm undertones. For a richer flavor, you can sweeten the tea with Mint Syrup (page 57) or Berry Syrup (page 62).

PLANNING AHEAD The iced tea can be made up to 8 hours in advance and stored in the refrigerator.

Place the tea bags in a large glass pitcher.

Peel the lemon or orange. Cut the peel into very large pieces and add them to the pitcher.

Pour the boiling water into the pitcher and let steep for at least 10 minutes.

Remove the tea bags and discard. Refrigerate the tea until cool.

To serve, fill glasses with ice and add the tea. Sweeten, if desired, with syrup.

Grand Marnier Tea Cooler

Makes eight 10-ounce drinks

2 small oranges

3 tablespoons sugar

16 ounces Grand Marnier

Ice for serving

64 ounces Iced Tea (above)

GLASSWARE Iced-tea glasses
(see page 25)

A blend of Grand Marnier and iced tea creates a cooler perfectly suited for serving in the afternoon.

PLANNING AHEAD The iced tea can be made up to 8 hours in advance and stored in the refrigerator.

Using a zester, cut 8 strips of long zest from the oranges (see page 39) and set aside. Cut off the remaining zest and all the white pith from the oranges. Cut each fruit into 8 pieces and place them in a pitcher.

Sprinkle the sugar over the orange and muddle well (see page 22). Add the Grand Marnier and stir well.

Fill each glass halfway with ice. Divide the reserved zest among the glasses, then fill the rest of the way with ice. Fill the glasses with iced tea and serve.

Green Tea Toddy

Makes four 8-ounce drinks

Hot and soothing, this drink is the ultimate cure for the common cold.

Place the tea bags in a pitcher. Add the boiling water and let steep for 4 minutes.

Divide the lime rounds and orange zest among the mugs. Add 2 pieces ginger to each mug.

Add the sugar and the rum to the mugs and stir well. Add the tea and serve.

4 green tea bags

24 ounces boiling water

1 lime, cut into ½-inch rounds

Long zest of 1 small orange (see page 39)

One 3-inch piece fresh ginger, peeled and cut into 8 pieces

4 teaspoons sugar

8 ounces white rum

GLASSWARE Mugs (see page 25)

239 LEMONADE

239 WATERMELON LEMONADE

241 BLUEBERRY LEMONADE

241 LIMEADE

242 COCONUT LIMEADE

242 MANGO LIMEADE

243 ALEXANDRA'S ESSENCE

243 ROSE WATER COCKTAIL

244 SUMMER SOLSTICE

244 FAUX MOJITO

244 FAUX MARGARITA

246 CRANBERRY SAUCE

246 MARASCHINO MUDDLE

247 MCINTOSH PUNCH

247 NONALCOHOLIC WATERMELON PUNCH

NON-
ALCOHOLIC
REFRESHERS

I ENTERTAIN QUITE A BIT, AND AT ANY GIVEN PARTY, I USUALLY HOST AT LEAST one person who is not drinking alcohol for one reason or another. Often enough, I choose not to imbibe, myself. However, I am no fan of sugary sodas that don't whet the appetite and rarely make a good accompaniment to the food I'm serving. Nonalcoholic beer can be quite good, but at times something less filling and more interesting is called for. It's also nice to offer something for kids.

With that in mind, I have included in this chapter traditional favorites such as a variety of three Lemonades (pages 239 to 241), and I have also included some new and more savory cocktails, such as the Summer Solstice (page 244) and the Rose Water Cocktail (page 243). These should satisfy the most discerning nonalcoholic consumer. Many are ideal summertime drinks, so refreshing that the missing alcohol is unlikely to be noticed by even the most diehard fans of hard drinks. Others, such as the McIntosh Punch (page 247) and Cranberry Sauce (page 246), are based on ingredients in season during fall and winter, which makes them ideal accompaniments to holiday festivities.

And don't forget that any one of these "cocktails" can be made alcoholic by simply adding a splash of your favorite liquor. So if you're trying to please a diverse group and you have only enough space or time for one festive drink, consider making one of the delicious selections from this chapter and arranging bottles of a few base liquors—rum, vodka, and brandy would be a fine start—so guests can spike their own. These nonalcoholic refreshers are delicious and elegant enough to be served at any event.

Lemonade

Makes ½ gallon or eight 8-ounce drinks
(photograph on page 236, bottom left)

Fresh lemonade does not have to be syrupy sweet. The sweetness level and body are up to you: For lighter body, add more water, and for more sweetness, add more syrup.

PLANNING AHEAD The lemonade can be made up to 8 hours in advance and stored in the refrigerator.

Place the lemon juice and 8 ounces each of syrup and water in a large pitcher. Stir well.

Taste and add more water or syrup, if necessary. Serve over ice with a mint leaf in each glass.

32 ounces fresh lemon juice
(from 24 to 30 lemons)

8 to 16 ounces
Simple Syrup (page 56)
or Vanilla Syrup (page 58)
or Pineapple Syrup (page 61)

8 to 16 ounces ice water

Ice for serving

8 mint leaves for garnish

GLASSWARE Iced-tea or cooler glasses (see page 25)

Watermelon Lemonade

Makes ½ gallon or eight 8-ounce drinks
(photograph on page 236, right)

This recipe combines two summer favorites: watermelon and fresh lemonade. If the melon yields a great deal of juice, you will not need to add water. If the melon is less juicy or less ripe, you may need to add more. Taste the lemonade before serving and adjust as needed.

PLANNING AHEAD The lemonade can be made up to 8 hours in advance and stored in the refrigerator.

Cut the watermelon into 2-inch cubes. Place the cubes into a colander set inside a bowl and sprinkle with sugar. Stir the watermelon to exude the juice. You will get anywhere from 8 to 24 ounces of juice depending on the ripeness of the melon. Reserve the leftover melon for another use.

Pour the lemon juice and the watermelon juice into a large pitcher. Add 8 ounces syrup and stir well.

Taste and add more syrup or water if necessary. Serve over ice.

1 small watermelon
(10 pounds or less)

¼ cup sugar

32 ounces fresh lemon juice
(from 24 to 30 lemons)

8 to 16 ounces Simple Syrup
(page 56)

Up to 16 ounces ice water

Ice for serving

GLASSWARE Iced-tea or cooler glasses (see page 25)

Blueberry Lemonade

Makes ½ gallon or eight 8-ounce drinks (photograph opposite and on page 236, top left)

Here, blueberries mellow the high acidity of the lemonade, making it more food friendly. This drink is the perfect refresher for summertime barbecues.

PLANNING AHEAD The lemonade can be made up to 8 hours in advance and stored in the refrigerator.

Place the blueberries into a large pitcher and sprinkle with the sugar. Use a wooden spoon to mash about half the blueberries against the sides of the pitcher to extract their juice.

Stir the lemon juice into the blueberries.

Add 8 ounces each of syrup and water and stir well.

Taste and add more syrup or water if necessary. Serve over ice.

1 cup fresh blueberries

2 tablespoons sugar

32 ounces fresh lemon juice (from 24 to 30 lemons)

8 to 16 ounces Simple Syrup (page 56)

8 to 16 ounces ice water

Ice for serving

GLASSWARE Iced-tea or cooler glasses (see page 25)

Limeade

Makes ½ gallon or eight 8-ounce drinks

When I first started selling limeade at Gramercy Tavern, it immediately outsold lemonade. At first I thought it was simply the novelty. Later I found out that two of my waiters were from Mexico and were weaned on limeade. They sold it and their wonderful life story to anyone fortunate enough to sit at their stations. Limes are often sweeter than lemons, so definitely taste the limeade as you make it. You might need less syrup than you would were you making an equal amount of lemonade.

PLANNING AHEAD The limeade can be made up to 8 hours in advance and stored in the refrigerator.

Place the lime juice and 8 ounces each of syrup and water in a large pitcher. Stir well.

Taste and add more water or syrup if necessary. Serve over ice.

32 ounces fresh lime juice (from 24 to 30 limes)

8 to 16 ounces Simple Syrup (page 56) or Vanilla Syrup (page 58) or Mint Syrup (page 57) or Pineapple Syrup (page 61)

8 to 16 ounces ice water

Ice for serving

GLASSWARE Iced-tea or cooler glasses (see page 25)

Coconut Limeade

Makes ½ gallon or eight 8-ounce drinks

32 ounces fresh lime juice
(from 24 to 30 limes)

Two 10-ounce cans unsweetened
coconut milk

8 to 16 ounces Simple Syrup
(page 56) or Pineapple Syrup
(page 61)

Up to 16 ounces ice water

Ice for serving

GLASSWARE Iced-tea or cooler
glasses (see page 25)

There's an old song from the '70s about a kind of island remedy that goes, "You put the lime in the coconut and drink it all up." I must have heard it hundreds of times, and I think it inspired me to make this drink. Use pineapple syrup for a more exotic treat.

PLANNING AHEAD The limeade can be made up to 8 hours in advance and stored in the refrigerator.

Place the lime juice, coconut milk, and 8 ounces syrup in a large pitcher. Stir well.

Taste and add more syrup or water if necessary. Serve over ice.

Mango Limeade

Makes ½ gallon or eight 8-ounce drinks

1 large ripe mango, peeled and
diced into 1-inch cubes

2 tablespoons sugar

32 ounces fresh lime juice
(from 24 to 30 limes)

8 to 16 ounces Simple Syrup
(see page 56) or Vanilla Syrup
(see page 58) or Mint Syrup
(see page 57) or Pineapple Syrup
(see page 61)

8 to 16 ounces ice water

Ice for serving

GLASSWARE Iced-tea or cooler
glasses (see page 25)

The mangoes alone make this a special summer refresher, but if you really want to wow your guests, use one of the suggested flavored syrups. Try peeling off the mango skin in long strips and floating it on top of the drink for a nice garnish.

PLANNING AHEAD The limeade can be made up to 8 hours in advance and stored in the refrigerator.

Place the mango in a large pitcher and toss with the sugar. Stir well with a wooden spoon, mashing some of the mango against the sides of the pitcher to extract the juice.

Add the lime juice to the mangoes.

Stir in 8 ounces each of syrup and water.

Taste and add more syrup or water if necessary. Serve over ice.

Alexandra's Essence

Makes eight 8-ounce drinks

One Thanksgiving my brothers and I held our family holiday meal in our restaurant, Dylan Roadhouse, in Granite Springs, New York. The restaurant was closed, and we did all the cooking for thirty-some people. While I was cooking, my daughter, Alexandra, snuck behind the bar and found some leftover squeeze bottles of fruit purees we used for cocktail making. Here is the result of her brief foray into the world of mixology. Melted sorbet is a quick and easy way to approximate fruit puree.

Fill two squeeze bottles with the melted sorbets.

Fill the iced-tea glasses with ice and the lemonade or limeade.

Into each glass, squirt some of the raspberry sorbet on one side. On the other side squirt the mango sorbet.

Watch all the kids smile.

½ pint raspberry sorbet, melted

½ pint mango sorbet, melted

½ gallon Lemonade (page 239) or Limeade (page 241)

GLASSWARE Iced-tea glasses (see page 25)

Rose Water Cocktail

Makes four 8-ounce drinks

This has become a favorite because of its food-friendly qualities and adult taste. For an interesting twist and more richness, add 2 ounces of cream or milk to the cocktail shaker. If you have roses in your garden and they haven't been sprayed with anything you wouldn't want to eat or drink, try floating one or two petals on the drink as a garnish. Rose water (see Mail-order Sources), like orange flower water, is very potent and aromatic. A little goes a long way.

Fill the highball glasses with ice.

Fill a cocktail shaker with ice. Add the sour mix, rose water, and bitters. Shake vigorously until the outside of the shaker is frosted and beaded with sweat.

Strain into the glasses. Add the lime zest and fill the glasses with mineral water. Stir well and serve.

Ice for serving

16 ounces Lemon Sour Mix (page 65)

4 teaspoons rose water

8 dashes Angostura bitters

Long zest of 1 lime (see page 39) for garnish

16 ounces slightly sparkling mineral water, very cold

GLASSWARE Highball glasses (see page 23)

Summer Solstice

Makes four 4-ounce drinks (photograph opposite, left)

3 ounces fresh lemon juice
(from approximately 2 lemons)

12 ounces verjus

8 dashes orange bitters

8 red grapes for garnish

GLASSWARE Cocktail glasses
(see page 24)

This nonalcoholic drink is the closest thing you'll find to an alcohol-based cocktail. Verjus, the juice of unripe grapes, lends a delicate flavor and a hint of sweetness.

Fill a cocktail shaker with ice and add the lemon juice, verjus, and bitters.

Shake vigorously until the outside of the shaker is frosted and beaded with sweat.

Strain into the cocktail glasses and garnish each with 2 grapes speared on toothpicks.

Faux Mojito

Makes four 6-ounce drinks (photograph opposite, right)

2 limes, cut into eighths

4 teaspoons sugar

12 mint leaves

Ice for serving

20 ounces club soda

GLASSWARE Rocks glasses
(see page 23)

The mojito is one of the world's great cocktails, even without the rum.

Place 4 pieces of lime into each rocks glass.

Add 1 teaspoon sugar and 3 mint leaves to each glass. Muddle together (see page 22).

Fill the glasses with ice, top with club soda, and serve.

Faux Margarita

Makes four 9-ounce drinks

4 limes

4 teaspoons sugar

8 dashes orange bitters

2 teaspoons orange flower water
(see Straight Up, page 94)

Kosher salt for rimming the glasses

Ice for serving

24 ounces slightly sparkling
mineral water, very cold

GLASSWARE Highball glasses
(see page 23)

This cocktail is more savory than sweet. Orange flower water is very potent so be careful not to use more than what is called for.

Using a zester, cut long zest (see page 39) from the limes and set aside. Cut off and discard all the white pith and any remaining zest from the limes, then cut the fruit into quarters and transfer all the pieces except one to a bowl.

Sprinkle the sugar over the limes and add the orange bitters and orange flower water. Muddle very well (see page 22).

Pour the salt onto a small plate. Rub the reserved piece of lime along the outer edge of the lip of each highball glass— not along the inside of the rim. Holding each glass at an angle, roll the outer edge of the rim in the salt until it is fully coated.

Fill each glass halfway with ice. Divide the lime mixture among the glasses. Fill the rest of the way with ice, then top off with the mineral water. Stir well.

Float some lime zest on top of each drink and serve.

Cranberry Sauce

Makes sixteen 5-ounce drinks

12 ounces fresh cranberries

16 ounces white grape juice

1 orange, cut into ¼-inch-thick rounds, each round cut into 4 pieces

2 liters ginger ale, chilled

GLASSWARE Punch cups or wineglasses and a punch bowl or large pitcher (see page 25)

This punch is more refined and less sugary than other punches, making it more palatable to serve with dinner. Using tonic water instead of ginger ale is a nice alternative.

PLANNING AHEAD The cranberry mixture should be made and set to chill at least 30 minutes before making the punch. It can be made up to 24 hours in advance and stored in the refrigerator. Chill the ginger ale for at least 30 minutes before making the punch.

Rinse the cranberries and place them in a saucepan with the grape juice. Bring to a boil over high heat. Stir and reduce the heat. Simmer just until you hear the cranberries begin to pop, about 5 minutes. Remove from the heat immediately. Transfer to a punch bowl or pitcher and chill for 30 minutes.

Add the orange pieces to the cranberries.

Add the ginger ale, stir well, and serve.

Maraschino Muddle

Makes six 4-ounce drinks

8 ounces fresh lemon juice (from 5 to 6 lemons)

8 ounces fresh lime juice (from approximately 8 limes)

4 ounces natural white grape juice

1 ounce orange flower water (see Straight Up, page 94)

8 Maraschino Cherries (page 53) or use store-bought

2 ounces maraschino syrup from cherries

3 teaspoons sugar

6 dashes bitters

6 half slices of orange

Ice for serving

Club soda

GLASSWARE Rocks glasses (see page 23)

I was making Maraschino Old-fashioneds (page 131) one evening when I noticed a pregnant friend was eating my whole batch of homemade maraschino cherries. I made her this drink in the interest of saving my stock of cherries. The beverage has winelike flavor and complexity, so I heartily recommend serving it with dinner as well as for an aperitif.

Fill a cocktail shaker or tall pitcher with ice and add the lemon and lime juices, grape juice, and orange flower water. Shake or stir vigorously.

Into each rocks glass, place 2 maraschino cherries with a healthy dose of the syrup, ½ teaspoon sugar, a dash of bitters, and an orange slice. Muddle thoroughly (see page 22).

Fill each glass with ice and pour in the juice mixture. Stir vigorously until well blended. Top off with club soda and serve.

McIntosh Punch

Makes twelve 4½-ounce drinks

Flavored with apples and maple sugar, this makes a great nonalcoholic punch to serve during the holidays when you are entertaining a large group. It also makes a nice aperitif and is a festive option for the kids.

Core the apples and cut them into 1-inch cubes. Place them in a punch bowl or large pitcher. Sprinkle the maple sugar and squeeze 1 lemon over the apples. Stir well.

Slice the other lemon and the lime into ¼-inch-thick rounds and add them to the apples.

Add the orange zest to the apples.

Add the cider, stir well, and serve.

2 McIntosh apples

¾ cup maple sugar

2 lemons

1 lime

Long zest of 1 orange (see page 39)

Three 750-milliliter bottles nonalcoholic sparkling apple cider

GLASSWARE Punch cups or wineglasses and punch bowl or large pitcher (see page 25)

Nonalcoholic Watermelon Punch

Makes twenty 4-ounce drinks

Here is a nonalcoholic variation of rum-spiked Watermelon Punch (page 193).

PLANNING AHEAD The watermelon cubes must be frozen for at least 30 minutes.

To prepare the watermelon, cut the rind away from the flesh and discard. Cut the flesh into 1-inch cubes (you should have 6 to 8 cups) and place them in a colander set inside a bowl. Stir the cubes gently to extract as much juice as possible. The more you stir, the more juice will be extracted; just be careful not to overdo it and break down the melon. You should have at least 8 ounces and up to 16 ounces of juice. Set the watermelon juice aside.

Place the watermelon cubes in a freezer bag and freeze at least 30 minutes.

Mix the syrup, lemon juice, lime juice, vanilla extract, and orange bitters with the extracted watermelon juice. Chill the mixture while the watermelon cubes are freezing.

When ready to serve, place the watermelon cubes in a punch bowl with the blueberries and mint. Add the watermelon juice mixture and stir well. Add the ginger ale and serve.

1 small (about 10 pounds) watermelon

16 ounces Simple Syrup (see page 56)

8 ounces fresh lemon juice (from approximately 6 lemons)

8 ounces fresh lime juice (from approximately 8 limes)

1 teaspoon vanilla extract

1 teaspoon orange bitters

½ cup blueberries for garnish

4 mint sprigs for garnish

1 liter ginger ale

GLASSWARE Punch cups and punch bowl (see page 25)

251 HOT AND SWEET MAPLE PECANS

251 NOT YOUR ORDINARY TRAIL MIX

252 PUMPKIN SEED POPCORN

252 SPICY ROASTED CHICKPEAS

253 GRILLED ROSEMARY AND SUN-DRIED TOMATO FLATBREAD

254 CHIPOTLE CHEDDAR CHIPS

256 GUACAMOLE

256 ROASTED EGGPLANT DIP

257 BOURBON-BACON BEAN DIP

258 SESAME GRILLED ASPARAGUS

259 ROMAN ARTICHOKES

260 BAKED STUFFED FINGERLING POTATOES

261 HOLLOW BREAD FONDUE

262 SMOKED MOZZARELLA AND SUN-DRIED TOMATOES IN GRAPE LEAVES

263 RICOTTA TART

265 PASTA FRITTATA

266 TEA-SOAKED EGGS WITH WASABI MAYONNAISE

267 SCALLOPS ON ROSEMARY SKEWERS

268 GRILLED SHRIMP COCKTAIL

268 CURRIED CHICKEN ON ENDIVE SPOONS

269 YOGURT-CRUSTED LAMB CHOPS

269 PROSCIUTTO, ARUGULA, AND GORGONZOLA ROLLS

271 BUTTERMILK BISCUIT CROSTINI WITH SMOKED HAM

272 BACON-WRAPPED CHESTNUT-STUFFED DATES

273 **COCKTAILS AND CHEESE**

SNACKS AND HORS D'OEUVRES

WHEN I HAVE A GROUP OVER FOR DINNER, I VERY OFTEN USE THE COCKTAIL HOUR as a first course instead of serving a more traditional appetizer. From there, we may have a salad or simply proceed to our main course and dessert. This approach works particularly well during the summer, when grilling outdoors. It gives guests time to mingle, relax, imbibe, and nibble all at once. This can often be the best part of the meal.

Wide-ranging and diverse influences have inspired the recipes in this chapter. The Spicy Roasted Chickpeas (page 252) hail from the eastern Mediterranean. The Buttermilk Biscuit Crostini with Smoked Ham (page 271) are a play on a southern favorite. Chipotle Cheddar Chips (page 254) get their inspiration from the American Southwest and the Tea-Soaked Eggs with Wasabi Mayonnaise (page 266) from Asia.

I like to coordinate my snacks and hors d'oeuvres with the main course I am serving. For example, serve Plum Sake (page 186) with Sesame Grilled Asparagus (page 258) and Curried Chicken on Endive Spoons (page 268) before an Asian-style striped bass. Planning the whole dinner—including the cocktails and hors d'oeuvres—around a single theme makes it easy for guests to enjoy the food.

The recipes on the following pages are some of my tried-and-true favorites. Whether you use them as a snack, as hors d'oeuvres, or as a first course, have fun mixing and matching.

Hot and Sweet Maple Pecans

Makes 2 cups pecans (photograph on page 248, bottom)

Here is a great snack to keep on hand. The combination of heat, salt, and sweet makes these addictive. They go well with most cocktails, although I prefer them with dark liquor drinks such as the Rum and Plum (page 223), the Grape and Grain (page 134) or the classic Old-fashioned (page 96). You can substitute simple syrup or even ginger syrup (this gives the nuts an extremely spicy and exotic flavor) for the maple syrup.

PLANNING AHEAD The hot and sweet pecans can be made 1 day ahead and stored in a cool, dry place.

In a small bowl, mix together the sugar, salt, black pepper, cayenne pepper, and paprika. Set aside. Place the syrup in a bowl large enough to hold the pecans and set aside.

Place the pecans in a nonstick skillet over high heat. Cook, stirring or shaking the pan constantly, until the pecans are hot and slightly toasted, about 5 minutes.

Immediately transfer the pecans to the bowl of syrup. Stir well to coat.

Add the spice mixture and stir well. Immediately spread the pecans on a cookie sheet in a single layer. Allow to cool before transferring to a bowl and serving.

¼ cup turbinado sugar
(see page 41)

1 teaspoon salt

¼ teaspoon ground black pepper

¼ teaspoon cayenne pepper

¼ teaspoon paprika

3 tablespoons maple syrup
or Simple Syrup (page 56) or
Ginger Syrup (page 59)

2 cups pecans

Not Your Ordinary Trail Mix

Makes 5 cups trail mix (photograph on page 248, right)

This trail mix—a pleasantly cacophonous combination of sweet, spicy, chewy, crunchy, and creamy—pairs well with almost any cocktail. No one flavor dominates, so feel free to toss this together for almost any occasion when handfuls of snacks are appropriate. Wasabi peas are available in most Asian or specialty markets.

PLANNING AHEAD The mix can be made 24 hours in advance and stored at room temperature.

Mix all ingredients in a large serving bowl and toss gently to combine. Dig in.

1 cup Hot and Sweet Maple Pecans
(above)

1 cup toasted pumpkin seeds
(see page 252)

½ cup safflower seeds

½ cup wasabi peas

½ cup dried blueberries

½ cup dried cranberries

½ cup peanut butter chips

½ cup chocolate chips

Pumpkin Seed Popcorn

Makes 6 cups popcorn (photograph on page 248, left)

FOR THE PUMPKIN SEEDS

1 teaspoon salt

½ teaspoon paprika

½ teaspoon ground black pepper

¼ teaspoon garlic powder

¼ teaspoon cayenne pepper

2 cups raw hulled pumpkin seeds

1 tablespoon olive oil

FOR THE POPCORN

3 tablespoons peanut oil

⅓ cup popcorn

½ teaspoon salt

With its combination of salt, spice, and crunch, this snack pairs well with a sweet-and-sour drink such as the Margarita (page 81) or Watermelon Cooler (page 184).

Mix the salt, paprika, black pepper, garlic powder, and cayenne pepper in a small bowl and set aside.

Place the pumpkin seeds and olive oil in a large bowl and toss well to coat.

Spread the pumpkin seeds evenly in a nonstick skillet over high heat. Toast, shaking the pan and tossing the seeds constantly until they are browned and puffed, about 5 minutes. Immediately transfer the seeds back to the large bowl, add the spice mix, and toss to coat.

Heat a large heavy-bottomed saucepan with a tight-fitting lid over medium heat. Add the peanut oil and popcorn and shake the pan to spread the popcorn and oil evenly over the bottom of the pan. Partially cover the pan, allowing a crack for the steam to escape. Cook the popcorn, constantly shaking the pan, until the popping has stopped.

Immediately remove the pan from the heat, sprinkle the popcorn with salt, and toss to coat. Add the popcorn to the pumpkin seeds. Serve warm in a basket or bowl lined with a nice paper or cloth napkin.

Spicy Roasted Chickpeas

Makes 3 cups chickpeas (photograph on page 248, top)

Two 15½-ounce cans chickpeas

¼ cup olive oil

1 teaspoon kosher salt

1 teaspoon ground cumin

1 teaspoon ground black pepper

½ teaspoon cayenne pepper

2 teaspoons fresh thyme leaves

1 cup shelled pistachios or cashews (optional)

These savory chickpeas go well with a Bloody Mary (page 215) or any of the vodka infusions, such as the Rosmarino (page 129) or Basil Martini (page 126).

PLANNING AHEAD These can be made up to 5 hours in advance and stored at room temperature.

Preheat the oven to 400°F.

Rinse and drain the chickpeas well. Place them on a rimmed baking sheet. Add the olive oil, salt, cumin, black pepper, and cayenne pepper. Stir well to mix.

Bake, stirring occasionally, until the chickpeas are golden and crisp, about 20 minutes.

Remove from the oven and stir in the thyme and the nuts, if using. Return to the oven and bake, watching carefully that they don't overcook or scorch, until crunchy, about 10 minutes. Serve in a bowl or basket lined with a napkin.

Grilled Rosemary and Sun-Dried Tomato Flatbread

Makes 2 small flat loaves, enough for 12 servings

Serve this delicious flatbread plain or with Bourbon-Bacon Bean Dip (page 257). If you are short on time, you can use store-bought pizza or bread dough and simply grill or bake as directed.

PLANNING AHEAD The dough must rise for 1 to 2 hours at room temperature or for 8 hours in the refrigerator. Once it has risen, it can be coated with olive oil, wrapped in plastic, and frozen for 1 month. Thaw it overnight in the refrigerator before forming the loaves.

Combine the yeast, flour, and 2 teaspoons salt in the bowl of a food processor. Turn the machine on and add 1 cup of water, 2 tablespoons olive oil, and the sun-dried tomatoes.

Process for about 30 seconds, adding more water a little at a time, until the mixture forms a ball and is slightly sticky to the touch. If it is too dry, add another tablespoon of water and process for another 10 seconds. If the mixture is too sticky, add a little more flour and process for another 10 seconds.

Turn the dough onto a lightly floured work surface and knead for a few seconds until smooth.

Pour 1 tablespoon olive oil into a large bowl, add the dough, and turn it to coat it evenly with the oil. Cover the bowl with plastic wrap and let the dough rise in a warm place until it doubles in size, 1 to 2 hours. Alternatively, you can place it in the refrigerator for 8 hours.

When the dough has risen, divide it in half. Roll each half out on a floured surface until it is about ½ inch thick.

Divide the remaining olive oil between the loaves, rubbing the oil on both sides of the dough, then sprinkle them with salt and rosemary.

To grill: Prepare a hot grill and brush the rack with oil. Carefully transfer the dough to the rack and cook until each side is puffed, firm, and well browned, about 2 minutes per side. To bake: Preheat the oven to 500°F. Bake on a cookie sheet until puffed and firm, 6 to 12 minutes. You will not get the same crispness or brownness in the oven.

Serve hot on a cutting board, either cut in pieces or left whole so your guests can tear it apart themselves.

1 teaspoon instant yeast

3 cups all-purpose flour

2 teaspoons kosher salt, plus extra for sprinkling

1 to 1¼ cups water

6 tablespoons olive oil

½ cup finely chopped sun-dried tomatoes (from 12 to 15 whole sun-dried tomatoes)

1 tablespoon very coarsely chopped fresh rosemary leaves

Chipotle Cheddar Chips

Makes approximately 30 chips

6 ounces shredded sharp Cheddar cheese

½ teaspoon chipotle pepper powder or cayenne pepper

Chopped parsley or cilantro for garnish (optional)

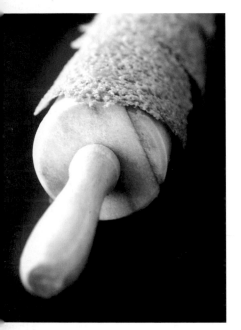

These chips are delicious on their own or served with salsa, Guacamole (page 256), or Bourbon-Bacon Bean Dip (page 257). Serve them before a main meal of fajitas with a Margarita (page 81) or Banana Rum Frappé (page 121).

Toss together the Cheddar and chipotle pepper powder.

Preheat a nonstick pan or griddle over low heat until fairly warm to the touch.

Using a tablespoon for a rough measure, place 2- to 2½-inch rounds of cheese in the pan, about 2 inches apart. Cook without disturbing until the cheese bubbles and is firm enough to lift, about 4 to 5 minutes.

Quickly remove the rounds from the pan with a metal spatula and drape over a rolling pin. Allow to cool completely, then place the chips on paper towels to drain.

Wipe any excess fat from the pan and repeat until all the cheese is cooked. Arrange the chips on a flat tray or dish lined with doilies or paper napkins. Avoid piling them too high, or they will break. Sprinkle with chopped parsley or cilantro and serve immediately.

Guacamole

Makes 12 servings

6 ripe avocados

1 lime

2 tablespoons finely minced red onion

1 tablespoon finely minced pimiento

1 teaspoon kosher salt

½ teaspoon minced garlic

¼ teaspoon cumin powder

¼ teaspoon cayenne pepper

¼ teaspoon ground black pepper

The secret to great guacamole is ripe avocados. Choose ones that are generally firm to the touch but give under slight pressure, particularly at the ends. Try serving the Kaffir Lime Kocktail (page 119) with this dip. For an entrée to follow, skip the obvious quesadillas and try serving Chilean sea bass roasted with a squeeze of lime over a tomato and cilantro salad.

Slice the avocados in half and remove the pit. Scoop out the flesh and place in a bowl. Squeeze the lime over the avocados and mash them together with a wooden spoon until they are as smooth or chunky as desired.

Add the rest of the ingredients. Stir to mix and serve immediately in a bowl with a platter of tortilla chips or fresh cut vegetables.

Roasted Eggplant Dip

Makes about 10 servings

2 large eggplants

½ cup grated Parmesan cheese

2 ounces fresh lemon juice (from approximately 2 lemons)

¼ cup extra virgin olive oil

1 teaspoon minced garlic

Kosher salt and ground black pepper to taste

This dip is wonderful with Grilled Rosemary and Sun-Dried Tomato Flatbread (page 253), or simply served with crackers or pita bread. There are no better drinks to serve with this than the Basil Martini (page 126) or Greenmarket Gibson (page 123).

Preheat the oven to 500°F.

Pierce the eggplants all over with a knife. Roast the eggplants, turning occasionally, until they collapse and the skin blackens, 15 to 30 minutes depending on their size. Remove them from the oven and let them cool.

When the eggplants are cool enough to handle, split them in half and scoop out the flesh. Finely chop the flesh and place in a large bowl.

Stir in the cheese, lemon juice, oil, garlic, salt, and pepper. Serve at room temperature.

Bourbon-Bacon Bean Dip

Makes 12 servings

Serve this dip with Chipotle Cheddar Chips (page 254), raw veggies, tortilla chips, or grilled slices of crusty bread. Because of the density of the dip, I prefer to serve it with a light, effervescent beverage, such as the Tenberry Highball (page 180) or GT Buck (page 122).

PLANNING AHEAD The beans must soak overnight.

The dip can be made up to 2 days in advance and stored in the refrigerator.

Rinse the beans under cold water and remove any foreign particles. Place the beans in a large saucepan and cover with cold water by several inches. Let sit overnight.

Drain the beans, rinse thoroughly, and drain again. Return the beans to the saucepan and cover by 2 inches with cold water. Add the onion, carrot, thyme, and bay leaf and stir well. Partially cover the pan and bring to a boil over high heat.

Reduce the heat to medium and cook until the beans are tender, about 40 minutes, adding more water if necessary.

While the beans are cooking, place the bacon strips in a skillet and cook over medium heat until crisp. Drain on paper towels, then crumble.

Pour off the fat from the skillet and place over medium heat. Add the crumbled bacon, bourbon, and Worcestershire sauce. Cook, scraping up the brown bits on the bottom of the skillet, until the liquid thickens slightly; remove the pan from the heat.

When the beans are soft, drain them thoroughly, discarding the bay leaf and thyme. Transfer them to a bowl and add the bacon mixture and the salt, pepper, cumin powder, and cayenne pepper. Mash the mixture together until smooth. Serve in a bowl with chipotle cheddar chips, tortilla chips, or freshly cut vegetables on the side.

VEGETARIAN BOURBON BEAN DIP Prepare the bourbon-bacon bean dip, substituting 1 pound of mushrooms for the bacon. Chop the mushrooms into small dice. Sauté them in 2 tablespoons of olive oil until very soft, about 10 minutes. Add the bourbon and Worcestershire sauce to the mushroom mixture, then add this mixture to the beans.

1 pound dried pinto beans

1 onion, peeled and coarsely chopped

1 carrot, peeled and cut into 1-inch pieces

1 branch fresh thyme

1 bay leaf

¼ pound sliced smoked bacon

¼ cup bourbon

1 teaspoon Worcestershire sauce

1 tablespoon salt

1 teaspoon pepper

½ teaspoon cumin powder

¼ teaspoon cayenne pepper

Sesame Grilled Asparagus

Makes 6 servings

12 to 18 thick asparagus spears

One 1-inch piece fresh ginger, peeled and very finely minced

¼ cup soy sauce

¼ cup peanut or other light vegetable oil

1 ounce lime juice
(from approximately 1 lime)

1 tablespoon sesame seeds

Grilling is an excellent way to serve asparagus, since it holds its shape and crunch. It takes on a smoky note and its rich flavors caramelize. This recipe is great with the Plum Sake (page 186), as the Asian flavors marry well. It also goes very well with almost any of the bubbly cocktails, especially the Ginger Champagne Punch (page 195) or the Blood Orange Sparkler (page 146).

Using a vegetable peeler, remove the tough outer skin from the bottom half of asparagus. Place the asparagus in a square glass baking dish.

Mix together the ginger, soy sauce, oil, and lime juice and pour over the asparagus. Let stand at room temperature for 15 minutes.

Meanwhile, preheat the grill or broiler. Grill the asparagus on high heat until slightly charred on one side, 1 to 2 minutes. Turn once and grill for 1 to 2 minutes more.

Transfer the asparagus to plates and top with sesame seeds. Serve warm.

Roman Artichokes

Makes 12 servings

Artichokes contain an acid called cynarin that makes them notoriously wine "unfriendly," often causing wine to taste flat, acidic, or simply off. They are great, however, with cocktails. This would be a perfect time to serve the bittersweet and bubbly Sparkling Campari Cocktail (page 118). Serve these with a dish of aged balsamic vinegar for dipping.

PLANNING AHEAD The artichokes can be made up to 1 hour in advance and stored at room temperature. Warm them in a 500°F oven for 5 minutes before serving.

To prepare the artichokes, use a vegetable peeler to peel the stems, then trim the stems to about 1 inch. Pull off the tough green outer leaves to reach the tender yellow leaves underneath. Cut off about 1 inch from the tops of the artichokes. Spread the leaves open and use a spoon to scoop out the tough fibers. Rub all the surfaces of the artichokes with the lemon.

Fill a heavy-bottomed pot with about 3 inches of oil. Heat over medium-high heat until the oil is hot but not smoking. (To ensure that the oil is ready, toss an artichoke leaf in the oil. The oil is ready when the leaf is surrounded by briskly moving bubbles and begins to move on its own around the pan.) Add 3 artichokes and cook, turning them frequently so that they brown evenly, about 8 minutes. Drain them on paper towels. Repeat with the other artichokes.

Working with one artichoke at a time, place it on a plate stem end up and press a second plate on top to flatten it.

Return 2 or 3 artichokes to the hot oil and cook, turning frequently so that they brown evenly, about 6 minutes. Drain them on paper towels. Repeat with the remaining artichokes. Cut each artichoke in half and sprinkle with salt to taste.

Arrange the artichoke halves on a platter large enough to fit them all. Serve hot, with balsamic vinegar for dipping, if desired.

6 long-stemmed artichokes

½ lemon

Up to 4 cups oil (a combination of 2 cups peanut oil and 2 cups olive oil)

Kosher salt to taste

Balsamic vinegar (optional)

Baked Stuffed Fingerling Potatoes

Makes 24 potatoes

24 fingerling potatoes (choose generally smooth potatoes that are at least 1½ to 2 inches long and 1 inch wide) or small new bliss potatoes

1 strip bacon

1 tablespoon butter, softened, plus 1 tablespoon, melted, for browning

1 tablespoon milk

1 teaspoon chopped chives

½ teaspoon salt

¼ teaspoon black pepper

These potatoes are a reason to break a low-carbohydrate diet. They are very hearty, so avoid serving them with a heavy entrée. If you cannot find fingerlings, substitute small new bliss potatoes. The richness of the potatoes and the buttery flavors call for something refreshing and acidic to bring balance to the dish, so try serving this with any of the Sangrias (pages 171 to 176) or a Blackberry Daiquiri (page 114).

PLANNING AHEAD The stuffed potatoes can be assembled 24 hours in advance and stored in the refrigerator. Bake for 20 minutes before serving.

Preheat the oven to 425°F.

Wash the potatoes and place in a single layer in a shallow baking pan. Bake until a skewer can easily pierce them, 25 to 30 minutes. Remove from the oven and let cool.

Meanwhile, cook the bacon until crisp and drain it on paper towels. Crumble it and set it aside.

When the potatoes are cool enough to handle, cut each one in half lengthwise and scoop out the insides, reserving the skins. Place the scooped-out potato in a bowl. Add the bacon, 1 tablespoon butter, milk, chives, salt, and pepper. Mash together thoroughly, adding more milk or butter if the mixture is too dry.

Spoon the stuffing into the scooped-out potato skins and arrange them stuffed side up in the baking pan. Brush the tops with the melted butter and bake just long enough to brown the tops, about 10 minutes. Serve immediately.

Hollow Bread Fondue

Makes about 12 servings

This isn't so much a fondue as an ersatz grilled-cheese sandwich. However you look at it, it is easy and delicious. By using several cheeses in layers, you get a more interesting and varied flavor. Feel free to experiment using cheeses different from those suggested here. Serve this with a strongish cocktail to wash down the richness of the cheeses, such as a Shaggy Dog (page 133) or Montecristo Muddle (page 133).

½-pound wedge Brie or Camembert

One 12-inch round boule loaf

1 tablespoon olive oil

1 tablespoon minced garlic

½ pound shredded Swiss cheese

1 tablespoon grated Parmesan cheese

1 teaspoon cracked black pepper

Set a rack about 6 inches from the broiler and preheat the broiler.

Cut the Brie into long slices, running the length of the wedge, and set aside.

Cut the top off the boule so that the base is about 2 inches high. Hollow out the inside of the bread, allowing ½ inch to 1 inch of thickness all the way around. Spread the olive oil and garlic evenly around the inside of the bread bowl.

Place the bread bowl on a cookie sheet and toast under the broiler just until the bread has crisped up below the edges, about 1 to 2 minutes. Watch it closely and remove immediately when ready.

Spread the Swiss cheese evenly inside the bread bowl and place under the broiler just until the cheese begins to soften, 15 to 20 seconds. Remove immediately.

Sprinkle the Parmesan cheese over the Swiss cheese, then arrange the Brie over the Parmesan. Sprinkle the cracked pepper over the Brie. Place the bread under the broiler, checking frequently, until the cheeses have softened considerably but the Brie still holds its shape, 20 to 40 seconds. Remove immediately and transfer the bread bowl to a cutting board. Let cool for 1 minute.

Using a large kitchen knife, cut the bowl into wedges and arrange them on a cutting board or large plate for serving.

Smoked Mozzarella and Sun-Dried Tomatoes in Grape Leaves

Makes 16 hors d'oeuvres

1 pound smoked mozzarella

16 large grape leaves

16 sun-dried tomatoes

2 tablespoons olive oil

Serve this with a vibrant cocktail that will stand up to the earthiness of the grape leaves and the smokiness of the mozzarella cheese. The Greenmarket Gibson (page 123), Manhattan (page 77), and Sazerac (page 91) all work well. Substitute feta cheese for the smoked mozzarella for a less creamy but still delicious alternative.

PLANNING AHEAD The hors d'oeuvres can be made up to 6 hours in advance and stored in the refrigerator. Broil just before serving.

Set a rack about 6 inches from the broiler and preheat the broiler.

Cut the mozzarella into 4 even slices, then cut each slice into quarters. This will give you 16 cubes—it is fine if the cubes are not perfectly even.

Rinse the grape leaves under cold water and dry them on paper towels. Lay the grape leaves vein side up on a work surface.

Place a piece of mozzarella and a sun-dried tomato on each leaf, slightly closer to the stem end.

Roll the stem end of each leaf over the filling, then fold in the sides and continue rolling up the leaf to make a little square package. Lay the package on a broiler pan or cookie sheet with the seam side down. Brush each package with olive oil.

Broil just until the cheese inside is soft, 45 to 60 seconds. Stack in a pyramid on a plate (this helps keep the inner and bottom rolls warm) and serve immediately.

Ricotta Tart

Makes 12 servings

This simple savory dish is an excellent stand-alone hors d'oeuvre or a perfect first course accompanied by a salad. The tart is firm enough for your guests to use their fingers, or you may serve it with forks. Its creamy yet dry texture works well with a sweet-sour drink such as the Park Avenue (page 146) or a sparkling drink such as the Adelina (page 150).

Preheat the oven to 350°F.

Place the ricotta, egg whites, salt, 1 teaspoon pepper, oregano, and lemon zest in a mixing bowl. Mix well with a spoon or whisk.

Lightly oil an 8-inch springform pan. Pour in the ricotta mixture and smooth the top. Sprinkle the remaining pepper on top.

Bake until the tart is visibly dry, about 30 minutes.

Remove the tart from the oven and let cool for 5 minutes. Run a thin-bladed knife around the edge of the pan, being careful not to nick the side of the tart. Release and remove the side of the pan. Cut the tart into 12 wedges.

Arrange on individual plates and serve.

18 ounces ricotta cheese

2 large egg whites

1 teaspoon salt

2 teaspoons ground black pepper

¼ teaspoon dried oregano

Grated zest of 1 lemon

1 tablespoon olive oil for greasing the pan

Pasta Frittata

Makes 12 servings

This is my favorite way to use leftover spaghetti or linguine. The key is to use six eggs per pound of pasta, so if you have less pasta, use proportionally fewer eggs. This dish is easily thrown together for an easy brunch dish and makes a great hors d'oeuvre or first course served hot or at room temperature.

Heat 1 tablespoon oil in a skillet over medium heat. Add the onion and cook, stirring, until softened, about 8 minutes. Transfer the onion to a large bowl and add all of the remaining ingredients except the remaining oil. Stir thoroughly to combine.

Preheat a 12-inch nonstick skillet over high heat and add 1 1/2 tablespoons oil. Spread the pasta mixture evenly in the pan, pressing down to flatten the mixture as much as possible. Reduce the heat to medium.

Cook the pasta until the underside is crispy and brown, about 10 minutes.

Place a large plate on top of the frittata in the pan. Place one hand firmly on the plate and the other firmly on the handle of the pan. Over a sink, flip the pan to transfer the frittata to the plate.

Place the pan back on the heat and add the remaining oil. Return the frittata to the pan, cooked side up. Cook until the bottom is firm and crispy, about 10 minutes more.

Remove the pan from the heat and slide the frittata onto a large platter or wooden cutting board. Cut the frittata into wedges and serve immediately, or let it cool to room temperature before serving.

4 tablespoons olive oil

1 onion, chopped

1 pound cooked spaghetti or other long pasta

6 eggs, lightly beaten

1 cup Parmesan cheese

1 teaspoon salt

1 tablespoon ground black pepper

1/4 teaspoon grated nutmeg

1 cup cooked and drained spinach (4 to 5 cups uncooked)

1/2 cup chopped sun-dried tomatoes

Tea-Soaked Eggs with Wasabi Mayonnaise

Makes 12 servings

12 large eggs

4 cups water

¾ cup soy sauce

2 tablespoons sugar

4 bags black tea,
such as Lapsang Souchong

½ cup mayonnaise

1 teaspoon rice wine vinegar,
plus more to taste

1 teaspoon wasabi powder

The subtle smoky flavor that the Lapsang Souchong tea imparts makes these ideal as part of a Sunday brunch buffet with the Asian Mary (page 217). Wasabi powder is widely available in Asian or specialty markets. If you cannot find it, use mustard powder or prepared mustard instead. Feel free to use any black tea in place of Lapsang Souchong.

PLANNING AHEAD The eggs must cool to room temperature and then be chilled for 2 hours.

The unpeeled eggs can be stored in the refrigerator in their poaching liquid for up to 2 days.

Place the eggs in a 2- to 3-quart saucepan and cover with cold water by 1 inch. Bring to a rolling boil, partially covered. Remove the pan from the heat and let stand, covered, for 10 minutes. Transfer the eggs with a slotted spoon to a bowl of ice water and let stand 5 minutes.

With the back of a spoon, gently tap each egg all over, just enough to lightly crack the shell. Do not peel the eggs and do not tap too hard or the tea will seep into the shell and completely dye the egg, as opposed to just staining it between the cracks.

Bring the 4 cups water, soy sauce, and sugar to a boil in a saucepan, stirring regularly. Once the sugar has fully dissolved, reduce the heat and add the tea bags. Simmer, covered, for 10 minutes. Remove and discard the tea bags. Add the eggs and more water, if necessary, to completely cover the eggs. Simmer the eggs, covered, for 10 minutes.

Remove the pan from the heat, uncover the pan, and let the eggs and liquid cool to room temperature. Once they are cool, chill in the refrigerator for 2 hours.

Remove the eggs from the poaching liquid and discard all but ¼ cup of the liquid. Peel the eggs carefully, discarding the shells.

Whisk together the reserved ¼ cup poaching liquid, mayonnaise, rice wine vinegar, and wasabi powder.

To serve, halve the eggs and arrange them flat side down on a platter. Serve with the wasabi mayonnaise for dipping.

Scallops on Rosemary Skewers

Makes 8 servings

Fresh scallops are sweet, firm, and succulent, with a slightly salty edge. They go with a wide array of beverages, and since they are light, they will not fill you up before your main meal. Serve with a citrusy drink such as the Salty Dog (page 132) or Rum Sling (page 179).

Preheat an outdoor grill or the broiler.

Strip the rosemary leaves off the bottom half of the branches. Chop 1 teaspoon of the leaves for the scallops. Reserve the rest for another use. Soak the branches in warm water for approximately 15 minutes; this will help keep them from burning.

In a small bowl, mix the olive oil with the chopped rosemary, garlic, salt, and pepper. Squeeze the lemon into the olive oil and mix well.

Slide 1 scallop onto each branch and brush with the olive oil mixture.

Grill just until the scallops are firm to the touch, with nice grill marks, but not tough, about 1 to 2 minutes per side. Or broil just until the scallops are firm to the touch and the edges have browned a bit, about 1 to 2 minutes per side. Serve warm, simple, and unadorned.

8 branches fresh rosemary

2 tablespoons olive oil

½ teaspoon minced garlic

½ teaspoon kosher salt

¼ teaspoon ground black pepper

1 ounce fresh lemon juice (from approximately 1 lemon)

8 large sea scallops

Grilled Shrimp Cocktail

Makes 8 servings

FOR THE SHRIMP

8 skewers

24 large shrimp,
peeled and deveined

2 tablespoons olive oil

1 tablespoon minced garlic

1 teaspoon kosher salt

FOR THE COCKTAIL SAUCE

1/2 cup ketchup

2 ounces fresh lemon juice
(from approximately 3 lemons)

1 tablespoon prepared horseradish

1 tablespoon capers

1 teaspoon smoked paprika

1/2 teaspoon hot sauce

1/2 teaspoon ground black pepper

Serve this grilled version of the classic hors d'oeuvre with a Poire Frappé (page 205), as the fruit flavor complements the clean taste of the shrimp and stands up to the smoky taste from the grill.

PLANNING AHEAD Wooden skewers must be soaked in water for at least 1 hour or up to overnight.

Soak 8 skewers in water for at least 1 hour. Thread 3 shrimp onto each skewer and place on a plate or in a bowl. Coat the shrimp with the olive oil and sprinkle with the garlic and salt. Cover with plastic wrap and refrigerate for 30 minutes.

Meanwhile, to prepare the cocktail sauce, place all the sauce ingredients in a bowl. Stir well to combine and set aside.

Preheat the grill or broiler to high heat. Grill or broil the shrimp until firm to the touch and slightly charred outside, approximately 2 minutes per side. Serve with the cocktail sauce.

Curried Chicken on Endive Spoons

Makes 2 dozen spoons

4 boneless, skinless chicken breast halves (about 1 1/2 pounds)

1 rib celery, very finely minced

1/2 small red onion, very finely minced

1 tablespoon honey

2 teaspoons curry powder

1/4 cup mayonnaise

1/4 cup raisins or golden raisins, or a combination

3 Belgian endives

The flavor of curry is perfect for cocktails and goes particularly well with drinks that include mint, such as the Mojito (page 88) or the Lime Tequila Frappé (page 177).

PLANNING AHEAD Can be assembled up to 3 hours in advance.

Bring 4 cups water to a boil in a pot large enough to submerge the chicken breasts. Add the chicken, reduce the heat, and simmer the breasts for 10 minutes. Remove the pan from the heat and let the chicken cool to room temperature in the water.

Meanwhile, place the celery and onion in a bowl. In a separate bowl, whisk together the honey and curry powder. Add the honey mixture, mayonnaise, and raisins to the onion and celery. Mix well and set aside.

When the chicken breasts have cooled, remove them from the water and pat them dry with paper towels. Finely dice the chicken and stir it into the mayonnaise mixture.

Cut the root end off the endives. Separate the leaves (you should have 24 whole leaves). Rinse well and pat dry.

Place a heaping teaspoon of chicken salad at the base of each endive leaf and arrange on a platter to serve.

Yogurt-Crusted Lamb Chops

Makes 12 servings

Since you are spoiling your guests with lamb chops, serve the dish with something celebratory such as the Blood Orange Sparkler (page 146) or Autumn Punch (page 149).

PLANNING AHEAD The lamb chops must be marinated at least 6 hours, but are best if marinated for 48 hours.

In a flat high-sided glass baking dish, place the yogurt, shallots, lemon juice, oregano, and pepper. Stir well to blend.

Add the lamb chops and coat them well on both sides with the yogurt mixture. Cover and refrigerate for 48 hours (you can marinate for as little as 6 hours if you're short on time, but the longer the better), turning the chops once or twice a day.

Arrange a rack about 6 inches from the heat source and preheat your grill or broiler to high. Shake the excess yogurt off the chops and grill or broil until the yogurt is crusted, about 2 minutes per side for medium-rare. Arrange on a platter and serve with an extra bowl on the side for discarding the finished ribs.

8 ounces plain yogurt

2 shallots, very finely minced

1 ounce fresh lemon juice
(from approximately 2 lemons)

1 teaspoon dried oregano

1 teaspoon ground black pepper

12 rib lamb chops, trimmed

Prosciutto, Arugula, and Gorgonzola Rolls

Makes 12 rolls

The saltiness of the prosciutto and strength of the Gorgonzola call for something sweeter and stronger to wash them down. The Negroni (page 95) and the Pear Cobbler (page 111) are good options. Try substituting salami for the prosciutto, and ricotta cheese flavored with Parmesan cheese for the Gogonzola.

PLANNING AHEAD The rolls can be made up to 4 hours in advance. Cover with plastic wrap and store in the refrigerator.

Lay the prosciutto on a clean surface.

Lay an arugula leaf on each slice of prosciutto.

Place 1 piece of Gorgonzola crosswise across each arugula leaf.

Roll each into a neat little package and arrange on a platter. Serve with sliced crusty bread.

12 thin slices prosciutto
(about ¼ pound)

12 large leaves arugula, destemmed if necessary, well rinsed, and dried

1 pound Gorgonzola cheese,
cut into 12 pieces

Buttermilk Biscuit Crostini with Smoked Ham

Makes 20 small biscuits and 40 crostini halves

I've topped these crostini with smoked ham and honey mustard, but they are fantastic with just about anything you can imagine. Try a bit of olive tapenade or smoked salmon with crème fraîche. As biscuits and ham are a southern specialty, there's no better way to enjoy these little bites than with a silver mug filled with a Mint Julep (page 97). They are a bit filling, so serve them before a light main course, such as simple grilled or roasted fish or chicken.

PLANNING AHEAD The biscuits can be made 24 hours in advance and stored in the refrigerator in a sealed plastic bag. Warm them in a 200°F oven for 10 minutes before assembling.

Preheat the oven to 450°F.

In a bowl, whisk together the flour, baking powder, baking soda, and salt. Sprinkle the butter over the mixture and cut it into the flour with a pastry blender. Continue until some bits of the mixture are the size of peas and the rest look like coarse bread crumbs.

Alternatively, use a food processor: Process the dry ingredients for a few seconds to mix. Sprinkle the butter over the mixture and pulse until some bits of the mixture are the size of peas and the rest look like coarse bread crumbs. Be careful not to overprocess.

Using a large wooden spoon, stir in the buttermilk just until the mix forms a ball. Turn the dough out onto a lightly floured surface and knead 8 to 10 times. Do not worry if the dough is still sticky.

Press the dough into a ¾-inch-thick rectangle and cut it into 1-inch rounds with a biscuit cutter or inverted shot glass.

Bake on an ungreased cookie sheet until the biscuits are golden brown, 7 to 9 minutes.

Remove the biscuits from the oven and split them crosswise in half. Spread each biscuit half with a touch of honey mustard, place a strip of ham on top of each, and garnish with celery leaves or parsley, if desired. Arrange on a platter or tray and serve.

2 cups all-purpose flour

3 teaspoons baking powder

1 teaspoon baking soda

1 teaspoon salt

5 tablespoons cold butter, cut into small pieces

¾ cup plus 2 tablespoons buttermilk

2 tablespoons honey mustard

¼ pound smoked ham, cut into strips 2 inches long by ½ inch wide

Celery leaves or flat-leaf parsley leaves for garnish (optional)

Bacon-Wrapped Chestnut-Stuffed Dates

Makes 24 dates

24 chestnut halves

24 large pitted dried dates

2 ounces ricotta cheese

12 slices bacon

These have become a holiday favorite at my house and are delicious any time of year. If you cannot find chestnut pieces, substitute almonds, filberts, pecans, or your favorite nuts. Serve these with the Thanksgiving Sparkler (page 150) or a Rum and Madeira Cooler (page 137).

Preheat the oven to 500°F.

Stuff a chestnut half into each date.

Fill a pastry bag, fitted with a ¼-inch tip, with the ricotta cheese. Pipe just enough ricotta into each date to fill it. Set aside.

Lay the bacon slices on a cutting board and cut each slice in half crosswise.

Place one date on each of the bacon halves, then roll up the bacon to wrap the date. Arrange the rolls on a cookie sheet seam side down, spacing them about 1 inch apart.

Bake until the bacon is golden and crispy, 7 to 9 minutes. Let cool 1 minute before serving on a tray lined with a napkin to absorb any excess grease.

Cocktails and Cheese

Cheese is welcome at any point during a meal: with hors d'oeuvres, in a salad, as a course after the entrée, and sometimes even as a light lunch or supper by itself or with a salad.

Cocktails go very well with cheese, as their alcohol content and acidity cut through the fat, richness, and saltiness of most cheeses. When a cocktail is matched to a cheese, the drink in question needs to either contrast or echo certain qualities of the cheese. Sweet-tart drinks such as the Cosmopolitan (page 89) contrast nicely with Parmigiano-Reggiano and similarly salty cheeses. Strong drinks such as the Manhattan (page 77) can hold their own with full-flavored, semi-firm cheeses, such as Morbier. And sweeter, fruit-flavored drinks such as the Blackberry Daiquiri (page 114) are a good counterpoint to Gorgonzola and other aggressive cheeses.

Preparing a cheese board can be as simple as arranging a hunk of sharp Wisconsin Cheddar with apples and crusty bread. A variety of cheeses made from cow's, goat's, and sheep's milk and in different styles is especially nice if the cheese board is the main premeal attraction. Ideally, include a variety of soft, semifirm, firm, and hard cheeses for different tastes and textures. I prefer bread with my cheese, though many people prefer crackers and some need nothing but the cheese. Serving an array of breads and crackers, such as a fresh crusty white bread, a firmer whole-grain bread, and an assortment of both whole-grain and white crackers, means that all guests can find what they like. Also note that contrasting sweet flavors against savory cheeses can greatly enhance the flavor of the latter. Try serving a bread made with dried fruit, such as a date-nut or fennel-raisin bread. Quince paste or a little bowl of honey can be an interesting pairing with strong cheese, such as Manchego, as can blackberry jam or apple chutney.

Pictured on the following page is an ideally varied cheese plate, though it is certainly not necessary to serve nine cheeses. Choose three or four styles and textures for your cheese offering. Cheese can be stored a fairly long time, so if you do not use it all in one night, wrap each cheese loosely with plastic wrap, to allow it to "breathe." Really soft, moist cheeses fare better when wrapped with wax paper, as the plastic wrap hugs too closely to the outside of the cheese and causes faster deterioration.

1. **SWISS EMMENTALER** A semifirm cheese with a natural rind, Emmentaler is made in huge wheels and cut into wedges. It is made from cow's milk and is about 45 percent butterfat, which makes it richly textured and full of flavor.

2. **APPLEBY'S CHESHIRE** Cheshire is a farmhouse cow's milk cheese from England. It is savory, with nice salty notes and a firm texture like that of Cheddar. It has a tangy yet smooth finish.

3. **MANCHEGO** This is a delicious and widely available Spanish sheep's milk cheese. The inedible rind is generally black and the texture is firm yet crumbly. Its flavor is nutty and briny yet mild. Try serving it for dessert with a big dollop of honey on top and dried fruit on the side.

4. **GORGONZOLA DOLCE** My favorite blue cheese is Gorgonzola dolce, a powerful cow's milk blue cheese with an assertive flavor. *Dolce,* or "sweet" in Italian, does not mean the cheese is actually sweet, but indicates that it is aged less than the Gorgonzola naturale. Gorgonzola dolce is soft and almost sticky, with the pronounced aggressiveness common to blue cheeses and a very nutty finish.

5. **PARMIGIANO-REGGIANO** The king of cheese, Parmigiano is a hard, piquant, nutty, fairly salty cow's milk cheese with huge flavor. It is perfect "chipped" into bite-size pieces and served with hard salami.

6. **MORBIER** This semisoft cow's milk cheese from France is extremely seductive. Its two layers are separated by a layer of vegetable ash. This layering is a holdover from the time when a farmer would make one layer of the cheese with the morning milk and cover it with ash to protect it until he could add the second layer, which was made from the evening milk. Its flavor is assertive, with lots of nutty, fruity undertones.

7. **PIERRE ROBERT** This triple-cream cow's milk cheese from France is richly textured and full of fresh milk flavor with a hint of butter. The white rind on the outside is edible and delicious. While its flavor is fresh and bright, Pierre Robert is more about its incredibly sumptuous texture.

8. **STE. MAURE DE TOURAINE** The outside of the log of this very white, soft, yet crumbly goat's milk cheese from France is coated in edible ash. Ste. Maure is piquant yet very creamy, with a pronounced acidity that is quite appealing.

9. **LE CHEVROT** This wonderful goat's milk cheese from France is generally soft, though firmer, aged versions are occasionally available. I prefer the soft styles. The flavor is sweet, mild, and incredibly nutty. Like most goat cheeses, it has a pronounced acidity, and this one has an almost spreadable texture.

MAIL-ORDER SOURCES

FOR BITTERS, SYRUPS, AND MIXES:
Fee Brothers
800-961-FEES (800-961-3337)
585-544-9530
www.feebrothers.com

FOR PEYCHAUD'S BITTERS AND RUMS:
The Sazerac Company
504-831-9450
www.sazerac.com

FOR COCKTAIL MIXES AND SYRUPS:
Trader Vic's
877-7-MAI-TAI (877-762-4824)
www.tradervics.com

FOR BAR SUPPLIES, TOP TO BOTTOM:
Big Tray
800-BIG-TRAY (800-244-8729)
www.bigtray.com

**FOR A DIVERSE SELECTION OF BAR
SUPPLIES—JIGGERS, STIRRERS, MIXING
GLASSES, YOU NAME IT:**
Bar Supply Warehouse
877-673-7676
www.barsupplywarehouse.com

FOR SPICES AND YEASTS:
BulkFoods.com
419-324-0032
www.bulkfoods.com

**FOR YEASTS AND BREAD-BAKING
SUPPLIES:**
King Arthur Flour
800-827-6836
www.kingarthurflour.com

FOR SPICES AND DRIED HERBS:
Penzeys Spices
800-741-7787
www.penzeys.com

**FOR DRIED FRUITS, NUTS, AND
PRESERVES:**
American Spoon Foods
800-222-5886 (for information)
888-735-6700 (to order)
www.spoon.com

**FOR MEXICAN INGREDIENTS, SPICES, AND
HOT SAUCES:**
Kitchen Market
888-HOT-4433 (800-468 4433)
212-243-4433
www.kitchenmarket.com

FOR ASIAN INGREDIENTS:
The Oriental Pantry
800-828-0368
978-264-4576
www.orientalpantry.com

**FOR MIDDLE EASTERN SPECIALTIES AND
INGREDIENTS INCLUDING ROSE WATER
AND ORANGE FLOWER WATER:**
Sultan's Delight
800-852-5046
www.sultansdelight.com

**FOR ALL SORTS OF THINGS, FROM BAR
SUPPLIES TO PAPER SUPPLIES TO JUICES:**
Food Service Direct
www.foodservicedirect.com

FOR LIME JUICE AND OTHER SPECIALTIES:
Nellie and Joe's
800-LIME-PIE (800-546-3743)
www.keylimejuice.com

**FOR LEMON JUICE AND OTHER
SPECIALTIES:**
Melissa's/World Variety Produce
800-588-0151
www.melissas.com

**FOR QUALITY SYRUPS AND MIXERS,
COFFEES, AND SPECIALTY INGREDIENTS:**
RONA, Inc.
800-JAVA-123 (800-528-2123)
www.ronainc.com

**FOR SUPERIOR COFFEES WITH HIGH-
QUALITY ORGANICS:**
Kaffe Magnum Opus
800-652-5282
www.1cafe.com

**FOR SYRUPS, COCKTAIL MIXES, AND
SPECIALTY INGREDIENTS:**
The Peas & Corn Co.
912-654-9596
www.peasandcornco.com

**FOR COCOA NIBS, COCOA POWDER, AND
OTHER CHOCOLATE ITEMS:**
Scharffen Berger Chocolate
800-930-4528 (retail orders)
www.scharffenberger.com

**FOR CAPER BERRIES AND ALL SORTS OF
SPECIALTY INGREDIENTS:**
Scandinavian Spice Company
877-783-7626
www.scandinavianspice.com

**FOR SHISO LEAF AND OTHER JAPANESE
AND ASIAN SPECIALTIES:**
Sushi Foods Co.
888-81-SUSHI (888-817-8744)
www.sushifoods.com

**FOR KAFFIR LIME LEAVES AND OTHER
THAI INGREDIENTS:**
ImportFood.com
888-618-THAI (888-618-8424)
www.importfood.com

**FOR SEA SALTS FROM ALL OVER THE
WORLD:**
SaltWorks
425-885-7258
www.saltworks.com

FOR GLASSWARE:
Ravenscroft Crystal
212-463-9834
www.ravenscroftcrystal.com

BIBLIOGRAPHY

BERGERON, VICTOR. *Trader Vic's Bartender's Guide.* New York: Doubleday, 1947.

———. *Trader Vic's Book of Food and Drink.* New York: Doubleday, 1946.

BIRMINGHAM, FREDERICK A., ED. *The Esquire Drink Book.* New York: Harper and Brothers, 1956.

BITTMAN, MARK. *How to Cook Everything: Simple Recipes for Great Food.*
    New York: Macmillan, 1998.

CRADDOCK, HARRY. *The Savoy Cocktail Book.* London: Constable and Company, 1930.

CROCKETT, ALBERT STEVENS. *Old Waldorf Bar Days.* New York: Aventine Press, 1933.

EMBURY, DAVID. *The Fine Art of Mixing Drinks.* New York: Doubleday, 1948.

GRIMES, WILLIAM. *Straight Up or On the Rocks: The Story of the American Cocktail.*
    New York: North Point Press, 2001.

HARRINGTON, PAUL, AND LAURA MOORHEAD. *Cocktail: The Drinks Bible for the 21st Century.*
    New York: Viking, 1998.

JENKINS, STEVEN. *The Cheese Primer.* New York: Workman, 1996.

MASON, DEXTER. *The Art of Drinking.* New York: Farrar and Rinehart, 1930.

OLD MR. BOSTON DE LUXE OFFICIAL BARTENDER'S GUIDE. Compiled and edited by Leo Cotton.
    Boston: Ben Burk, 1935.

OLD TAVERNS OF NEW YORK. New York: Frank Allaben Genealogical Company, 1915.

PACULT, F. PAUL. *Kindred Spirits: The Spirit Journal Guide to the World's Distilled Spirits and
    Fortified Wines.* New York: Hyperion, 1997.

PENDERGRAST, MARK. *Uncommon Grounds: The History of Coffee and How It Transformed Our
    World.* New York: Basic Books, 1999.

ROBERT OF THE AMERICAN BAR. *Cocktails, and How to Mix Them.* London:
    Herbert Jenkins, Ltd., ca. 1927.

ROBERTS, JONATHAN. *The Origins of Fruit and Vegetables.* New York: Universe, 2001.

TAYLOR, DAVID. *Martini.* London: Hamlyn, 2002.

THOMAS, JERRY. *The Bon Vivant's Companion or How to Mix Drinks.* New York: Knopf, 1929.

WHITFIELD, W. C. *Here's How—Mixed Drinks.* Asheville, N.C.: Three Mountaineers, 1941.

ACKNOWLEDGMENTS

There are many people to thank, both for being part of this book and part of my life. I got into the restaurant business because I truly love people. To that end, I have made many, many friends over the years, many of whom I'd like to thank. Fernando Saralegui, my bar back buddy, thanks, but remember, my margarita is better. Alfredo Ruiz, one day we will get that tapas/wine-bar thing going. Bill and MaryLu, Joe and Kim, Gretchen, Amy, John Thomas, Will and Nancy, thanks for many fun days and nights and, of course, all the hours of juicing. Tom and Amy Paris, thanks for all the great dinners and beach bonfires over the years. Graceanne Jordan, every day was a good day working together. Don Pintabona, it's been a blast starting our partnership. Michael Waterhouse, my Irish half of the family, thanks for the help, inspiration, and Guinness. Larry Halperin, thanks for keeping me straight and sharing many a great meal. Rich Marshal, there is almost no one I would rather drink a great bottle of wine with than you. Karen Schloss and Frank Diaz, thanks for always being in my corner. Rick Dembeck, wherever you are, we had fun. Alfred Portale, the first great chef I worked with, thank you for setting my path of excellence. Bill Telepan, one day it will happen. . . . Waldy Malouf, thanks for all the great game. Danny Meyer, thank you for all the encouragement. Claudia Fleming, you provided more inspiration for this book than you know. Paul Grieco, thanks for being so damn dogmatic, or is it stubborn? Kevin Tyldesley, thanks for being steady as a rock—and bringing Marah into the picture.

A special thank-you to the following people for their contribution to the book: Stephen Falango and Robyn Silvestri of Ravenscroft Crystal, thanks for allowing me to use such extraordinary glassware. Alan Englander from Haas Restaurant Supply, thanks for the helping hand with everything. Robert Kreuter of Kaffe Magnum Opus, your coffee is extraordinary.

To David Black, my agent and friend, thanks for being so damn you! To my tough, whip-cracking, slave-driving, and simply brilliant editor, Pamela Cannon—wow. Thanks for teaching me how to do it right, and thanks to the entire creative team at Artisan. To my photographer, Mette Randem, for your progressive vision and talent. Thank you, thank you, thank you to Marah Stets, the best co-writer in the world.

I am blessed to have the most wonderful family. My three brothers—my best friends, closest confidants, and running mates—Neil, John, and David, what would life be without you? My three sisters, Carol, Cathy, and Clair—each has added spice to my life. Cathy, thanks for bringing me "behind the stick" for the first time. I must thank my mom, Adele, for a lifetime of inspiration. My sister-in-law Linda Mautone, thanks for keeping Dave in line and giving the world Isabella and Luke. Kristin, thanks for being your dad's life.

My daughter, Alexandra, once daddy's girl, always daddy's girl.

And last but certainly not least, Terri. My wife, my partner, my best friend, you are my world. I could not have done this without you.

INDEX

A

Adelina, 150
Alexandra's Essence, 243
amaretto, 98
   Mai Tai, 98
   Rum and Cherry Punch, 196
   Rum and Madeira Cooler, 137
Americano, 102
amontillado sherry, *see* sherry,
   amontillado
Angostura bitters, 32
applejack, 31, 112
   Apple Crisp, 111
   Apple Crush, 112
   Cider Highball, 182
   Hot Spiked Cider, 158
   Jack Rose, 95
   Pumpkin Cider, 159
   Rum Raisin Cider, 159
apricot brandy, *see* brandy, apricot
Apricot Mulled Wine, 160
Apricot Sunday, 144
Armagnac, 30–31
   Lapsang and, 233
Artichokes, Roman, 259
Asian Mary, 217
Asparagus, Sesame Grilled, 258
Autumn Punch, 149

B

Bacardi Limón: Triple Rum Martini,
   132
Bacon-Wrapped Chestnut-Stuffed
   Dates, 272
Baileys Irish Cream: Nevisian Smile,
   187
Baked Stuffed Fingerling Potatoes,
   260
Banana:
   Buttered Rum, 166
   Rum Frappé, 121
   Rum Punch, 121
Barbeque Cocktail, 218
Basil Martini, 126
Bean Dip, Bourbon–Bacon, 257
Belle de Brillet: Pear Cider Cooler, 184
Bénédictine: Between the Sheets, 107

berries, 42–45
Berry Syrup, 62
   Adelina, 150
   Bitter Pill, 183
   Gloom Chaser, 211
   Morning Glory Daisy, 221
   Park Avenue, 146
   Sazerac, 91
Between the Sheets, 107
Bitter Pill, 183
bitters, 32
blackberry brandy: Blackberry
   Daiquiri, 114
blackberry liqueur:
   Blackberry Caramels, 208
   Blackberry Cooler, 185
   Blackberry Daiquiri, 114
   Goose Berry, 210
   Tenberry Highball, 180
Black Currant Daiquiri, 117
Black Russian, 90
Blended Cream-Sicle, 205
blended whiskey, 28
Bloodless Mary, 101
Blood Orange:
   Sparkler, 146
   Sunrise, 220
Bloody Mary, 215
Blueberry Lemonade, 241
bourbon, 28–29
   -Bacon Bean Dip, 257
   Daisy, 104
   Dry Manhattan, 79
   Fix, 104
   Fizz, 104
   Flip, 87
   General Washington's Grog, 158
   Ginger Zip, 223
   Grape and Grain, 134
   Holiday Eggnog, 155
   Kentucky Cappuccino, 230
   Lemon Julep, 176
   Manhattan, 77
   Maraschino Old-fashioned, 131
   Mint Julep, 97
   Old-fashioned, 96
   Perfect Manhattan, 79

Sazerac, 91
Sours, 104
Sunday Ham, 136
Tea & Whiskey Highball, 180
Thanksgiving Nog, 156
Trina, 104
Vanilla Coffee, 232
Ward 8, 103
Whiskey and Ginger Muddle, 135
Whiskey and Ginger Punch, 198
brandy, 30–31, 66
   Alexander, 83
   Between the Sheets, 107
   Blackberry, 114
   Blackberry Caramels, 208
   Brandywine Sour, 151
   Café Brulot, 232
   Café Frappé, 230
   Champagne Sangria, 171
   Cherry Heaven, 221
   Chestnut Hot Chocolate, 164
   Chocolate Alexander, 203
   Christmas Eve Chocolate, 163
   Classic Sangria, 171
   Flip, 87
   French 75, 145
   Hard Berry Syrup, 62
   Holiday Eggnog, 155
   Old-fashioned, 96
   Park Avenue, 146
   Peach, 68
   Pear Cobbler, 111
   Philadelphia Fish House Punch,
      199
   Polaris, 136
   Port Punch, 196
   Sazerac, 91
   Sidecar, 91
   Stinger, 89
   Thanksgiving Nog, 15
   Thanksgiving Sparkler, 150
   Vanilla Alexander, 203
brandy, apricot:
   Frozen Mango Smash, 189
   Pineapple Punch, 197
   Valencia, 103
   Whiskey and Ginger Muddle, 135

brandy, cherry:
  Cherry Heaven, 221
  Chocolate Covered Cherry, 208
  Raspberry Ten, 125
  Singapore Sling, 84
  Summer Sunset, 123
brandy, plum, 68
  Island Rose, 207
  Rum and Plum, 223
brandy, Spanish: Prickly Pear
  Sangria, 176
Brandywine Sour, 151
Bronx, The, 93
Brown Sugar Syrup, 56
  Blackberry Caramels, 208
  Kentucky Cappuccino, 230
Buttered Rum, 166
Buttermilk Biscuit Crostini with
  Smoked Ham, 271

C

cachaca: Caipirinha, 104
Café:
  Brulot, 232
  Cacao Blend, 228
  Frappé, 230
  Shakarata, 233
Caipirinha, 104
calvados, 31, 112
  Apple Crisp, 111
  Apple Crush, 112
  applejack, 31
  Cider Highball, 182
  Hot Spiked Cider, 158
  The Normandy, 143
  Pumpkin Cider, 159
  Rum Raisin Cider, 159
Campari:
  Americano, 102
  Bitter Pill, 183
  Negroni, 95
  Sparkling Cocktail, 118
Canton Ginger Liqueur, 100
  Debonaire, 100
caper berries, 45, 129
Cappuccino, Kentucky, 230
Carrot Pickles, Quick, 50

Champagne Sangria, 171
cheese:
  Appleby's Cheshire, 275
  Le Chevrot, 275
  Chipotle Cheddar Chips, 245
  Gorgonzola Dolce, 275
  Hollow Bread Fondue, 261
  Manchego, 275
  Morbier, 275
  Parmigiano-Reggiano, 275
  Pierre Robert, 275
  Prosciutto, Arugula, and
    Gorgonzola Rolls, 269
  Ricotta Tart, 263
  Smoked Mozzarella and
    Sun-Dried Tomatoes in Grape
    Leaves, 262
  Ste. Maure de Touraine, 275
  Swiss Emmentaler, 275
Cherries, Maraschino, 53
cherry brandy, see brandy, cherry
Cherry Heering, 84
  Cherry Heaven, 221
  Chocolate Covered Cherry,
    208
  Pineapple Sling, 179
  Polaris, 136
  Rum Sling, 179
  Singapore Sling, 84
Cherry Sugar Fizz, 141
Chestnut Hot Chocolate, 164
Chicken, Curried, on Endive
  Spoons, 268
Chickpeas, Spicy Roasted, 252
Chipotle Cheddar Chips, 254
Chips, Chipotle Cheddar, 254
  Oven-Dried Tomato, 49
chocolate:
  Alexander, 203
  Covered Cherry, 208
  Hot Chocolate, 163
Chocolaty Whipped Cream, 54
  Chestnut Hot Chocolate, 164
Christmas Eve Chocolate, 163
Cider:
  Highball, 182
  Syrup, 159

cider, sparkling pear: Pear Cider
  Cooler, 184
Cinnamon Cardamom Blend, 229
citron vodka: Cosmopolitan, 89
citrus:
  -Flavored Vodka Syrup, 60
  Gin, 130
  juice, fresh, 38
  swirls, 40
  twists, 39
  wedges, 40–41
  zest, 39–40
Clove Martini, 136
Cocktail Onions, 52
cocktail pitchers, 21
Coco Lopez cream of coconut:
  Lava Flow, 188
  Nevisian Smile, 187
  Piña Colada, 90
Coconut Limeade, 242
coconut rum, see rum, coconut
Coco Yauco Blend, 227
coffee:
  Café Brulot, 232
  Café Cacao Blend, 228
  Café Frappé, 230
  Café Shakarata, 233
  Christmas Eve Chocolate, 163
  Cinnamon Cardamom Blend, 229
  Coco Yauco Blend, 227
  Iris's Coffee Nog, 157
  Kentucky Cappuccino, 230
  Millennium Blend, 227
  Mocha Rum Toddy, 230
  The Nick-o-cino, 189
  Pumpkin Spice Blend, 229
  Vanilla Spice Blend, 228
cognac, 30
Cointreau:
  Apple Crisp, 111
  Between the Sheets, 107
  Classic Daiquiri, 83
  Frothy Margarita, 81
  Frozen Margarita, 81
  Frozen Prickly Pear Margarita, 82
  Magnificent Mimosa, 142
  Margarita, 81

Moscato Cooler, 185
Rum and Cherry Punch, 196
Salty Dog, 132
Sidecar, 91
conversions and measurements, 46
cordial(s), 66–67
Blackberry, 66
Cranberry, 67
Cosmopolitan, 89
cranberry liqueur:
Cranberry Daiquiri, 116
Cranberry Daiquiri Punch, 116
Cranberry Sauce, 246
cream of coconut, Coco Lopez, 90
Cream–Sicle, 205
crème de cacao, dark, 163
Chocolate Covered Cherry, 208
Christmas Eve Chocolate, 163
Mocha Rum Toddy, 230
crème de cacao, white:
Brandy Alexander, 83
Grasshopper, 211
White Chocolate Martini, 204
crème de cassis:
Kir Royale, 145
Raspberry Ten, 125
crème de fraise:
Strawberry Kiwi Sangria, 175
Tenberry Highball, 180
crème de framboise, 125
Frozen Raspberry Daiquiri, 187
Raspberry Ten, 125
crème de menthe, green, Kentucky
Cappuccino, 230
crème de menthe, white:
Fresh Mint Sangria, 173
Kentucky Cappuccino, 230
Stinger, 89
curaçao, 32
Curried Chicken on Endive Spoons,
268

D

Daiquiri:
Blackberry, 114
Black Currant, 117
Classic, 83

Cranberry, 116
Cranberry, Punch, 116
Frozen Raspberry, 187
Daisy, 104
Dark and Stormy, 94
Dark and Stormy II, 195
Dates, Bacon-Wrapped
Chestnut-Stuffed, 272
Debonaire, 100
dessert wine, 151
dips, 256–57
Bourbon-Bacon Bean, 257
Guacamole, 256
Roasted Eggplant, 256
Drambuie, 109
Rusty Nail, 106
Warm and Rusty, 233
Dry Sac sherry: Prickly Pear
Sangria, 176
dry vermouth, *see* vermouth, dry

E

eau-de-vie, 174
Hard Berry Syrup, 62
Peach Sangria, 174
Echte Kroatsbeere Blackberry
liqueur:
Blackberry Caramel, 208
Blackberry Daiquiri, 114
Eggs, Tea Soaked, with Wasabi
Mayonnaise, 266

F

Faux Margarita, 244
Faux Mojito, 244
Fig Mulled Wine, 162
Fix, 104
Fizz, 104
Flatbread, Grilled Rosemary and
Sun–Dried Tomato, 253
Floridita, 102
Flutter, 211
43 Licks, 210
framboise: Tenberry Highball, 180
Frangelico:
Blackberry Caramels, 208
Chestnut Hot Chocolate, 164

Frappé:
Banana Rum, 121
Café, 230
Coconut Rum, 178
Lemon, 122
Lime Tequila, 177
Poire, 205
Vanilla, 204
French 75, 145
Frittata, Pasta, 265
Frozen:
Mango Smash, 189
Margarita, 81
Prickly Pear Margarita, 82
Raspberry Daiquiri, 187
fruits, 42–45

G

Galliano, 203
Cream-Sicle, 205
Grand, 207
Vanilla Alexander, 203
Vanilla Coffee, 232
garnishes, 38–39
homemade, 49–54; *see also*
specific garnishes
General Washington's Grog, 158
Gibson, 75
Greenmarket, 123
Gimlet, 86
gin, 27–28
The Bronx, 93
Citrus, 130
Classic Martini, 73
Daisy, 104
Dirty Martini, 74
Fix, 104
Fizz, 104
Fizz, Ramos, 94
French 75, 145
Gibson, 75
Gimlet, 86
Gin-ger & Tonic, 130
Lemon Frappé, 122
Maiden's Prayer, 98
Martinez, 74
Negroni, 95

gin (*continued*)
  Pineapple Sling, 179
  Pompano, 131
  Raspberry Ten, 125
  Rickey, 100
  Salty Dog, 132
  Silver Bullet, 76
  Singapore Sling, 84
  Sours, 104
  Summer Buck, 183
  Tenberry Highball, 180
  Tom Collins, 84
  Trina, 104
  Vesper, 76
gin, Tanqueray No. Ten:
  Gin-ger & Tonic, 130
  Pompano, 131
  Raspberry Ten, 125
ginger:
  Champagne Punch, 195
  Zip, 223
ginger beer, 94
  Dark and Stormy, 94
  Dark and Stormy II, 195
  Moscow Mule, 102
  Whiskey and Ginger Punch, 198
Ginger Syrup, 59
  Gin-ger & Tonic, 130
  Ginger Champagne Punch, 195
  Ginger Zip, 223
  Singapore Sling, 84
glassware, 23–25
Gloom Chaser, 211
Godiva Liqueur: Chocolate
    Alexander, 203
Godiva White Chocolate Liqueur:
  43 Licks, 210
  Vanilla "Cocoa," 164
Goose Berry, 210
Gosling's Black Seal Rum, *see* rum,
    Gosling's Black Seal
Grand, The, 135
Grand Galliano, 207
Grand Marnier:
  Blackberry Cooler, 185
  Café Brulot, 232
  Fig Mulled Wine, 162

The Grand, 135
Grand Galliano, 207
Grand Margarita, 81
Grand Mimosa, 142
Park Avenue, 146
Rhett Butler, 107
Tea Cooler, 234
Grand Mimosa, 142
Grape and Grain, 134
Grape Leaves, Smoked Mozzarella
    and Sun-Dried Tomatoes in,
    262
grappa:
  Christmas Eve Chocolate, 163
  Limoncello, 69
Grasshopper, 211
Greenmarket Gibson, 123
Green Tea Toddy, 235
Grenadine, 64
  Brandywine Sour, 151
  Floridita, 102
  Gloom Chaser, 211
  Island Rose, 207
  Jack Rose, 95
  Knickerbocker, 103
  Lava Flow, 188
  Morning Glory Daisy, 221
  Park Avenue, 146
  Planter's Punch, 87
  Zombie, 86
Grey Goose La Vanille:
  Clove Martini, 136
Grey Goose Le Citron:
  Goose Berry, 210
Grey Goose vodka:
  Clove Martini, 136
Grilled Rosemary and Sun-Dried
    Tomato Flatbread, 253
Grilled Shrimp Cocktail, 268
GT Buck, 122

H

Ham, Smoked, Buttermilk Biscuit
    Crostini with, 271
Hard Berry Syrup, 62
herbs, 45–46
Holiday Eggnog, 155

Hollow Bread Fondue, 261
Hot and Sweet Maple Pecans:
    Not Your Ordinary Trail Mix,
    251
Hot Chocolate Chocolate, 163
hot sauces, 33
Hot Spiked Cider, 158

I

ice, 37
Iced Tea, 234
  Grand Marnier Tea Cooler, 234
Irish whiskey, 28
Iris's Coffee Nog, 157
Island Rose, 207

J

Jack Rose, 95
Jalapeño Vodka, 219
  Barbeque Cocktail, 218
Jamaican rum: Swizzle, 106
juice, fresh citrus, 38

K

Kaffir Lime Kocktail, 119
Kahlúa:
  Black Russian, 90
  Christmas Eve Chocolate, 163
  Flutter, 211
  Iris's Coffee Nog, 157
  The Nick-o-cino, 189
Kentucky Cappuccino, 230
Kir Royale, 145
Knickerbocker, 103

L

Lamb Chops, Yogurt–Crusted, 269
lapsang souchong:
  and Armagnac, 233
  Tea Soaked Eggs with
      Wasabi Mayonnaise, 266
Lava Flow, 188
Lemonade, 239
  Alexandra's Essence, 243
  Blueberry, 241
  Watermelon, 239
Lemon Frappé, 122
Lemon Julep, 176

Lemon Sour Mix, 65
   Brandywine Sour, 151
   Fizz, 104
   Pear Cobbler, 111
   Ramos Gin Fizz, 94
   Rose Water Cocktail, 243
   Sours, 104
   Summer Sunset, 123
   Tom Collins, 84
   Trina, 104
Licor 43, 114
   Blackberry Daiquiri, 114
   Black Currant Daiquiri, 117
   43 Licks, 210
   Vanilla "Cocoa," 164
   Vanilla Coffee, 232
Lillet Blanc, 76
   Dry Manhattan, 79
   Vesper, 76
Limeade, 241
   Alexandra's Essence, 243
   Coconut, 242
   Mango, 242
lime leaves, Kaffir, 119
Lime Sour Mix, 65
   Blackberry Daiquiri, 114
   Black Currant Daiquiri, 117
   Classic Daiquiri, 83
   Cranberry Daiquiri, 116
   Frothy Margarita, 81
   Frozen Prickly Pear Margarita, 82
Lime Tequila Frappé, 177
Limoncello, 69
   Citrus-Gin, 130
   Lemon Frappé, 122
   Maraschino Highball, 182
   Pear Cider Cooler, 184
liqueurs, *see specific liqueurs*

M

McIntosh Punch, 247
Madeira, 137
   Flip, 87
   General Washington's Grog, 158
   Pineapple Nog, 156
   Rum and Madeira Cooler, 137

Magnificent Mimosa, 142
Maiden's Prayer, 98
Mai Tai, 98
Maker's Mark bourbon: Whiskey
   and Ginger Punch, 198
Mandarine Napoleon liqueur:
   Gloom Chaser, 211
   Pomegranate Punch, 194
Mango Limeade, 242
Manhattan, 77–79
   classic, 77
   Dry, 79
   Perfect, 79
   sweet, 77
Maple Pecans, Hot and Sweet, 251
Maraschino:
   Highball, 182
   Muddle, 246
   Old-fashioned, 131
Maraschino Cherries, 53
Maraschino liqueur, 74
   Floridita, 102
   Maraschino Highball, 182
   Martinez, 74
Margarita, 81–82
   Faux, 244
   Frothy, 81
   Frozen, 81
   Frozen Prickly Pear, 82
   Grand, 81
Martinez, 74
Martini:
   Basil, 126
   Classic, 73
   Clove, 136
   Dirty, 74
   Martinez, 74
   Triple Rum, 132
   White Chocolate, 204
Massanez Poire: Poire Frappé, 205
measurements and conversions, 46
Mediterranean Mary, 216
Millennium Blend, 227
Mint Syrup, 57
   Limeade, 241
   Mango Limeade, 242
   Tea & Whiskey Highball, 180

mocha:
   Rum Cooler, 177
   Rum Toddy, 230
Mojito, 88
   Faux, 244
Montecristo rum: Montecristo
   Muddle, 133
Morning Glory Daisy, 221
moscato:
   Cooler, 185
   Sparkling Campari Cocktail, 118
Moscow Mule, 102
Myers's rum: Piña Colada, 90

N

Negroni, 95
Nevisian Smile, 187
Nick-o-cino, The, 189
nonalcoholic, 239–247
   Pineapple Punch, 197
   Watermelon Punch, 247
Normandy, The, 143
Not Your Ordinary Trail Mix, 251

O

Old-fashioned, 96
olives, 45
   Vermouth-Soaked, 51
100 percent agave tequila, 29–30, 122
151 proof rum: Zombie, 86
onions, 45
   Cocktail, 52
Orange:
   Negroni, 95
   Rob Roy, 93
orange bitters, 32
orange vodka: Island Rose, 207
orgeat syrup, 98
   Mai Tai, 98
Oven-Dried Tomato Chips, 49

P

Park Avenue, 146
Pasta Frittata, 265
Peach:
   Sangria, 174
   Sunday, 144

peach brandy: Philadelphia Fish House Punch, 199
pear liqueur:
Cider Cooler, 184
Pear, Poire, 151
Pear Cobbler, 111
Pear Sunday, 144
Pecans, Hot and Sweet Maple, 251
Pedro Ximenez sherry, *see* sherry, Pedro Ximenez
peppermint schnapps: Fresh mint Sangria, 173
Pernod, 108
Morning Glory Daisy, 220
Rosmarino, 129
Sazerac, 91
Peychaud's bitters, 32
Philadelphia Fish House Punch, 199
Pickle Mary, 217
Piña Colada, 90
pineapple:
Punch, 197
Sangria, 172
wedges, 42
Pineapple Syrup, 61
Coconut Limeade, 242
Fix, 104
Lemonade, 239
Limeade, 241
Mango Limeade, 242
Pineapple Nog, 156
Pineapple Sling, 179
Singapore Sling, 84
pinot noir: Fig Mulled Wine, 162
pitchers, cocktail, 21
Planter's Punch, 87
plum brandy, *see* brandy, plum
Plum Sake, 186
plum wine, *see* wine, plum
Poire Frappé, 205
Polaris, 136
Pomegranate Punch, 194
Pompano, 131
Popcorn, Sesame Seed, 252
port:
Brandywine Sour, 151

Fig Mulled Wine, 162
Flip, 37
port, ruby:
Port Punch, 196
Summer Sunset, 123
Potatoes, Baked Stuffed Fingerling, 260
Prickly Pear Sangria, 176
Prosciutto, Arugula, and Gorgonzola Rolls, 269
Pumpkin:
Cider, 159
Spice Blend, 229
Pumpkin Seed Popcorn, 252
punch:
Autumn, 149
Banana Rum, 121
Cranberry Daiquiri, 116
Dark and Stormy II, 195
Ginger Champagne, 195
McIntosh, 247
Nonalcoholic Pineapple, 197
Nonalcoholic Watermelon, 247
Philadelphia Fish House, 199
Pineapple, 197
Planter's, 87
Pomegranate, 194
Port, 196
Rum and Cherry, 196
Sloe Comfortable, 199
Watermelon, 193
Whiskey and Ginger, 198
Zombie, 86

R
Ramos Gin Fizz, 94
raspberry syrup:
Daisy, 104
Knickerbocker, 103
Raspberry Ten, 125
red wine: Classic Sangria, 171
Red Wine Syrup, 60
Brandywine Sour, 151
Park Avenue, 146
Rhett Butler, 107
Ricard: Sazerac, 91

Ricotta Tart, 263
riesling:
Apricot Mulled Wine, 160
Peach Sangria, 174
Roasted Eggplant Dip, 256
Rob Roy, 93
Roman Artichokes, 259
Rose's Lime Juice: Gimlet, 86
Rose Water Cocktail, 243
rosé wine, *see* wine, rosé
Rosmarino, 129
ruby port, *see* port, ruby
rum, 29
and Cherry Punch, 196
Daisy, 104
Fix, 104
Fizz, 104
Flip, 87
and Madeira Cooler, 137
and Plum, 223
Sours, 104
Syrup, 59
Tenberry Highball, 180
Trina, 104
rum, coconut:
Frappé, 178
Lava Flow, 188
Nevisian Smile, 187
rum, dark, 59
Banana Buttered Rum, 166
Banana Rum Frappé, 121
Blackberry Cordial, 66
Blackberry Daiquiri, 114
Black Currant Daiquiri, 117
and Cherry Punch, 196
Coconut Rum Frappé, 178
Collins, 84
Holiday Eggnog, 155
Hot Spiked Cider, 158
Iris's Coffee Nog, 157
Knickerbocker, 103
and Madeira Cooler, 137
Mai Tai, 98
Mocha Rum Cooler, 177
Mocha Rum Toddy, 230
Philadelphia Fish House Punch, 199
Planter's Punch, 87

Pumpkin Cider, 159
Raisin Cider, 159
Summer Sunset, 123
Thanksgiving Nog, 156
Watermelon Cooler, 184
Zombie, 86
rum, Gosling's Black Seal:
Dark and Stormy, 94
Dark and Stormy II, 195
Triple Rum Martini, 132
rum, Jamaican: Swizzle, 106
rum, light, 59
Classic Daiquiri, 83
Cranberry Daiquiri, 116
Floridita, 102
Frozen Mango Smash, 189
Green Tea Toddy, 235
Hard Berry Syrup, 62
Lava Flow, 188
Mojito, 88
Piña Colada, 90
Pineapple Nog, 156
Pineapple Sangria, 172
Planter's Punch, 87
and Plum, 223
Sling, 179
Sparkling Rum Runner, 143
Strawberry Kiwi Sangria, 175
Watermelon Punch, 193
Zombie, 86
rum, Montecristo: Montecristo
Muddle, 133
rum, Myers's: Piña Colada, 90
rum, 151 proof: Zombie, 86
rum, spiced: Piña Colada, 90
Rum Syrup, 59
Sparkling Rum Runner, 143
Triple Rum Martini, 132
Rusty Nail, 106
rye, 29
Classic Manhattan, 77
Dry Manhattan, 77, 79
Old-fashioned, 96
Perfect Manhattan, 77, 79
Sazerac, 91
Whiskey and Ginger Punch,
198

S
sake, 186
Asian Mary, 217
Plum Sake, 186
salt, 42
Salty Dog, 132
Sangria:
Champagne, 171
Classic, 171
Fresh Mint, 173
Peach, 174
Pineapple, 172
Prickly Pear, 176
Strawberry Kiwi, 175
sauces, hot, 33
Sazerac, 91
Scallops on Rosemary Skewers,
267
Scarlett O'Hara, 107
schnapps, peppermint: Fresh Mint
Sangria, 173
schnapps, strawberry: Strawberry
Kiwi Sangria, 175
scotch, 28
Old-fashioned, 96
Rob Roy, 93
Rusty Nail, 106
Silver Bullet, 76
Tea & Whiskey Highball, 180
Warm and Rusty, 233
Whiskey and Ginger Peach, 198
scotch, Highland malt: Debonaire,
100
sea salt, 42
Sesame Grilled Asparagus, 258
Shaggy Dog, 133
Shakarata, Café, 233
sherry, amontillado:
The Grand, 135
Mediterranean Mary, 216
Port Punch, 196
Prickly Pear Sangria, 176
sherry, Dry Sac: Prickly Pear
Sangria, 176
sherry, Pedro Ximenez:
Autumn Punch, 149
Black Currant Daiquiri, 117

Shrimp Cocktail, Grilled, 268
Silver Bullet, 76
Simple Syrup, 56
Adelina, 150
Blueberry Lemonade, 241
The Bronx, 93
Café Shakarata, 233
Coconut Limeade, 242
Fizz, 104
Iced Tea, 234
Jack Rose, 95
Lemonade, 239
Lemon Sour Mix, 65
Limeade, 241
Lime Sour Mix, 65
Mango Limeade, 242
Mint Julep, 97
Mojito, 88
Nonalcoholic Watermelon
Punch, 247
Park Avenue, 146
Poire Frappé, 205
Rum Sling, 179
Sazerac, 91
Singapore Sling, 84
Sours, 104
Swizzle, 106
Trina, 104
Vanilla Alexander, 203
Vanilla "Cocoa," 164
Ward 8, 103
Watermelon Cooler, 184
Watermelon Lemonade, 239
Singapore Sling, 84
sloe gin:
Sidecar, 91
Sloe Comfortable Punch, 199
Smirnoff vodka: Moscow Mule, 102
Smoked Ham, Buttermilk Biscuit
Crostini with, 271
Smoked Mozzarella and Sun-Dried
Tomatoes in Grape Leaves,
262
Sour Mix:
Lemon, 65
Lime, 65
Sours, 104

Southern Comfort, 233
  Ginger Zip, 223
  Rhett Butler, 107
  Scarlett O'Hara, 107
  Sloe Comfortable Punch, 199
Spanish brandy, 31
sparkling wine, *see* wine, sparkling
spiced rum: Piña Colada, 90
Spiced Syrup, 62
  Sunday Ham, 136
Spiced Whipped Cream, 54
  Thanksgiving Nog, 156
spices, 42
Spicy Roasted Chickpeas, 252
Spiked Pear Cider, 158
Stinger, 89
Strawberry Kiwi Sangria, 175
strawberry liqueur: Adelina, 150
strawberry schnapps: Strawberry
  Kiwi Sangria, 175
sugar, 41–42
Summer Buck, 183
Summer Solstice, 244
Summer Sunset, 123
Sunday Ham, 136
Sun-Dried Tomato(es):
  in Grape Leaves, Smoked
    Mozzarella and, 262
  and Grilled Rosemary Flatbread,
    253
sweet vermouth, *see* vermouth,
  sweet
swirls, citrus, 40
Swizzle, 106
Sylk Cream Liqueur, 189
  The Nick-o-cino, 189
syrups, 55–64
  see also specific syrups

T

Tabasco sauce, 33
Tangerine Dream, 220
Tanqueray No. Ten Gin, see Gin,
  Tanqueray No. Ten
Tart, Ricotta, 263
Tea:
  Cooler, Grand Marnier, 234

Green, Toddy, 235
Iced, 234
Soaked Eggs with Wasabi
  Mayonnaise, 266
& Whiskey Highball, 180
techniques, 21–22
Tenberry Highball, 180
tequila, 29–30
  Blood Orange Sunrise, 220
  Frothy Margarita, 81
  Frozen Margarita, 81
  Frozen Prickly Pear Margarita, 82
  Frozen Raspberry Daiquiri, 187
  Grand Margarita, 81
  Margarita, 81
  Tangerine Dream, 220
tequila, 100 percent agave, 29–30,
  122
  GT Buck, 122
  Kaffir Lime Kocktail, 119
tequila, silver, 29
  Flutter, 211
  Lime Tequila Frappé, 177
Thanksgiving Nog, 156
Thanksgiving Sparkler, 150
Tia Maria: Nevisian Smile, 187
Toddy:
  Green Tea, 235
  Mocha Rum, 230
Tom Collins, 84
Trail Mix, Not Your Ordinary, 251
Trina, 104
Triple Rum Martini, 132
triple sec:
  Apple Crisp, 111
  Cosmopolitan, 89
  Floridita, 102
  Frozen Mango Smash, 189
  Frozen Raspberry Daiquiri, 187
  Gloom Chaser, 211
  Knickerbocker, 103
  Maiden's Prayer, 98
  Mai Tai, 98
  Pear Cobbler, 111
  Planter's Punch, 87
  Sangria, Classic, 171
twists, citrus, 39

U
utensils, 18–21
V
Valencia, 103
Vanilla:
  Alexander, 203
  "Cocoa," 164
  Coffee, 232
  Frappé, 204
vanilla liqueur:
  Mocha Rum Cooler, 177
  Watermelon Cooler, 184
  Watermelon Punch, 193
Vanilla Spice Blend, 228
  Vanilla Coffee, 232
Vanilla Syrup, 58
  Lemonade, 239
  Limeade, 241
  Mango Limeade, 242
  Vanilla "Cocoa," 164
vanilla vodka, *see* vodka, vanilla
Vanilla Vodka Syrup, 60
  Goose Berry, 210
  Vanilla Alexander, 203
  Vanilla "Cocoa," 164
vegetables, 45
verjuice: Summer Solstice, 244
vermouth, 31
  Vermouth-Soaked Olives, 51
vermouth, dry, 31
  Barbecue Cocktail, 218
  Basil Martini, 126
  The Bronx, 93
  Citrus Gin, 130
  Classic Martini, 73
  Cocktail Onions, 52
  Dirty Martini, 74
  Dry Manhattan, 77, 79
  Gibson, 75
  Greenmarket Gibson, 123
  Perfect Manhattan, 79
  Pompano, 131
  Rosmarino, 129
  Shaggy Dog, 133
  Silver Bullet, 76

vermouth, sweet, 31
 Americano, 102
 Bitter Pill, 183
 Blood Orange Sparkler, 146
 The Bronx, 93
 Classic Manhattan, 77
 Martinez, 74
 Negroni, 95
 Perfect Manhattan, 79
 Polaris, 136
 Raspberry 10, 125
 Rob Roy, 93
 Salty Dog, 132
 Sparkling Campari Cocktail, 118
Vesper, 76
vodka, 27
 Apple Crush, 112
 Asian Mary, 217
 Basil Martini, 126
 Black Russian, 90
 Bloodless Mary, 101
 Bloody Mary, 215
 Cider Highball, 182
 Classic Martini, 73
 Cranberry Cordial, 66
 Cream-Sicle, 205
 Daisy, 104
 Dirty Martini, 74
 Fix, 104
 Fizz, 104
 Grasshopper, 211
 Greenmarket Gibson, 123
 Hard Berry Syrup, 62
 Jalapeño, 219
 Lemon Frappé, 122
 Limoncello, 69
 Mediterranean Mary, 216
 Morning Glory Daisy, 221
 Negroni, 95
 Pickle Mary, 217
 Pomegranate Punch, 194
 Pompano, 131
 Rosmarino, 129
 Salty Dog, 132
 Shaggy Dog, 133
 Silver Bullet, 76
 Sloe Comfortable Punch, 199
 Sours, 104

 Sparkling Campari Cocktail, 118
 Syrup, 60
 Tenberry Highball, 186
 Trina, 104
 Vesper, 76
vodka, citron: Cosmopolitan, 89
vodka, Grey Goose, see Grey Goose
vodka, orange: Island Rose, 207
vodka, Smirnoff: Moscow Mule,
 102
vodka, vanilla:
 Poire Frappé, 205
 White Chocolate Martini, 204
Vodka Syrup, 60
 see also Vanilla Vodka Syrup

W

Ward 8, 103
Warm and Rusty, 233
water, 37
watermelon:
 Cooler, 184
 Lemonade, 239
 Punch, 193
 Punch, Nonalcoholic, 247
wedges, citrus, 40–41
wedges, pineapple, 42
Whipped Cream, 54
 Chestnut Hot Chocolate, 164
 Christmas Eve Chocolate, 163
 Kentucky Cappuccino, 230
 Mocha Rum Toddy, 230
 Spiced, 54
 Vanilla "Cocoa," 164
 Vanilla Coffee, 232
Whipped Cream, Chocolaty, 54
 Chestnut Hot Chocolate, 164
Whipped Cream, Tangy, 54
 Hot Chocolate Chocolate, 163
whiskey, 28–29
 Daisy, 104
 Fix, 104
 Fizz, 104
 and Ginger Muddle, 135
 and Ginger Punch, 198
 Sours, 104
 Trina, 104
White Chocolate Martini, 204

white crème de cacao, see crème
 de cacao, white
white crème de menthe, see crème
 de menthe, white
wine, dessert: Brandywine Sour, 151
wine, pinot noir: Fig Mulled Wine, 162
wine, plum:
 Champagne Sangria, 171
 Plum Sake, 186
 Rum and Plum, 223
wine, red: Classic Sangria, 171
wine, riesling:
 Apricot Mulled Wine, 160
 Peach Sangria, 174
wine, rosé:
 Peach Sangria, 174
 Pineapple Sangria, 172
 Prickly Pear Sangria, 176
 Strawberry Kiwi Sangria, 175
wine, sparkling:
 Adelina, 150
 Apricot Sunday, 144
 Autumn Punch, 149
 Blood Orange Sparkler, 146
 Champagne Sangria, 171
 Cherry Sugar Fizz, 141
 French 75, 145
 Ginger Champagne Punch, 195
 Grand Mimosa, 142
 Kir Royale, 145
 Magnificent Mimosa, 142
 The Normandy, 143
 Park Avenue, 146
 Pear, Poire, 151
 Pineapple Punch, 197
 Sparkling Rum Runner, 143
 Thanksgiving Sparkler, 150
wine, white: Fresh Mint Sangria, 173
Worcestershire sauce, 33
 Bloodless Mary, 101
 Bloody Mary, 215
 Bourbon-Bacon Bean Dip, 257

Y

Yogurt-Crusted Lamb Chops, 269

Z

zest, citrus, 39–40
Zombie, 86

Published by Artisan
A Division of Workman Publishing, Inc.
708 Broadway
New York, New York 10003–9555
www.artisanbooks.com

Library of Congress
Cataloging-in-Publication Data

Mautone, Nick.
Raising the bar : better drinks better
entertaining / Nick Mautone with
Marah Stets; photographs by
Mette Randem.
p. cm.
Includes index.
ISBN 1-57965-260-3
1. Cocktails. I. Title. II. Marah Stets.
TX951.M32 2004
641.8'74—dc22   2004052877

Printed in Singapore
10 9 8 7 6 5 4 3 2 1

Book design by Nicholas Caruso
This book was set in Chalet,
Cheltenham, and Din